JOHN PAUL COOPER

Figure 1. John Paul Cooper, 1890s. Cooper Family Archives.

JOHN PAUL COOPER

Designer and Craftsman of the
ARTS & CRAFTS MOVEMENT

N. NATASHA KUZMANOVIĆ

SUTTON PUBLISHING

First published in the United Kingdom in 1999 by
Sutton Publishing Limited · Phoenix Mill
Thrupp · Stroud · Gloucestershire · GL5 2BU

British Library Cataloguing in Publication Data
A catalogue record for this book is available from the British Library

ISBN 0 7509 2088 2

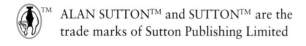 ALAN SUTTON™ and SUTTON™ are the
trade marks of Sutton Publishing Limited

Typeset in 10/13 pt Sabon
Typesetting and origination by
Sutton Publishing Limited
Printed in Great Britain by
Butler & Tanner, Frome, Somerset

*For my parents
and for Ursula, whose
perseverance never wavered.*

CONTENTS

LIST OF ILLUSTRATIONS

All measurements in the text and captions are given in centimetres.

BLACK AND WHITE ILLUSTRATIONS

Page No.

FOREWORD

BY GILLIAN NAYLOR

Born in 1869, John Paul Cooper belonged to the second generation of artist/craftsmen inspired by the idealism of John Ruskin and William Morris. He was a contemporary of Archibald Knox, and although the lives and achievements of many of his Art Worker colleagues have been recorded in monographs and in exhibitions and publications celebrating the canons of the Arts and Crafts Movement, Cooper has remained a shadowy figure. He is frequently mentioned – especially by his contemporaries – but the extent, nature and significance of his work has never been fully acknowledged by historians of the Movement.

Natasha Kuzmanović's study, therefore, is a vital contribution to Arts and Crafts scholarship. Cooper's designs are identified and documented, and because of the extensive archive material that was available to her, Dr Kuzmanović has been able to record the processes and practicalities of their production. At the same time, access to Cooper's letters and diaries (as well as family memoirs and memories) has enabled her to describe the ideas and the idealism that motivated him. Cooper's work, whether in gesso, precious metals or shagreen, was painstaking and perfectionist, and we learn how many hours were devoted to each project, what costs were involved, who his patrons were and what they required of him. At the same time, we hear Cooper 'thinking aloud' as he works: the translucency of the skins he is using for shagreen give him 'the feeling of looking deep down into a pool of sea green water'; mother-of-pearl is so brilliant that 'the danger is of the worker forcing his material & working his subject in such a high key that it shrieks', while stones in jewellery, he believed, should 'play on one another as two notes of music'.[1]

It is not surprising, therefore, to learn that the young Cooper had hoped to be a writer; faced with his father's disapproval he decided to train as an architect because he 'did not know of any other profession except literature that I preferred'. John Paul Cooper then became an archetypal Arts and Crafts initiate. Like Ruskin and Morris, and like his friend and contemporary Ernest Gimson, he had an enterprising father who had founded the family's fortune. When John Paul embarked on his career in the 1880s, architecture, because of the proselytizing of Ruskin and Morris, was an honourable profession, and architecture at that time meant commitment, especially for a young man apprenticed to J.D. Sedding. Sedding, according to W.R. Lethaby, 'drew tenderly in a Ruskinian way' and 'saw as few in his time had seen that architecture was workmanship rather than paper, and that spirit came before forms'.[2] Working in Sedding's office was an ideal education for Cooper: it brought him into contact with kindred spirits – especially Henry Wilson, who became his friend and mentor – and it launched him on his career as an Art Worker.

Dr Kuzmanović's text commemorates a long working life. John Paul Cooper studied art as well as architecture, but he learned through doing. Henry Wilson introduced him to plasterwork, which led to his interest in gesso; when he discovered shagreen in 1898 he also followed Arts and Crafts precedent, since, according to Henry Wilson, he was reviving 'one of the lost arts . . . the only handicraft which has escaped the notice of the other members of the Arts and Crafts Exhibition Society'. Cooper became a member of the Arts and Crafts Exhibition Society and the Art-Workers' Guild, he wrote and lectured about the crafts, and for a brief period he taught metalwork at the Birmingham Municipal School of Art. This experience not only prompted him to work in metal, it also introduced him to Arts and Crafts politics – the manoeuvring for power and position to further the Craft Crusade.

Cooper was preoccupied with craft and idealism, however, rather than with position and politics. His days were ordered and orderly, devoted to work, reading, correspondence, contemplation and writing, and such free time as he had was dedicated to drawing and painting. Throughout his life, Cooper was concerned with meaning; like his Art Worker contemporaries he needed to understand the nature of the materials he was working with and he was also obsessed with their psychic and symbolic properties. Dr Kuzmanović's account of Cooper's personal interpretations of myth, symbols and symbolism confront the complexities of interpretative connoisseurship, and acknowledge the interaction between substance, style and interpretation.

Cooper shared his values as well as his approach to the creative process with his Art Worker colleagues. This monograph, therefore, celebrates a designer who produced a wide range of significant work, and at the same time provides a 'case study' of Arts and Crafts idealism in action. John Paul Cooper was a survivor. He was exhibiting with the Arts and Crafts Exhibition Society throughout the 1920s, and while his contemporaries were accused of producing 'worn out motives', Cooper's work was always singled out for praise. 'In silver alone,' wrote one critic, 'Mr Cooper is about the only English craftsman who consistently rivals the Danes – chiefly because, like them, he appears to think in silver.'

Dr Kuzmanović's close analysis of Cooper's design and craftsmanship demonstrates his professionalism. He was a dedicated craftsman, and at the same time he was sensitive to change. He was never satisfied with 'worn out motives'; those involved in the handicrafts, he maintained, 'should learn what they can do well, improve their methods & invent new ones'. It is the capacity to invent and re-invent that distinguishes Cooper. Dr Kuzmanović has done well to rediscover him and to reassess his achievements; by doing so she has advanced the historian's understanding of Arts and Crafts attitudes, and she has also thrown new light on developments within the craft movement in the 1920s and 1930s.

Gillian Naylor
2 October 1998

ACKNOWLEDGEMENTS

The magnitude of this project has necessitated the assistance and cooperation of countless scholars and colleagues. Among these many collaborators, however, a number of individuals deserve special mention.

My initial thanks go to Shirley Bury, former Keeper of Metalwork at the Victoria and Albert Museum, who first suggested Cooper as a possible subject, and to Peyton Skipwith of The Fine Art Society, who introduced me to Cooper's family and tirelessly answered my numerous questions and requests. The generosity and gracious cooperation of the Cooper family have been of pivotal importance to this project. Cooper's late daughter Ursula and her children enthusiastically supported and aided my studies of the Cooper archive and the publication of this book.

Among the faculty of the University of Michigan, where my research originated, I would particularly like to thank Marvin Eisenberg for his endless encouragement of my studies in the decorative arts and Gene Pijanowski for his metalsmithing expertise. I am also deeply grateful to Gillian Naylor of the Royal College of Art for sharing her expansive knowledge of the Arts and Crafts Movement and for writing such an excellent foreword to the book.

Likewise, for sharing their scholarship of late nineteenth-century and twentieth-century English history and art, I am indebted to: Martin Eidelberg, Mary Greensted, Charlotte Gere, William Hennessey, Halina Graham, Geoffrey Munn, John Swift, Michael Whiteway, and Glennys Wild. I am also grateful for assistance given by the staffs of the National Archive of Art and Design, the British Library, the Goldsmiths' Company, National Art Library, Royal College of Art, and the Royal Institute of British Architects.

The following individuals have generously cooperated in giving me access to and information about various Cooper pieces: Tracey Albainy and Peter Barnet of The Detroit Institute of Arts; David Alexander of St Paul's Church, Covent Garden; Vincent Ashwin of St James's and St Basil's Church, Fenham; Caroline Bacon of the Cecil Higgins Art Gallery, Bedford; David Beasley and Malcolm Barrett of The Worshipful Company of Goldsmiths, London; Sheila Beber of St Mary's Cathedral, Edinburgh; Peter Berry and Robert Howes of St Philip's Cathedral, Birmingham; Derek Charnock and Martin Day of St John the Baptist's Church, Whitwick; Colin Corke and Marjorie Horwood of St Mary's Church, Tatsfield; John Darrall of Oakham School, Rutland; Dame Eanswith of Stanbrook Abbey, Worcester; Richard Edgcumbe of the Victoria and Albert Museum, London; Robin Emmerson and Julian Treuherz of the National Museums and Galleries on Merseyside; Godfrey Evans of the

Royal Museum of Scotland, Edinburgh; David Formby of Lacock Abbey, Wiltshire; Elaine Grieg of the Huntly House Museum, Edinburgh; Robert Hamilton and Christopher Cocksworth of the Royal Holloway, University of London, Egham; John Hardacre and Pat Mather of Winchester Cathedral; Nicholas Harris; Neil Harvey and Anita Gross of The Wolfsonian, Miami Beach; Tim Hatwell of St Peter's and St Paul's Church, Cudham; Ralph Holt of Hancocks & Co., London; John Humphries of All Saints' Church, Kings Cliffe; Peter Jeffs of Aesthetics, London; John Jesse; Janet Johnstone of the Cheltenham Ladies' College; Andrew Lambert of Trinity College, Cambridge; Allison Ledes and Lynya Floyd of The Magazine Antiques, New York; Sally Leeson of St Andrew's Church, Limpsfield Chart; David Macey and Paul Lockyes of Canterbury Cathedral; Jane May of Leicester City Museums Service; I.H. McCausland of the Royal Green Jackets, Winchester; Arnold Naylor of the Royal Aeronautical Society, London; Sonya and David Newell-Smith of Tadema Gallery, London; Barbara Penman and Paul Plumley of St Paul's Church, Four Elms, Kent; Julia Poole of the Fitzwilliam Museum, Cambridge; Sandra Pragnell and Jonathan French of St John Divine, Richmond; Ruth and Joseph Sataloff; Deborah Shinn and Todd Olson of the Cooper-Hewitt National Design Museum, New York; Tony Stone of June and Tony Stone Fine Antique Boxes, London; Charles Truman and Michael Wiggins of Asprey, London; Brian Watchorn of Pembroke College, Cambridge; Margaret Weare of the Ellen Terry Memorial Museum, Tenterden; and John Witheridge of Eton College, Windsor.

I am indebted to Alan Crawford for his attentive reading of my typescript and for making several thoughtful suggestions for improvement that were subsequently incorporated into the book. My gratitude also extends to the capable staff of Sutton Publishing: Peter Clifford and Jaqueline Mitchell, who first recognized the project's potential, and Sarah Moore, who deftly and copiously edited my text. The successful completion of this project was further aided by Joan Susskind's skilful translation of my manuscript into typed copy and by Robert Cotton's photographic talent.

Finally, my thanks go to Joseph Chiarello, whose faith, humour and compassion gave me stamina; and to my parents, whose life-long support has at last attained a small degree of fulfilment.

INTRODUCTION

Metal work and jewellery in the past were always looked upon as holding a peculiar intermediate position between the Fine and Industrial Arts. The fine arts were those primarily occupied with the expression of ideas, the industrial arts had for their primary object utility, but the expression of ideas was still considered of importance, it was that which gave them their humanizing influence. The Arts and Crafts movement was perhaps above all things a humanizing movement on the part of artists to give back to the handicrafts the humanitarian aspect which they had lost.

John Paul Cooper (1869–1933)[1]

Great Britain was not only the first country to become industrialized but also the first to query the consequences of industrialization.[2] One of the creative responses to this self-analysis was the Arts and Crafts Movement which gave British decorative arts and design theory unprecedented international prestige at the end of the nineteenth century. Concurrent with this reaction against industrialism were numerous attempts by British government officials to improve the aesthetic quality of 'art-manufactures', that is, trade-produced, decorative objects. According to *The Art Journal*, the impetus for this reform was commercial and market oriented:

. . . while the mechanical skill which had raised the producing capabilities of Britain to a height unexampled in the world's history, was appreciated and rewarded, the skill which would have made production more beautiful and more valuable had sunk under neglect as to have become a thing all but forgotten, if not a long lost source of wealth. . . . The Art-knowledge of France, combined with its growing powers of production, began to threaten the undisputed superiority of England in the world's market.[3]

Throughout the second half of the nineteenth century, similar British periodicals acknowledged French superiority in the artistic design of art-manufactures and attributed this to the French system of art education, which stressed practical training. Even in 1893, while reviewing the Chicago international exhibition, *The Art Journal* concluded that the French commercial decorative objects were still aesthetically far superior to those of any other European country.[4]

In fact, from the moment of its foundation in 1839, *The Art Journal* was an early, self-appointed campaigner for artistic reform in the decorative design of manufactured goods. However, its conservative outlook inclined it to always press for reform within established governmental institutions rather than to support radical action as subsequently proposed by the Arts and Crafts movement:

> It was in the crisis of the industrial Art-History of England that the *Art Journal* launched forth to do battle on behalf of the dispirited and sinking cause; and, in the national elevation of industrial Art, this Journal has, from then until now, been a powerful and conspicuous agent . . . the *Art Journal* seized the great truth, and raised it as an ensign for the nation – that beauty is cheaper than ugliness, that knowledge of Art is essential to successful industry, and that, so applied, it not only bears a high commercial value, but diffuses a reforming and elevating influence throughout the masses of population.[5]

A House of Commons Select Committee was appointed in 1835 'to inquire into the best means of extending a knowledge of the Arts and Principles of Design among the people (especially the manufacturing population) of the country'.[6] Its findings reported that 'the Arts had received little encouragement in this country', that there was a 'great want of instruction in design among our industrial population', and that 'for merely economical reasons, it equally imports us to encourage Art in its loftier attributes, since it is admitted that the cultivation of the more exalted branches of design tends to advance the humblest pursuits of industry, while the connection of Art with manufacture has often developed the genius of the greatest masters in design'.[7] In 1837, the fear of market loss and the findings of this committee resulted in the establishment of the first British School of Design at Somerset House in London, later renamed the Royal College of Art.

The influence of this government education programme on the art industry was to be judged at the first international exhibition. Held in London during 1851, it was viewed by its organizers as a 'gathering together of the results of that Art-education and Art-agitation, which had been progressing during the previous twenty years . . . a means of allowing a national stock-taking in Art-industries'.[8] Discouragingly, the entire 1851 Crystal Palace exhibition:

> . . . as with one voice of overwhelming impressiveness, demonstrated the extraordinary fact that the great mass of producers throughout the world . . . were profoundly ignorant of the true character and value of Art, and of the relation which Art is competent to bear, and is ever ready and desirous to bear, to Manufacture.[9]

However, more encouragingly, the exhibition also served to place firmly the 'subjects of Art, Art industry, and Art education into the [public] debating arena'.[10] In reply to a report compiled by Lord Canning concerning the activities of the 1851 exhibition juries, Prince Albert stated: 'There is no direction its [the 1851 exhibition's] effects will be more sensibly and immediately perceived than in the improvement which it may be expected to produce in taste, and in the impulse it has given to the arts of design.'[11]

By 1852, it was obvious that the government's schools of design, now established in all the major industrial cities of Britain, had failed to bring about any perceptible improvement in the design of art-manufactures. As a result, the management of the schools was reorganized under Henry Cole (1802–82), a tireless bureaucrat dedicated to improving industrial design. Cole supported a practical alliance between the fine artist and the manufacturer based on the design principle of functionalism: the fitness of form and decoration to the function of an object. Under Cole's management, the London School of Design was reorganized and moved to South Kensington, the new location giving its name to the government's network of design schools which henceforth became known as the South Kensington system. But Cole's attempts at industrial reform through design education likewise proved futile. By 1884, the condemnation of the South Kensington system had received official sanction:

> The Report of the Royal Commission on Technical Education confirms the opinions of those who have not hesitated to pronounce as unsatisfactory in its results, the system of Art teaching, as applied to industries of this kingdom, which has been pursued by South Kensington authorities during the past thirty years.[12]

In attempting to produce students of immediate use to industry, the South Kensington schools provided a strictly vocational form of education which endeavoured to rationalize and categorize design theory. The artist Owen Jones (1809–74) was one of the most influential figures in the formation of the decorative theories promoted by Cole's schools of design that advocated a flat, geometrized ornament and restrained, sober forms dictated by an object's utility. Even Lewis F. Day (1845–1910), a founding activist of the Arts and Crafts Exhibition Society, paid tribute to Jones:

> No man did more than he towards clearing the ground for us, and so making possible the new departures which we have made since his time. The influence of Ruskin, and of Pugin before him, counts also for something, but I attribute even more weight to the teaching of Owen Jones, because he appealed to and touched the manufacturers, whom he somehow succeeded in persuading to believe in him, much to the improvement of their productions.[13]

The students at the South Kensington schools learned rigidly defined ornamental principles and studied historic precedent by slavish copy drawing. In other words, artistic creativity and individuality were discouraged, and students received no practical training in the application of these abstract theories: '. . . the opinion is general that the teaching of the schools is of no use beyond the elementary stages of drawing; and that as regards the application of Art to material, and to general trade purposes the schools are utterly inefficient.'[14] This lack of practical application of design theory to actual materials and to the unique requirements of specific industries doomed Cole's schools to remain largely ineffectual in producing designers capable of reforming British art-manufactures.

Concurrent with this trend to improve industrial goods, there evolved a contrasting movement that rejected, in principle, any alliance between the fine arts and manufacture. Based on the theoretical writings of John Ruskin (1819–1900), this opposing viewpoint questioned the very morality of the machine and the value of an industrialized society. It saw artistic creativity and industrial production as two mutually exclusive endeavours, incapable of joining forces to produce aesthetically pleasing objects. Ruskin's rejection of the machine, his praise of manual labour – stressing individual creativity – and his belief in the equal importance of both the fine and decorative arts formed the theoretical basis for the Arts and Crafts Movement.

Professor Oscar Lovell Triggs (1865–1930), a vocal proponent of the Arts and Crafts Movement in Chicago, pointed out that it was the essayist Thomas Carlyle (1795–1881) who first aroused Ruskin's interest in contemporary social issues and who inspired Ruskin to a condemnation of the machine-oriented, capitalist society of Victorian England.[15] A.W.N. Pugin (1812–52) was another Ruskin precursor whose linkage of morality with aesthetic quality and preference for medieval art and society likewise influenced Ruskin's thinking. It was under Pugin's influence that the Gothic revival school of architects evolved, and the offices of such architects as Edmund Street (1824–81) became the cradle of so many future Arts and Crafts artists, including William Morris, (1834–96), Philip Webb (1831–1915), J.D. Sedding (1838–91), and Richard Norman Shaw (1831–1912). These architects, in turn, provided the nursery for the second generation of craft artists, including Henry Wilson (1864–1934), and William Lethaby (1857–1931), as well as John Paul Cooper.

John Ruskin's chapter on 'The Nature of Gothic', published in the second volume of *The Stones of Venice* (1853), provides one of the most complete disclosures of his views about design. Here, Ruskin emphasized nature as the only true source of artistic inspiration, the need of the designer to master the practical techniques and understand the specific capabilities of his materials, and the morality of such design, all characteristics he associated with Gothic art. This chapter had a seminal influence on William Morris. Describing its text, Morris stated:

> To my mind . . . it is one of the most important things written by the author, & in future days will be considered as one of the very few necessary and inevitable utterances of the century . . . it seemed to point out a new road on which the world should travel . . . [the only] way out of the folly and degradation of Civilization. For the lesson which Ruskin here teaches us is that art is the expression of man's pleasure in labour; that it is possible for man to rejoice in his work.[16]

Inspired by his teachings, Morris proceeded to give practical application to Ruskin's theories. As Morris's contemporaries were quick to point out, he

> was but a pupil of Ruskin, for he originated almost nothing in point of theory, the socialism with which he identified himself being but the

socialism of Ruskin's. . . . Of narrower range than Ruskin, but more intensive in his own direction, he [Morris] gave his life to the determination of the relation between art and labour, and made himself, therefore, the chief exponent of the idea of the arts and crafts. Ruskin theorized; Morris demonstrated: henceforth the problem of other workers is that of extension and inclusion.[17]

As Ruskin's and Morris's influence expanded during the second half of the nineteenth century, their ideas served to undermine the attempts of Cole and his followers to reconcile art with industry in order to raise the quality of trade goods. The emphasis of Morris and his supporters on the manual production of decorative objects in which the idiosyncrasies of handwork contributed to overall aesthetic success was fundamentally incompatible with machine-executed work. Instead of actively trying to reform design within established commercial factories, such artists founded independent firms, guilds, and studios to produce handwork whose execution and aesthetic criteria neglected the artistic possibilities of the machine. Morris, in 1861, was the first to establish such a firm for the designing and execution of interior furnishings. As a loose collaborative of similar-minded artists who had helped Morris furnish and decorate his Red House in Bexleyheath, Kent, the group included painters Dante Gabriel Rossetti (1828–82) and Edward Burne-Jones (1833–98), and the architect Philip Webb. A circular advertising the firm stated:

> The growth of Decorative Art in this country, owing to the efforts of English Architects, has now reached a point at which it seems desirable that Artists of reputation should devote their time to it. . . . These Artists, having for many years been deeply attached to the study of Decorative Arts of all times and countries, have felt more than most people the want of some one place they could either obtain or get produced work of genuine and beautiful character. They have therefore now established themselves as a firm.[18]

This prospectus recognized the decorative arts as worthy of the highest artistic attention, equal to that due to painting and architecture. According to the prevailing attitude of the Royal Academy and in the teaching methods of the South Kensington system, the decorative arts were considered of lesser aesthetic importance than the fine arts. They were considered less artistically demanding than painting and therefore ideally suited to practitioners of inferior artistic talent. The artistic importance given by Morris's circle to the decorative arts stressed the actual manual participation by the designer in the execution of his work. Consequently, in order to create a design deserving and capable of artistic execution, the designer had to be familiar with the various technical processes and inherent properties of his materials, a concept ignored by the training given at the government-sponsored schools of design.

Morris, himself, spent much time personally mastering various craft techniques, particularly those related to the dyeing and weaving of textiles. In 1875, he wrote to Mrs Burne-Jones:

I shall be glad enough to get back to the dye-house at Leek tomorrow. I daresay you will notice how bad my writing is; my hand is so shaky with doing journey-man's work the last few days: delightful work, hard for the body and easy for the mind. . . . Leek, Monday. . . . I have been dyeing in her [the blue vat] all the afternoon, and my hands are a woeful spectacle in consequence. . . . I lost my temper in the dye-house for the first time this afternoon . . . I wish I hadn't been such a fool; perhaps they will turn me out to-morrow morning, or put me in the blue-vat.[19]

With the formation of the Art-Workers' Guild in 1884, the teachings of Ruskin and Morris began to be institutionalized. This club-like organization, founded by a young group of architectural pupils and assistants, was similarly interested in raising the quality of decorative design based on a respect for hand craftsmanship and for the mutual importance of the fine, architectural, and decorative arts. According to its second annual report, the 'Guild was formed for the purpose of bringing into closer union all classes of Art Workmen, and for the furtherance of practical knowledge of various crafts'.[20] With 'Art is Unity' as its motto, the Guild became the theoretical nucleus of the Arts and Crafts movement. Its meetings provided an open forum for the exchange of information, ideas, and opinions between its elected members who were regarded as 'craftsmen in Architecture, Painting, Sculpture, and the kindred Arts'.[21] Though the Guild did not actively publicize its views, the scholastic appointments of its members dispersed the Arts and Crafts creed among the emerging generation of decorative artists.

The Arts and Crafts Exhibition Society was founded in 1888 as the exhibiting arm of the Art-Workers' Guild. It evolved from an unsuccessful scheme for a national exhibition which was to challenge the Royal Academy's élitism and disinterest in the decorative arts. Remarkably, Morris took no active part in the formation of either the Art-Workers' Guild or the Arts and Crafts Exhibition Society. In fact, he is recorded as having distinct misgivings about both ventures.[22] Though both organizations acknowledged him as their spiritual leader and gave him honorary memberships, Morris had by then decided that in order to reform art, one had first to reform society politically. Only a socialist society could provide an environment condusive to the aesthetic improvement of the decorative arts. Ruskin preached much the same ideology.

The aims of the new Arts and Crafts Exhibition Society were summarized by one of its founding members, Lewis F. Day:

To assert the possibilities of Art in design, applied even to the least pretentious purpose, and in every kind of handicraft; to protest against the absolute subjection of Art in its applied form to the interests of that extravagant waste of human energy which is called economic production; to claim for the artist or handicraftsman, whose identity it has been the rule to hide, and whose artistic impulse it has been custom to curb . . . some recognition and some measure of appreciation.[23]

The theoretical basis for the Society, which gave its name to the entire artistic movement dedicated to its goals, was published in the preface to the catalogue of its first exhibition:

> The root and basis of all Art lies in the handicrafts. If there is no room or chance of recognition for really artistic power and feeling in design and craftsmanship – if Art is not recognized in the humblest object and material, and felt to be as valuable in its own way as the more highly rewarded pictorial skill – the arts cannot be in sound condition; and if artists cease to be found among the crafts there is a great danger that they will vanish from the arts also, and become manufacturers and salesmen instead.[24]

The Society's exhibits, accompanied by lectures and practical demonstrations, sought to raise the standard of decorative arts by educating the public and by providing useful models and technical information for interested artists to emulate. Between 1888 and 1899 these exhibitions attracted great public and critical interest. They received wide international acclaim for their progressive emphasis on technique, material, and utility which joined together to produce a new, simpler,

Figure 2. Page from Cooper's Stockbook I showing objects completed in 1907. Item no. 373 is illustrated in Figure 114. Cooper Family Archives.

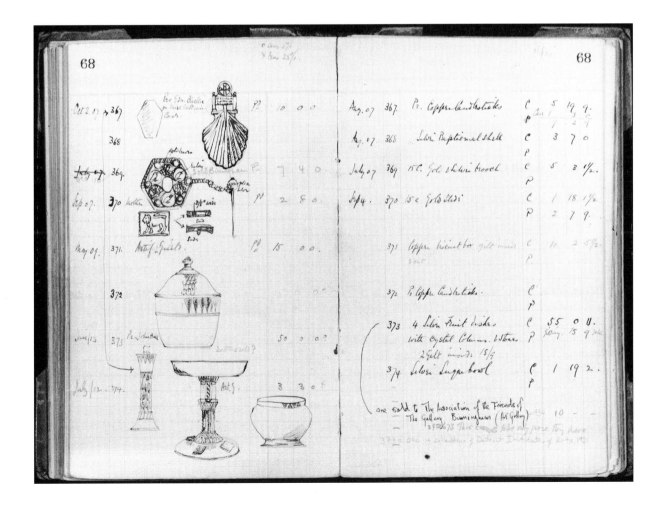

more functionally oriented, nature-inspired style in contrast to the ponderous, complex, ornament-laden historicizing style of contemporary art-manufactures.

As stated earlier, the influence of the Arts and Crafts principles was most strongly felt in British art education. During the 1880s and 1890s, members of the Art-Workers' Guild began accepting appointments at various South Kensington schools. For example, in 1890 Lewis Day, founder and later Master of the Guild, became an examiner at the South Kensington School of Design. In 1893, Walter Crane (1845–1915), third master of the Guild and President of the Arts and Crafts Exhibition Society, became Director of Design at the Manchester School of Art; in 1898 he was appointed Principal of the Royal College of Art. William Lethaby, one of the dominant founders of the Art-Workers' Guild, became joint director of the London County Council's newly formed Central School of Arts and Crafts in 1896; in 1900 he was made sole Principal there and became the first professor of ornament and design at the Royal College of Art. These educators introduced practical training into their classrooms and acquainted students with technical processes and materials. However, this technical knowledge was now applied to the execution of hand-crafted objects rather than to industrial design, the original aim for establishing such schools.

It was not until the 1910s that prominent designers once again focused serious attention on machine-made wares. With the foundation of such organizations as the Design and Industries Association in 1915 and with the renewed threat of foreign dominance in British markets – this time by Germany instead of France – British artistic interests once again turned to the improvement of industrial design. As a result, institutions like the Art-Workers' Guild and the Arts and Crafts Exhibition Society gradually declined in popularity and social relevance, no longer spearheading the reform of decorative design. A detailed discussion of the effects that this renewed concern for industrial design had on the Arts and Crafts movement appears in Chapter Three.

However, in 1888 when John Paul Cooper arrived in London, the Arts and Crafts Movement was approaching the height of its popularity and influence. As a young architectural student, Cooper fell under the spell of what was then considered the most progressive and innovative school of artistic thought not only in Britain but also in Europe and America. Cooper was apprenticed to J.D. Sedding, second master of the Art-Workers' Guild and founding member of the Arts and Crafts Exhibition Society, and his artistic development was inevitably influenced by the principles of this Movement: the hand manufacture of objects whose design reflected their materials and uses, and relied on nature for decorative inspiration. This craft ethic shaped both Cooper's artistic judgements and executed work.

In common with other craft artists mentioned earlier, Cooper came from an affluent, non-artistic family, and his interest in the decorative arts evolved while he was training to become an architect. This resemblance to contemporary artists combined with the immense wealth of Cooper's extant personal papers and documents make him an ideal subject for a case study concerning the training, aesthetic outlook, and physical achievements of second-generation Arts and Crafts artists. A detailed study of his career

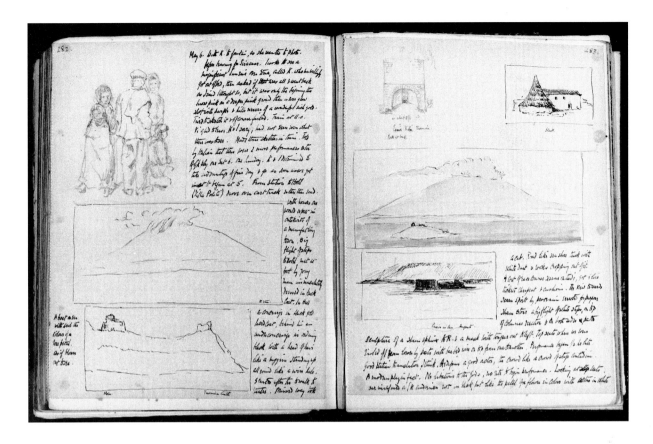

is justified not only by the availability of factual material, but also by the aesthetic quality of Cooper's objects. His executed works in gesso, mother-of-pearl, shagreen and metal reveal a high level of artistic achievement; their careful and subtle designs give even his most utilitarian objects a sense of creative expression and artistic importance.

Figure 3. Page from Cooper's Journal II describing a trip he took to Sicily in 1922. Cooper Family Archives.

ARCHIVAL SOURCES

The main body of the book, detailing Cooper's career and stylistic development, is based on archival material never before examined. Though Cooper is known and admired by British art scholars, their information concerning his career and work has hitherto been fragmentary and often incorrect. His personal papers have not been thoroughly studied nor has there been a comprehensive analysis of his work in gesso, mother-of-pearl, shagreen, or metal.[25]

To assure maximum factual accuracy, my research has focused on Cooper's extant personal papers and documents held by Cooper's surviving family. This material contains four groups of the most important documents concerning Cooper's career: his stockbooks, journals, costing books and exhibition/approval books. The three volumes of stockbooks, which assign a number to each completed object, carefully record the appearance, completion dates, and sales information of each object Cooper executed between 1899 and 1933 (Figure 2). The five volumes of

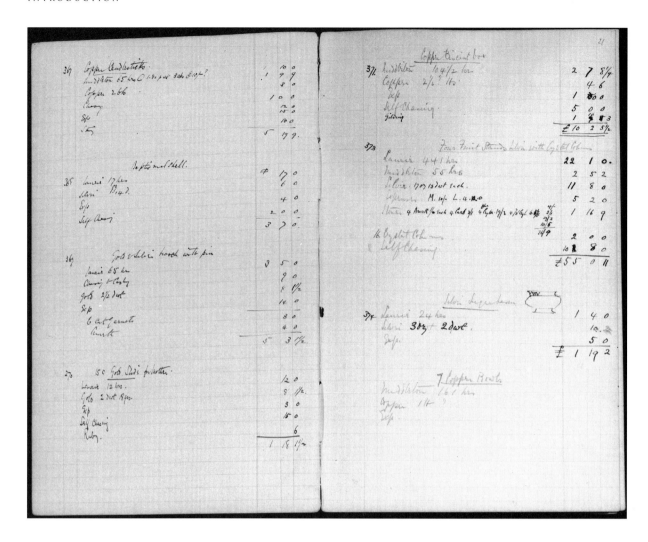

Figure 4. Page from Cooper's Costing Book II showing the expenses for making item no. 373 illustrated in Figure 114. Cooper Family Archives.

journals contain actual and copied pages from Cooper's contemporary diaries and holiday notebooks, along with reminiscences of his childhood and early artistic career (Figure 3). The four volumes of costing books supplement the stockbooks by listing the exact cost of making each piece, including the materials and workmen employed to execute them (Figure 4). The three volumes of exhibition/approval books list objects Cooper sent to various exhibitions, sales galleries, and clients.

Extensive reference is made to this archival material in the notes to each chapter. The initials JPC are used to designate this material in each cited reference.

BIOGRAPHY

I think one might sum up my father's life as one of 'searching'. He always seemed to be seeking for something, whether in 'Art,' 'Religion' or 'Literature,' the three subjects that interested him most. He never seemed contented to accept things as they were, to accept the accepted without deeply delving into many books.

Francis Cooper[1]

PRE-1888

Born on 3 October 1869 into an affluent Leicester family, John Paul Cooper was the eldest of four children (Figure 5). His father, John Harris Cooper (1832–1906), was a self-made man who rose meteorically from apprentice to senior partner in a large, prosperous Leicester machine knitting company which by the 1880s carried the name Messrs Cooper, Corah and Sons (Figures 6, 8). The firm still exists today under the name of Corah Plc and is still headquartered at St Margaret's Works in Leicester. In the 1920s, the firm began supplying knitted goods to Marks & Spencer, Corah's own St Margaret trademark evolving into the St Michael trade name under which all of Marks & Spencer goods were sold.[2]

Paul's mother, Fanny Loder (1834–1921), was the daughter of a third-generation antiquarian bookseller whose shop in Woodbridge, Suffolk, was a gathering place for local authors to browse, read, and converse (Figure 7).[3] Fanny was John Harris's second wife. Cooper's first marriage had ended the very day of the wedding when his new bride informed him that she had only married him for his money; Cooper left her on the spot. The divorce procedure at the time was so protracted that Paul and his sister Violet (d. 1960) were born before John Harris was able to marry Fanny Loder. The law, at the time, did not legitimize children born out of wedlock no matter what the circumstance.[4]

Unlike her husband, Fanny Loder was well educated, well read, and spoke fluent French. John Paul Cooper reminisced about his contrasting parents:

With mother every excursion was an adventure. . . . With father it was cut & dried & carried out on rather a grandiose scale. We went out like an army and like an army after a hard field day returned tired in mind and body. Father seemed to be connected with business & political side of life, Mother with the artistic side & romance.[5]

Clearly, it was Fanny's literary and cultural connoisseurship that exerted the most influence on Paul:

> When [we were] small Mother used to see that we only read the best authors Scott, Dickens, Thackeray which I devoured. . . . She . . . only gave us the best books to read, keeping all trash away from us. . . . In fact, as far as she could she trained us to like the best in everything.[6]

In discussing his childhood exposure to the fine arts, Paul Cooper also included his father's marginal interest:

> Of painting and sculpture she [Cooper's mother] knew very little, & they did not come our way, except for the pictures Father collected, which were taken for granted, like the furniture. Father was interested in pictures, modern academic ones. Yearly he went to the R.A. & the Royal Institute of Water Colour Painters & came home with the catalogues well marked & notes such as 'Fine' or 'Rubbish' written on the margin.[7]

Perhaps the most effective description of the Cooper household came in later years from Paul's close friend, the stage designer Edward Gordon Craig (1872–1966):

Figure 5. John Paul Cooper, far right, with brothers, Gerald and Bernard, and sister, Violet, 1881. Cooper Family Archives.

His father was not an artist, but a manufacturer in the North of England, and in his house, hung with large, massive gilt-framed masterpieces by some R.A.'s to-day unknown (everything in the house was massive), it was strange to enter Paul's small room upstairs, and to come across the shelves laden with books on architecture, early and late editions of Ruskin, and all sorts of French, Italian, and Spanish books . . . and looking at his walls, I was not disappointed with myself, to feel that I knew someone who was studying the water-colours of John Frederick Lewis, Turner and Ruskin and others – and not only studying, but possessing himself of these things.[8]

As a result of his early exposure to literature, initiated by his mother, reading was to absorb much of Paul's time throughout his life. In fact, Cooper initially wanted to become a professional writer. His father's strong disapproval and

Figure 6. John Harris Cooper, wealthy industrialist and Paul Cooper's father, 1890s. Cooper Family Archives.

Figure 7. Fanny Loder Cooper, Paul Cooper's mother, whose artistic leanings had a strong influence on his early development, 1890s. Cooper Family Archives.

disappointment at Paul's refusal to join the family business, pushed him into the more reputable profession of architecture: 'I had started architecture, which I did not because I liked it, for I wanted to be a writer, but because I did not know of any other profession except literature that I preferred.'[9] More precisely, Cooper's acquaintance with architecture was initiated by the Leicester architect William Jackson. An old friend of Cooper's father's, Jackson had designed St Margaret's Works in 1865 and all its subsequent additions until his death in 1894.[10] The architect also shared Paul's interest in literature: 'He [Jackson] used to send Mother books at times . . . & it was through him that I went in for architecture, he gave me a copy of Ruskin's 'Stones of Venice,' when I started architecture.'[11] Paul's father never understood his son's love for books and learning and even threatened to cut off his allowance if he continued to spend so much money on books instead of buying much-needed clothes (Figure 9).[12]

Cooper's fervent interest in literature was also the initial impetus for his early friendships with Edward Gordon Craig, architect Henry Wilson, and furniture designer Ernest Gimson (1864–1919). Like Cooper, Gimson came from Leicester and his father, a wealthy iron-founder, had hoped that Gimson would enter the family business. Gimson, however, decided to become an architect and joined J.D. Sedding's office, where he met Cooper.

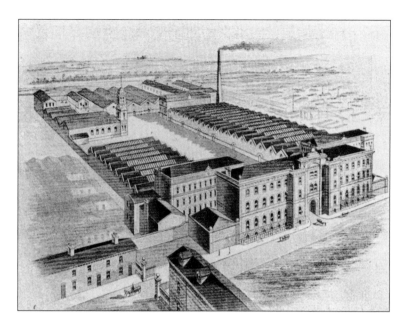

Figure 8. Drawing of St Margaret's Works, Leicester, where Paul Cooper's father was senior partner, 1892. Cooper Family Archives.

Cooper's attempts at literary prose occasionally emerge in his own journals. For example, in describing a scene near Menton, France, Cooper wrote: 'As I approached the Italian frontier I saw the sentinel standing out against the gathering light in the East like a huge bird with its wings folded . . . the sun rose over the promontory [*sic*] in front. A lovely golden ball, & as I looked it grew larger & fuller, & coats seemed to peel off it every moment leaving it brighter.'[13] In these same journals, Cooper recounted his London birth and early history: 'I was born a Cockney, within the sound of the Bow Bells, but was taken almost immediately to Bedford & then within about 6 months to Rotherby.'[14]

In Rotherby, a hamlet to the northeast of Leicester, the Cooper family settled into the old Manor House, which years later Paul described with typical Arts and Crafts scornful disgust: 'Parts of the house were old, but a new gabled front had been added of Early Victorian hideosity' (Figure 10).[15] Despite its architectural shortcomings, the house's rose garden and idyllic setting in the middle of meadows and fields had a profound naturalistic impact on Cooper. One of his 'earliest recollections is of being in a garden, on a summer morning with flowers in bloom & bees humming, and everything looking as if transformed, as if I suddenly found myself in fairyland'.[16]

At the age of eight, being weak and thin, Cooper was sent to a seaside school in Eastbourne for the sake of his health. The school was run by two sisters named Shoesmith. In retrospect, Paul characterized the teaching there as admirable: 'I was started on Latin grammar and received a good grounding.'[17] His summers were also spent at various English and French seaside resorts with the rest of the Cooper family, who now lived at Evington Hall, an Italianate villa on the eastern outskirts of Leicester (Plate 1).

In 1880 he was sent to Old Hall School, Wellington, Shropshire (Figure 11).[18] Though Cooper wrote, 'I wasted my time the 5 yrs. I was there', the school's headmaster, Dr Cranage, had a lasting influence on him.[19] It was at this school that Cooper was allowed to develop his interest in nature. He and another young budding ornithologist spent much of their free time in nearby fields watching for birds and searching for their nests.[20] One term, Dr Cranage offered a prize for the best collection of wildflowers: Paul entered the botany competition, diligently pressing specimens in hope of winning the contest.[21] To encourage Cooper's interest further, in 1883 the headmaster gave him a book entitled *Country Walks of a Naturalist With His Children*, which described various country flora and fauna.[22] This book remains among Cooper's personal effects. When the boy left the school, Dr Cranage presented Cooper with a pocket microscope which he also kept his entire life.[23]

It was while he was at this Shropshire school that Cooper first mentioned learning to draw from Vere Foster drawing exercise books (Figure 12). However, he found the drawing books dull and delighted when he 'was allowed to copy a Landseer'.[24] Dr Cranage examined the drawing books at the end of the term: 'we went up to his study in turn & he drew over the work with a very black pencil'.[25] In addition, Cooper briefly recalled in his journals that it was at school that he was taught china painting by a visiting French instructor.

While he was at the Wellington school Cooper began his first diary, which described holidays spent with his family in London.[26] The journal records visits in 1883 and 1884 to Kew Gardens, South Kensington Museum (now the Victoria and Albert Museum), the Natural History Museum, the British Museum, the National Gallery, and to the Lyceum Theatre to see Henry Irving and Ellen Terry in *Much Ado About Nothing*. Such itineraries were organized by his mother to educate her children in standards of taste and culture.

In September 1885, Cooper was transferred to Bradfield College in Berkshire.[27] Preferring to learn German to Greek and Latin, Cooper was dismayed when he was put into the classical rather than modern studies

Figure 9. Self-portrait depicting Cooper's uncut hair, frayed trousers and interest in books, 1890s. Cooper Family Archives.

Figure 10. Manor House, Rotherby, Leicestershire, where the Cooper family lived during the 1870s. Cooper Family Archives.

programme at the school.[28] Though his studies were hard and much time had to be devoted to compulsory cricket and football, Cooper still managed to read avidly, mainly during study breaks when the other boys amused themselves with sports.[29] His diaries and letters record the authors he was reading: Brontës, Shakespeare, Milton, Macaulay, and Trollope.[30] It was also now that Cooper began reading about architecture: unfortunately, he never recorded the authors or titles of these architectural books.[31]

For Cooper, the most significant event that occurred during his Bradfield days was his acquaintance and subsequent friendship with Edward Gordon Craig. According to Craig, this happened in 1887, two days before the end of term:[32] 'It was on the cricket field at Bradfield College that I first met J. Paul Cooper, studying English classics in a 4½ *d* edition published by Cassell's. I happened to be doing the same.'[33] Their mutual preference for reading over sports, a shared enthusiasm for architecture, and Cooper's fascination with Craig's famous actress mother, Ellen Terry (1847–1928), cemented their life-long friendship.[34] Craig characterized their relationship as firm and 'ever memorable', one of the few important events that happened to him at Bradfield.[35] In December 1887, Cooper left Bradfield for London. Craig, on the other hand, did not return to London until 1889 when he began acting with Ellen Terry and Henry Irving (1838–1905) at the London Lyceum Theatre. It was there that Cooper saw Craig in *The Dead Heart*, sent a note backstage, and thereby renewed their friendship.

Between 1889 and 1893, Cooper and Craig spent much time together exploring the artistic sights of the city, including James Abbott McNeill Whistler's Peacock Room (1876–7) in F.R. Leyland's house, and the countryside surrounding London (Figure 13). In addition, Cooper often visited Terry's Barkston Gardens home where he was introduced to her fashionable circle of friends, including the greatest English actor of the time, Henry Irving. Cooper began frequenting the Lyceum Theatre on opening nights and was allowed to watch the performance from behind the stage, seated on a chair in the stage wings with a peephole on to the audience. In his journals, Cooper described himself and Craig as young rebels, 'violently opposed to all things Academical, & generally in a stage of revolt, not seeing any good in 'suffering fools gladly'.[36]

LONDON: 1888–1900

In January 1888, Cooper recorded his address as 60 Belsize Road, South Hampstead. By April 1890, he had moved to 99 Fellows Road, South Hampstead.[37] He was receiving an allowance of £50 per year from his father and studying drawing at the Heddon Street atelier run by the architects Walter Millard (1853–1936) and Frank Baggallay (1855–1930), the only private architectural school in England at the time and a forerunner of the Architectural Association Schools.[38] Cooper remembered that the atelier 'was run, I believe, on French lines, no practical work was done there. Walter Millard was the artist, his partner a business man, who left very little impression on me. . . . I was set to copy architectural drawings, & learnt somewhat about the styles of architecture. I don't

Figure 11. Football team at Old Hall School, Wellington, Shropshire, with Cooper standing on the far right, 1884. Cooper Family Archives.

think I ever got on to design.'[39] Cooper was the only novice in the atelier where the architect Detmar Blow (1867–1939), later primarily associated with country house commissions, occasionally appeared to execute drawings.

Concurrently, Cooper enrolled in the Architectural Association's Class for the Study of Ornament and Colour Decoration, first offered in September 1887. The course consisted of studying the principles of and sketching ornamental and colour decoration, based on naturalistic models and historic design sources.[40] Cooper won first prize for his work in this class and was awarded Ruskin's *The Art of England*, which remains among his personal effects.

At the end of 1888, Cooper's father came to London to see about placing his son in Norman Shaw's architectural firm as an apprentice, no doubt on the advice of his close friend, Leicester architect William Jackson.[41] Shaw's office was full and W.R. Lethaby, his chief assistant who became one of Cooper's close friends, told Cooper's father 'the best man in London that you can send him [Paul] to, is Sedding. He's quite outside the ordinary run of architects, full of enthusiasm, very clever, . . . your son cannot do better.'[42] Shortly afterwards, Cooper and his father went to John D. Sedding's office at 447 Oxford Street, next door to the showroom of Morris & Company. Sedding looked at Cooper's drawings, executed at the Heddon Street atelier, and agreed to take him on as an apprentice for three years at a fee of £300 per year.[43]

As stated in the Introduction, J.D. Sedding was a pupil of G.E. Street. After leaving Street's office in 1863, he worked as an architect in Cornwall and Bristol before opening his own office in London. His architectural work was mainly ecclesiastical, with Holy Trinity Church, Sloane Street, London, being his best known commission. Sedding's style consisted of a free and simplified adaptation of English late Gothic forms. He also occasionally designed metalwork, embroideries, and wallpaper. In 1876 Sedding met Ruskin, who deeply influenced his ideas concerning the observation, depiction, and use of natural forms for ornamental work. Accordingly, Sedding was to state: 'For the professional stylist, the confirmed conventionalist, an hour in his garden, a stroll in the embroidered meadows, a dip into an old herbal, . . . is wholesome exercise, and will do more to revive the original instincts of a true designer than a month of sixpenny days in a stuffy museum.'[44] Sedding was Master of the Art-Workers' Guild in 1886 and 1887 and a founding member of the Arts and Crafts Exhibition Society. In 1892, Charles Rennie Mackintosh (1868–1928) chose the following statement by Sedding as a motto for Glasgow designers: 'There is hope in honest error: none in the icy perfections of the mere stylist.'[45]

The choice of Sedding's office was, in general, a happy one for Cooper, though he still had literary ambitions: 'My heart was only partly in my work. I read a great deal which Sedding did not wholly approve of, though he was himself well read. He caught me once reading a Victor Hugo & told me I was wasting my time.'[46] In the office, 'Sedding left the teaching largely to Wilson, who gave one a new outlook, but was a bad teacher. Sedding we all loved & admired, he would come in and talk for a short time I was going to say brilliantly, but it was hardly that it was more charmingly. He would come & sit on one's stool & work on one's drawing with one arm round one's shoulder.'[47]

Figure 13. Cooper sketching seated with Edward Gordon Craig looking on, Bradgate Park, 1890. Ink notations made by Craig. Cooper Family Archives.

Figure 14. Ink sketches of Cooper by Henry Wilson, on the left, and of Wilson by Cooper on the right, dated 1897. The intimacy of these renderings mirrors the closeness of their friendship. Cooper Family Archives.

In Sedding's office along with Cooper were: Henry Wilson, his chief assistant, who became one of Cooper's closest friends, initially through their mutual love of French novels (Figure 14); Arthur Grove (1870–1929), Wilson's chief assistant; Henry Finch (1869–1924); Alfred Powell (*c.* 1865–1960), who later achieved distinction as a pottery painter; and Charles Nicholson (1867–1949), apprenticed slightly after Cooper. Ernest Gimson, who had been an earlier pupil of Sedding's, came in occasionally.[48] He and Cooper also became good friends, initially through their mutual interest in poetry. Detmar Blow, whom Cooper had met at the Heddon Street atelier, also briefly worked in Sedding's office.[49] Another regular visitor was Christopher Whall (1849–1924), the stained glass artist, who executed various commissions for Sedding.[50] Describing Sedding's architectural firm, Cooper wrote: 'We called it "the office" in contradiction to all other offices. Sedding was much too original to please the other architects, & we followed him, in excess & looked upon the Academy [Royal Academy of Art], the Institute [RIBA], and The Architectural Association as composed of old fogies, without any life in them.'[51]

During their holidays, most of Sedding's office went on sketching expeditions, either in England or abroad, drawing buildings, making notes of special features, and sending illustrated letter 'reports' back to London. Cooper continued this practice of taking sketching trips and of sending illustrated letters throughout his life (Figures 15, 16). From the 1890s on, Cooper's journals mainly summarize his holidays abroad where he spent his time drawing and visiting local museums and churches. The margins of his journals are filled with quick sketches recording his observations (Figure 3). His interests in medieval art and architecture tended to govern his holiday destinations which, most often, were in either France or Italy.[52] The sites and artworks Cooper encountered during these sojourns, which lasted from a few days to a month, stimulated his imagination and often directly inspired his subsequent work. Several of his pieces exemplify such frank artistic adaptations.

During the 1890s, Wilson and Cooper spent nearly every Easter or Whitsun sketching together on the Continent. Cooper's summer holidays, while an apprentice in Sedding's office, were spent travelling and sketching in England. In addition, to further Cooper's architectural training, Sedding sent him with other members of the office's staff to measure and draw architectural sites specifically related to the firm's commissions.[53]

Aside from working in Sedding's office and taking sketching expeditions, Cooper was persuaded by Wilson in the autumn of 1889 to attend, with him, evening drawing classes at the Royal Architectural Museum, Tufton Street, Westminster. The museum was a huge repository of plaster figure and decorative ornament casts. The architectural

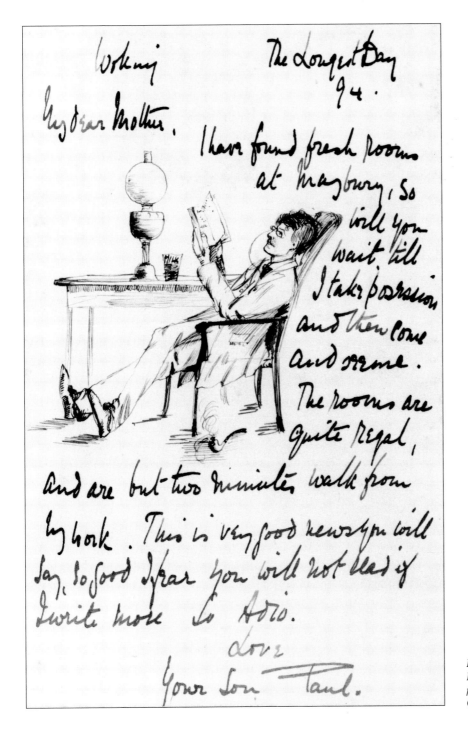

Figure 15. Illustrated letter sent by Paul to his mother, depicting his favourite pastime, dated 1894. Cooper Family Archives.

Figure 16. *Illustrated letter sent by
Paul Cooper to his son Francis,
depicting extensive letter-writing by
an exhausted Cooper,
c. 1922. Cooper Family Archives.*

historian John Summerson (1904–1992) characterized it as 'a strange
galaxy of plaster bits and pieces – a magnification of what Soane had
attempted on a smaller scale in his Museum.'[54] To these holdings,
Ruskin loaned his entire collection of Venetian as well as some French
casts. Describing the museum, Cooper wrote: 'There was a large
Entrance Hall full of plaster casts of Gothic caps [capitals] & ornament
& a lot of Greek figures and Italian heads by Donatello etc. . . . we
started work on modelling the nose and mouth of Michael Angelo's
"David".'[55]

At the museum, Cooper began by copying the plaster figures in clay.
Subsequently, he made drawings from the casts and only then was

allowed into life class (i.e. drawing from live models) where he 'worked in charcoal, in line with as fine a point as one could manage, no rubbing with the finger, & no highly-finished work, as was done at S. Kensington, & what we considered less advanced schools'.[56] The life class was taught by Frederick Brown (1851–1941), later professor at the Slade School of Art. Months spent drawing from casts was a Brown prerequisite before he would allow new students into the life class (Figure 18).

When Brown was appointed to the Slade School in 1892, Cooper and Wilson transferred to Heatherleys, an art school started in 1844 by a rebellious group of students from the government-sponsored School of Design at Somerset House. Subsequently, both Dante Gabriel Rossetti and Edward Burne-Jones worked at the school.[57] Under the school's principal, John Crompton (c. 1855–1927), Cooper began working in watercolours from draped models several nights a week.[58]

In April 1891, Sedding died suddenly of pneumonia. Cooper was devastated:

Figure 17. Wash drawing of a sculptural relief, dated 1891. Cooper Family Archives.

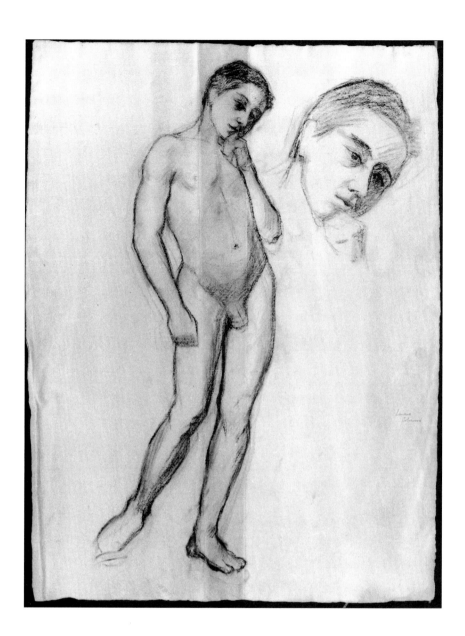

Figure 18. Charcoal drawing of Lorenzo Colarossi, who later became one of Cooper's studio workmen, done by Cooper in life class at the Royal Architecture Museum during the 1890s. Cooper Family Archives.

After Sedding's death it was a question as to whether I should continue my apprenticeship under Wilson or change it. It was decided that I should go on. Wilson took on the practice, & though one hardly noticed it at the time a great change gradually took place. It made the second great step in my life, the first being when I started Architecture. Sedding was a born architect & expected me to have no other leanings, whereas I had always wished to turn to literature. Wilson, on the contrary . . . went to a School of Art, learnt drawing as such, and worked in galleries copying old masters, & had a decided inclination to the decorative side. Architecture furnished him the means.[59]

Cooper further clarified this artistic shift: 'Shortly after Sedding's death Wilson started modelling & turned to the Craft Side.'[60] By 'modelling' Cooper also seems to be referring to his own aroused interest in

Figure 19. Drawing illustrated in
The Studio *of the first gesso box
Cooper sent to the 1893 Arts and
Crafts Society exhibition. Clipping
in Cooper Family Archives.*

plasterwork, which featured so prominently in Wilson's 1890s architectural commissions at Welbeck Abbey, Worksop, Nottinghamshire, for the Duke of Portland and at Maybury Cottage in Woking, Surrey, for the Duchess of Portland's aunt. Wilson's shift towards the crafts and Cooper's involvement with the execution of the plasterwork for certain Wilson commissions seem to have encouraged Cooper's experiments in gesso. Exhibiting for the first time, Cooper sent a gesso box (i.e. a box covered with a plaster-like low relief decoration) to the 1893 Arts and Crafts Society exhibition (Figure 19).[61]

Before joining Sedding's office, Henry Wilson had worked in the architectural firms of John Oldrid Scott (1841–1913) and John Belcher (1841–1913). However, it was in Sedding's office that Wilson's artistic talents fully flowered, enabling him to take over the practice when Sedding died.[62] During the 1890s, Wilson increasingly turned his attention to craft work, particularly metalwork. Cooper wrote that following Sedding's death, Wilson took up jewellery on Norman shaw's advice and began experimenting with wire 'on the lines that Alfred Gilbert had taken up'.[63] Furthermore, Wilson's father, who was rather skilful with his hands, began doing 'a lot of small jobs for his son',[64] executing portions of Wilson's designs. In 1897 Wilson established his own studio at 17 Vicarage Gate, which combined his architectural practice with a metal workshop. Wilson's approach to design was cross-disciplinary and architectural, displaying a highly articulate use of symbolism. In metalwork, his style combined Byzantine and late Gothic forms.

Pinpointing the actual beginning of Cooper's interest in jewellery is more difficult since the dating he gives in his journals is often confused and inaccurate. In discussing Wilson's interest in jewellery, Cooper had added: 'I had on a visit to Paris . . . been fascinated by a little gold chain with a flower design, which I had seen in a shop window, that was the first piece of jewellery I had really cared for. Perhaps that unconsciously acted as a ferment, which began to act when Wilson started that art at Vicarage Gate.'[65]

During 1892, Cooper entered the competition for the 1893 Pugin Studentship, a travelling stipend of £40 to be spent touring and sketching medieval architecture in England.[66] He had spent the summer months of 1892 travelling with Alfred Powell around England making architectural drawings to submit for the competition. At the same time, Powell was competing for the 1893 Owen Jones Studentship. Cooper did not win the Pugin, having submitted too few measured drawings along with his watercolour views (Plate 3).[67] Powell did win the Owen Jones and elected to spend his studentship travelling in Italy. Cooper wrote: 'Father was so pleased about my attempt that he gave me £50 to go with Powell.'[68]

Cooper wrote a detailed account of his trip with Powell to Italy;[69] Powell also wrote a partial account of the journey.[70] However, Cooper's account, indicative of his literary ambitions, is much more informative and entertaining. From September to December 1893, the tour took them from Ghent through Switzerland to Milan, Venice, Florence, Padua, Ravenna, Siena and Rome. Medieval architecture and art were of primary interest. Both of them spent most of their time examining, measuring and drawing such architecture and its decoration. From reading Cooper's account of the journey, it becomes immediately apparent that this was one of the most influential and formative trips he took abroad. Many of his written observations point to motifs which appear in his work after the turn of the century, such as the La Rabot fort in Ghent (Figures 20, 21). The shape and composition of the inkstand in Figure 22 closely imitates the architecture of the fort.[71] Likewise, a pendant Cooper executed in 1913 also copies the triple-tower design of the building.[72]

Most of the drawings Cooper completed during this tour were submitted for the 1894 Pugin Studentship. Even though he again failed to win – being chastised for submitting drawings of Italian rather than English medieval architecture – Cooper was awarded a Medal of Merit (Figures 23, 24).[73] Wilson congratulated Cooper on the quality of the drawings and was disappointed that he had not received a higher prize.[74]

Having completed his apprenticeship, in 1894 Cooper was appointed by Wilson as Clerk of Works at Maybury Cottage,

Figure 20. Ink sketch of La Rabot, Ghent, in Cooper's Journal III, 1893. Cooper Family Archives.

Figure 21. Postcard owned by Cooper depicting La Rabot, a fifteenth-century fortification in Ghent, c. 1893. Cooper Family Archives.

*Figure 22. Inkstand in silver,
H 9.5 × W 14 × D 12.7, 1914.
Birmingham City Museum and Art
Gallery.*

Woking, a large house being erected for Miss Graham, the aunt of the Duchess of Portland. Aside from overseeing the workmen and all the construction work, Cooper wrote, 'I did all the plasterwork',[75] indicating that he designed and actually modelled the crucial sections of the decorative plaster reliefs himself (Figure 25, Plate 2). In his diary, Cooper noted that one of the Maybury plasterers, on seeing him modelling a peacock in plaster, commented: 'Excuse my asking if you are going to be an architect . . . because if you should have to leave it you'd be able to earn a lot at that work. . . . There's not much chance of your goin' under whilst you can work like that.'[76]

During 1895, besides completing work at Maybury, Cooper was also doing plasterwork for two other Wilson commissions: Welbeck Abbey in Nottinghamshire and Walmsgate Hall, Langworth, Lincolnshire.[77] At Welbeck, where Wilson was completing a chapel and library wing started by Sedding for the 6th Duke of Portland, Cooper assisted with the plasterwork ceilings, particularly in the gallery corridor where he modelled the poppy reliefs (Figure 26).[78] At Walmsgate, now demolished, Cooper again worked on the plaster ceilings and designed the plasterwork panel over the fireplace in the sitting room of Mrs Dallas-Yorke, the mother of the Duchess of Portland (Figure 27). In addition to Welbeck and Walmsgate, Cooper also assisted Wilson with the plasterwork at St Martin's Church, Marple, Cheshire. Here Cooper modelled the swallows on the spandrels of the arches and a dove in the Lady Chapel (Figure 28).[79]

The year 1896 was a momentous one for Cooper. For the first time, he began keeping accounts of his work both in a stockbook and in a separate costing book, indicating the genesis of personal commissions and affirming his own artistic identity.[80] At the end of January, Cooper took a

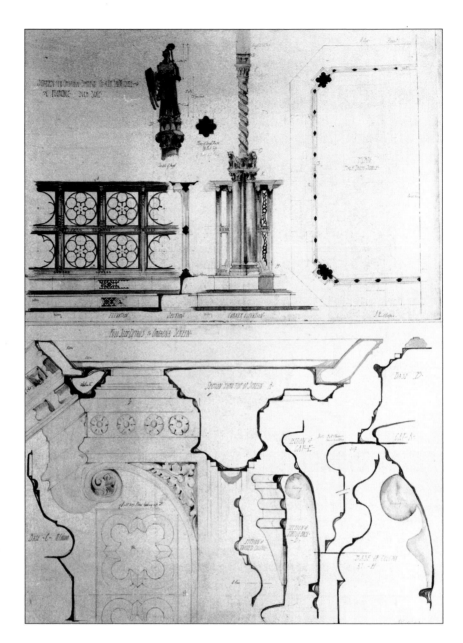

Figure 23. Architectural rendering of screen to the Andrea Orcagna Tabernacle, Or San Michele, Florence, submitted by Cooper for the 1894 Pugin Studentship. Cooper Family Archives.

studio with Finch and Wilson at 121 East Street Buildings, Manchester Square, London.[81] Here he was working on a Denoline (a premixed commercial gesso) box for the 1896 Arts and Crafts Society exhibition, and in metal. A journal entry made slightly earlier in the year on 7 January read: 'Made doorplate with heart tree, the beginning of my metalwork.'[82] During the same year, Wilson received an inscription commission for a surgeon's memorial. He gave Cooper, by then a good calligrapher, the job of chasing the lettering on to a 7.6 × 6.3 copper plate. Being one of Cooper's earliest attempts at chasing, the completed work was rather amateur and was rejected by the clients.[83] In 1896, Cooper was also working on a beaten copper altar frontal for Wilson's St Mark's Church, Brithdir, North Wales.[84] And also in 1896, Cooper received his second architectural commission – this time for alterations to Ellen Terry's cottage in Winchelsea, East Sussex.[85] By June of that year, Cooper had moved to 149 Cornwall Road, Notting Hill.[86]

In 1897, Cooper was introduced to the part-owner of *The Architectural Review*, Mr Abrams.[87] Wilson, the first editor of the magazine, was cognizant of Cooper's literary ambitions and arranged for him to write an article on J.D. Sedding for the periodical. With photographer S.E. Curtis, Cooper travelled to Cornwall and Devon to research the article. After the piece was completed, Abrams suggested a series on Sedding.[88] When Cooper finished the series, Abrams, impressed by its quality, asked him to continue writing articles for the magazine on any subject he wanted.[89] Between 1897 and 1900, Cooper published no fewer than eight pieces in *The Architectural Review* on a variety of subjects.[90] Often the articles appeared under the

Figure 24. Watercolour of font in the Cathedral Church of St Mark, Venice, submitted by Cooper for the 1894 Pugin Studentship. Cooper Family Archives.

Figure 25. Fireplace at Maybury Cottage, Woking, showing Cooper's harebell plasterwork above the mantle, c. 1894. Cooper Family Archives.

name of 'Khepr'. Cooper explained: 'I had signed my articles Khepr. Khepr being according to Gerald Massey [1828–1907] the name from which Cooper was derived. Khepr being the cycle god'.[91] By relating his name to the Egyptian god Khepri, Cooper also adopted one of the god's physical manifestations, the scarab, as his pictorial signature (Figure 29).[92] His sketches and watercolours often have a small drawn beetle instead of a written signature. Cooper also occasionally stamped his jewellery and silver work with a beetle mark.[93]

As Cooper matured, he became increasingly interested in spiritualism, mysticism, astrology, and the occult. On several recorded occasions, Cooper visited psychics and carefully noted the credibility of what they said and predicted. He even learned to chart horoscopes. Cooper also periodically attended occult lectures that explored reincarnation and cosmic consciousness. He came to believe that artistic inspiration derived from 'latent memory', a vast reserve of memories and experiences accumulated by an individual in past lives (i.e. previous existences on earth). By linking himself to one of the forms of the Egyptian sun god – the scarab specifically representing the sun god as creator at dawn – Cooper seemed subtly to affirm the cosmic inevitability of his own creative artistic powers.

At the end of 1897, Cooper moved from Cornwall Road to 16 Aubrey Walk, Kensington, no doubt to be closer to Wilson's own studio at 17 Vicarage Gate.[94] Here, Cooper not only set up his own studio but also started a small workshop.

The high point of Cooper's architectural commissions came in 1898, when he began designing the Infants' School at Whitwick, Leicestershire, eventually completed in 1903 (Plates 4, 5). He planned the office fittings and his first enlargement of St Margaret's Works in Leicester and designed six cottages in North Evington, Leicester, erected by his father as part of his charitable work.[95] Cooper's allowance from his father had by now increased to £300 per year, liberally enabling him to pursue his various artistic interests.[96]

An entry for 16 February 1898 in Cooper's Journal mentions a visit to Mrs Tuer.[97] Her husband, Andrew White Tuer (1838–1900), managing director of the Leadenhall Press and editor of the *Paper Printing Trades Journal*, regularly employed Arts and Crafts artists to illustrate his books. He was also experimenting with dyeing shagreen.[98] This was the first mention of Tuer by Cooper and indicates his burgeoning interest in shagreen. Cooper's diary entry for 23 October 1899 reads: 'About this date started practising in shagreen'.[99]

In April 1899, Cooper had already sent a shagreen stampbox to the International Society of Sculptors, Painters and Gravers exhibition.[100] He became a member of the society in 1901 and continued to exhibit regularly with it until 1920. In September of 1899 he sent four pieces of shagreen work to the sixth Arts and Crafts Society exhibition (Figure 30).[101] As this was the first time shagreen was ever exhibited with the Arts and Crafts Exhibition society, Cooper's work was considered rather innovative: 'Mr. J.P. Cooper . . . seems to have revived almost the only handicraft which has escaped the notice of the other members of the Arts and Crafts Society. The design and workmanship of these boxes are as delightful as their colour.'[102]

During the second half of the 1890s, Cooper was frequenting Wilson's studio at Vicarage Gate to execute various commissions for him.[103] These projects mainly consisted of plasterwork and metal inscriptions.[104] During these visits, Cooper must have seen the jewellery and metalwork that was being made and this inspired similar activities in his own studio. By February 1899, Cooper was employing Lorenzo Colarossi (1879–1965), a young silversmith from Wilson's studio, part-time at Aubrey Walk (Figure 18). Colarossi's execution of silver and shagreen work familiarized Cooper with the technical aspects of metalsmithing.[105] As a result, Cooper

Figure 26. Section of Cooper's plasterwork poppy relief for the gallery corridor of Welbeck Abbey, Worksop, Nottinghamshire, c. 1895. Photograph in Cooper Family Archives.

was able, for the first time to send a piece of metalwork to the 1899 Arts and Crafts Society exhibition (Figure 31).[106] On the merits of his pieces shown at the 1899 exhibition, Cooper was elected a member of the Arts and Crafts Exhibition Society in July of 1900.[107] On 26 March 1900, Cooper also completed his first recorded piece of jewellery, a silver and mother-of-pearl belt buckle (Figures 32, 33).[108]

By 1899, along with Colarossi, Cooper was also employing his future wife, May Morgan Oliver (1876–1954) (Figure 34). May, his second cousin, had excelled at drawing while still at school and had won all available art prizes. Her outstanding drawing ability is demonstrated by a few surviving portraits she sketched of her family. Determined to put her skill to use, she contacted Cooper who put her in touch with stained glass artist Christopher Whall, to whom she became an assistant in about 1896. In 1899, with Whall's permission, she began working part time in Cooper's Aubrey Walk studio.[109] Initially, she worked almost exclusively on the gesso boxes that preoccupied Cooper during this time. According to her children, May would patiently work on modelling the gesso on a box per Cooper's instructions while he was away from the studio. On his return, Cooper was never satisfied with the executed work and would have her remove all the gesso and begin again.[110]

Aside from gesso, Cooper's Costing Book I also records May working on mother-of-pearl pieces at the turn of the century. Furthermore, personal letters indicated that May managed Cooper's workmen when he was travelling and did silversmithing herself, including jewellery work. She became an accomplished silk weaver, exhibiting alongside her husband at the Arts and Crafts Society exhibitions. Their son Francis explained: 'My parents always seemed to me completely in agreement with each other in matters of taste. If one liked something, the other invariably did. . . . In the workshop my mother was known as "The Editor" (whose decision is final). If my father couldn't make up his mind . . . my mother would always be consulted.'[111]

By the end of 1900, George Romer, another Wilson workman, was also working part time in Cooper's studio.[112] George Romer was an older and more experienced workman than Colarossi. Consequently, he tended to execute Cooper's more complicated designs, particularly for jewellery.

The last significant event which

Figure 27. Design of overmantle plasterwork for the sitting-room in Walmsgate Hall, Langworth, Lincolnshire, c. 1895. The illustrated drawing is a copy by Francis Cooper after his father's original. Cooper Family Archives.

occurred at the end of the 1890s was Cooper's acquaintance with Montague Fordham (1869–1942). An entry for 23 October 1899 in Cooper's journal reads: 'Took work to Fordham who had just started Gallery. i.e. jewel box, octag. shagreen & small shag. stampboxes.'[113] This was the beginning of Cooper's long association with Fordham's Gallery and the subsequent Artificers' Guild which Fordham bought in 1903 and which eventually took over his shop.[114]

Montague Fordham's shop at 9 Maddox Street, London, sold the best contemporary decorative work executed by English Arts and Crafts artists, promoting the Arts and Crafts Movement in a fashion similar to Samuel Bing's encouragement of *Art Nouveau* in Paris. Initially, Cooper sold mainly shagreen work through Fordham, but by 1903, he was sending more metalwork than shagreen, mainly small, inexpensive items; the shop became the first commercial outlet for his work. On rare occasions, Cooper designed specific commissions for Fordham's clients. However, all Cooper-designed pieces sold by Fordham and later by the Guild were executed in Cooper's own workshops. Through both agencies, between 1899 and 1915, Cooper sold over 275 pieces of shagreen and metalwork.[115]

Figure 28. Designs for plasterwork swallows in the Lady Chapel, St Martin's Church, Marple, Cheshire, c. 1895. Cooper Family Archives.

BIRMINGHAM: 1901–6

In July 1901, Cooper was approached, on the recommendation of Henry Wilson, by the managing committee of the Birmingham art school to become a candidate for the headmastership of the Vittoria Street School for Jewellers and Silversmiths. Wilson had initially been approached to be a candidate for the post but he declined, recommending Cooper in his place: 'The only Artist who is to my knowledge suited for your post – apart from those who may already have applied – is Mr John Paul Cooper . . . His work is of great interest to me personally and I think it quite beautiful. It could do no harm to write him.'[116] Cooper accepted the invitation and went for an interview at Birmingham on 16 July, sending photographs and actual samples of his work for review. The submitted work was 'chiefly gesso & shagreen, with only one or two small things in metal'.[117]

During the interview, it became apparent that Cooper did not have enough direct metalwork experience to head such a technically oriented school. Cooper himself admitted: 'I had done very little metalwork . . . &

Figure 29. Ink self-portrait showing Cooper's beetle signature, dated January 1899. Cooper Family Archives.

had no certificates.'[118] The committee instead offered him the 'Teachership of Metalwork at the Central School at a salary of £275 per annum for attendance at 8 class meetings a week through out the Session: the appointment to date from the 1st of October, 1901.'[119]

Cooper accepted the post of metalwork and enamelling master at the Birmingham Municipal School of Art, then the most progressive member of the South Kensington educational system, on the understanding that the position would allow him enough time to continue his own private studio

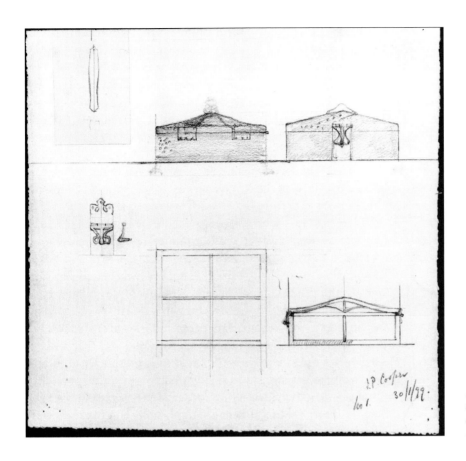

Figure 30. Cooper's earliest surviving shagreen design depicting a stampbox, dated 30 January 1899. Cooper Family Archives.

work. During the August and September before he took up his new appointment in Birmingham, Cooper 'went to Wilson's Studio at Vicarage Gate & had lessons in jewellery from his head man Innocent'.[120] He also had lessons there in metal raising from S. Cowell, another of Wilson's workmen.[121] By this date, Cooper considered himself fairly proficient in chasing: 'of chasing I knew sufficient to hold my own.'[122]

During the remainder of 1901, Cooper commuted between Birmingham and his Aubrey Walk studio, where he was completing various architectural commissions as well as working increasingly on jewellery and shagreen. On 28 December Cooper married May Oliver. After a brief honeymoon they settled in Birmingham, leasing a house, The Elms, in Castle Bromwich, a north-eastern suburb of the city. Cooper set up his private studio at Kyrle Hall, Sheep Street, Birmingham, which had been the home of the Birmingham Guild of the Handicraft until 1898.

Aside from having numerous teaching assistants, Cooper brought Colarossi with him to the Birmingham school;[123] simultaneously, Colarossi worked in Cooper's private studio at Kyrle Hall. By August 1902, George Romer, Cooper's other workman from his London studio, was also teaching at the school as well as working in Cooper's private studio.[124] William Hazlewood, a metalwork student himself, was appointed as 'Laboratory Attendant' to keep order among the boys in the classroom.[125] By 1904, Hazlewood was also one of Cooper's Kyrle Hall studio workmen and continued to work for him through the First World War.[126]

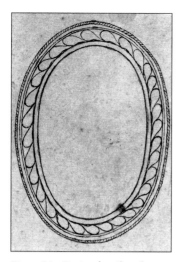

Figure 31. Design for silver frame, 1899, Cooper's earliest recorded piece of metalwork. Cooper Family Archives.

Cooper took up his teaching post in Birmingham, then considered the nineteenth-century mecca of tasteless trade jewellery, with a view to making drastic reforms.[127] The city's negative reputation stemmed from the geographical division of the metals industry in England at the time: the top end of the silver and jewellery trade was practised in London, centred around Clerkenwell, while Birmingham supplied the much larger, bottom-end market with inexpensive metalwork. In his journals Cooper frequently uses the then derogatory term 'Brummagen' to describe the city's trade-related inclinations: 'The Birmingham School of Art buildings are such as one would naturally imagine the Brummagen magnates would put up and be proud of. Very red, very fussy & very pretentious with carving & patterned tiles on the face, a building to make an artist shudder.'[128] The school authorities allowed Cooper the freedom to reorganize the classes and implement a teaching curriculum that followed the Arts and Crafts ideals of good craftsmanship and sensible design, which his predecessors had not done. In the classroom this meant a return to developing basic silversmithing skills and designing objects with a sensitivity to their materials and utility. Cooper admitted that these reforms alienated a lot of his students and many left. His goal in teaching students the rudiments of metalworking techniques was to train them as craftsmen capable of executing their own designs. No student design was permitted if the student himself was not able to execute it; before Cooper, the students had relied on their teachers to make up fanciful and complicated designs that were beyond their own manual skill. In addition, Cooper forced the students to create their own designs and would not allow them to 'borrow' ideas from their teachers as had previously been the practice.[129] Edward R. Taylor (1838–1912), Headmaster of the Municipal School of Art between 1885 and 1903, was impressed by Cooper's early achievements: '. . . [Cooper] has succeeded in a degree which appeared impossible in so short of time. He has won the confidence of the students although he has rightly insisted that unless they prove their ability they must begin at the beginning.'[130] In 1902, Lethaby came as General Examiner and was equally impressed with Cooper's accomplishments.[131]

However, the course of Cooper's teaching tenure at Birmingham did not run entirely smoothly. In February 1906 he resigned from the school, effective 31 August 1906.[132] The reasons for Cooper's departure were numerous. By the end of 1902, Cooper had already begun curtailing the number of hours he was actually spending in his classrooms, increasingly relying on teaching assistants like Romer and Colarossi to supervise the students. Moreover, Cooper's proposal that the students execute in the classroom, as practical exercises, his own studio work intended for private sale, and his suggestion that the school salaries of Romer and Colarossi should be paid through him agitated the school's managing committee.[133] In February 1906, the school's management strongly expressed displeasure at the entire situation. Cooper responded with his resignation: 'I have been informed by the Head Master, Mr Catterson-Smith, that you are not satisfied with the results of the work executed in the Metal Class of the Central School, and are of the opinion that the Master in charge should, in future, devote the greater amount of time to his class. As I think it would be unwise for me to offer to do this, I beg to tender my resignation.'[134]

During his years in Birmingham, Cooper's private studio began to prosper. Its metalwork output dramatically increased from three pieces in 1901 to forty in 1902 and fifty-nine in 1903.[135] Fordham's shop provided a steady demand for his work and members of Cooper's family, in particular his mother, were buying a large portion of his Birmingham output. The number of Cooper's workmen also increased. By 1905, he employed three skilled craftsmen: Colarossi, Romer, and Hazlewood. He also had two studio boys: 'Bob', an apprentice named Robert Clare; and 'Charlie,' possibly Charles Baker who later worked for the Artificers' Guild and for Cooper at Betsom's Hill.[136] In early 1906, George Middleton also joined the studio as a skilled craftsman.[137] In 1905 and 1906, Cooper received his first important public commission; it came from Birmingham Cathedral and was an order for two crosses and a pair of altar vases.

With such an active studio, it is obvious that the demands on Cooper's time were strenuous. Though genuinely interested in propagating Arts and Crafts reformist ideals in young, impressionable minds, Cooper's first passion was for his own studio work as well as for his growing family.[138] His first two children were born in Birmingham – Katharine in 1904 and Francis in 1906. Cooper saw his own children as future 'students' who would need careful artistic nurturing and thereby provide a private, non-bureaucratic outlet for his pedagogical leanings.[139]

In August 1906, Cooper's father died. Cooper was left a small inheritance that enabled him to abandon teaching, a profession he refused to return to even when Henry Wilson offered him his own position at the Royal College of Art: Cooper was determined to devote himself fully to his studio work.[140] Francis, his son, explained his father's financial situation further: '. . .what he [Cooper] made from his work could have barely paid the wages of his assistants, and that was more or less true during his whole lifetime. My father regarded his work as his mission; he felt it was necessary to the world, and it was to him a job worth doing for its own sake.'[141]

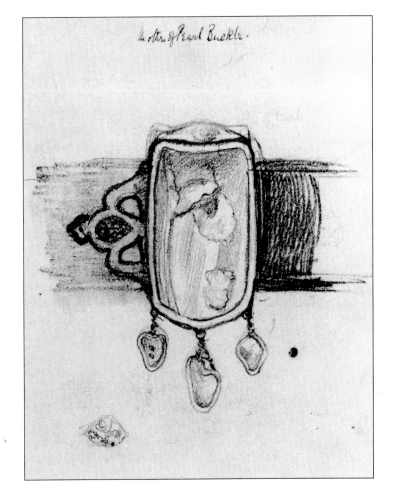

Figure 32. Design for belt buckle, 1899–1900, Cooper's earliest recorded piece of jewellery. Cooper Family Archives.

KENT: 1907–19

In May 1907, Cooper moved with his family from Birmingham to Hunton, near Maidstone, Kent. The choice of this location was not arbitrary. In 1902, Wilson had moved his studio from Vicarage Gate, London, to Kent where

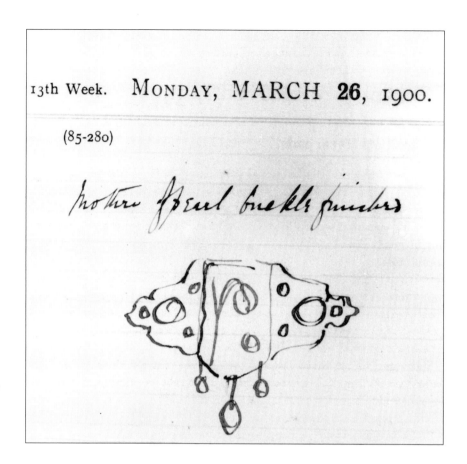

13th Week.   MONDAY, MARCH **26**, 1900.

(85-280)

Figure 33. Entry in Cooper's diary for 26 March 1900, depicting finished silver and mother-of-pearl belt buckle seen in Figure 32. Cooper Family Archives.

he concentrated on jewellery and metalwork and also began to sculpt seriously. Living in St Mary Platt near Sevenoaks, he wrote to Cooper in February 1906: 'Now there is a small house cottage vacant here, with a good garden – come & take it and take half of my workshop.'[142] By September, Wilson was even more strongly urging Cooper to move near him: 'Why not take the Thatched House [Wilson's own home] and the studio? Then I shall build another house at the end of the garden and we shall have a lovely colony.'[143] Cooper wanted to build his own house in Kent, but being wisely dissuaded by Wilson from rashly embarking on such a project, he decided instead to lease Grove House in Hunton (Figure 35).[144]

The Grove's coach house was converted into a workshop for Colarossi, Hazlewood and Middleton, who followed Cooper from Birmingham. Here, Cooper focused his efforts on designing more luxurious jewellery and metalwork, the increasing intricacy of which pointed to his growing artistic confidence. Shagreen pieces were also being made, increasingly becoming a staple product of his studio. Their elegant silver mountings, unusual material and cheaper price in comparison to silverwork and jewellery made them an 'artistic' commodity easily saleable to fashionable society.[145] This trend was to continue throughout his career, particularly in the 1920s and 1930s when shagreen accessories and toilet articles were popularized by Art Deco artists.

While at Hunton, Cooper began exhibiting his work on a more international scale. In the autumn of 1907 his work was part of displays that travelled to Detroit and Berlin.[146] In 1908 he sent pieces to Weimar and Leipzig and in 1909 to the Vienna International Exhibition, two of his exhibited pieces being simultaneously illustrated in *Deutsche Kunst und Dekoration*.[147] Vienna was not the first international exhibition in which Cooper participated: in 1902 he had sent a piece to the Turin exhibition and in 1906 to the Milan exhibition. In Milan, Cooper exhibited in the Arts and Crafts Exhibition Society section, receiving a gold medal that was awarded collectively to the Society.

In May 1908, Cooper became a member of the Art-Workers' Guild which provided an organized forum for all craft-oriented artists, including painters, sculptors and architects. Sedding had been one of its founders in 1884 and had taken Cooper to a few of its meetings. Cooper's move to Birmingham had delayed his membership. Now living within easy commuting distance of London, he could participate in its various activities.[148] His daughter Ursula remembered the regularity and enjoyment with which Cooper attended the Guild's meeting to see his artist friends and discuss creative ideas. Between 1907 and his death in 1933, Cooper delivered fourteen talks to the Guild. He also served on its executive committee from 1918 to 1920.

Suffering from severe indigestion and instructed by his doctor to live on higher ground composed of chalk or rock with a southern orientation,

Figure 34. May Morgan Oliver aged twenty-one, (centre), with two of her sisters, 1897. She became Cooper's wife in 1901. Cooper Family Archives.

Figure 35. Grove House, Hunton, Kent, where Cooper lived between 1907 and 1911. His daughter Kanty is standing in the drive, c. 1908. Cooper Family Archives.

Cooper began hunting for another residence in 1909.[149] The outcome of his search was gloomy: 'Old houses . . . are musty & fusty & new ones too ugly to live in.'[150] He resolved to build his own house. After another long search for a suitable site, a three-and-a-half acre plot on a hillside rising towards a disused chalk quarry to the north of Westerham, Kent, was purchased.

The erection of the house – Betsom's Hill – to Cooper's own designs was begun in October 1910.[151] The resulting two-storey house made of cement plaster, split oak boards and a clay tiled roof was Cooper's last major architectural undertaking. It consisted of ten rooms including a large studio and three bathrooms. A separate bungalow, already standing on the site, was converted into the workshop. In order personally to supervise the building of Betsom's Hill, Cooper moved his family from Hunton to Mariner's Cottage on the outskirts of Westerham.[152] On 30 June 1911 Cooper moved into Betsom's Hill, his Arts and Crafts homage to traditional rural architecture (Figure 36, Plate 6). His assistants Colarossi and Hazlewood followed him. By the end of 1911, Bernard Instone (1891–1987), a former student at the Birmingham Municipal School of Art, had also joined the workshop.[153]

The reminiscences of Cooper's children about Betsom's Hill indicate a rather regimented life style. According to Francis:

My father liked to plan his day. Meals had to be punctual, so there was no waiting for each other. We got up at 7 when my father occupied the bathroom for a longish time, while shaving. . . . He need not have taken nearly so long over shaving but in order to 'save time' and to do two jobs at once, he used to also learn a language. A dictionary being part of his shaving kit, 6 new words (was it?) had to be memorized each day, which spun the time out. After breakfast he would go into the studio for half an hour of quiet reading and meditation. . . . When this period of quiet was over, my father would go into the workshop to discuss the day's work with his assistants. About 11 o'clock he would go out of doors for exercise. . . . We had lunch at 12.30 – a vegetarian meal [the prescribed cure for Cooper's chronic stomach problems]. . . . After lunch my father relaxed with a pipe . . . while doing the practical side of his work, chasing, modelling, or making models for some future work in plasticine and wood. . . . We had tea to drink only at 4, high tea at 5 because it was thought by my parents not to be good to eat and drink at the same time. . . . In the evenings my father seemed to be busy letter writing or possibly writing papers to read at the Art Workers' Guild. . . . At the end of the evening he would settle down with a book, happy and oblivious to the rest of the world. . . . There were never any idle moments for him.[154]

Having settled into surroundings at Betsom's Hill, that reflected his own tastes and artistic preferences, Cooper now produced, during the 1910s, some of his most opulent, elaborately chased and elegantly lyrical designs (Plates 7, 8). This was the high point of the mature style that had begun to evolve in his Hunton studio. During these years, Cooper's reputation also

Figure 36. Various views of Betsom's Hill, Westerham, Kent, which Cooper completed in 1911 and where he lived and worked till his death in 1933. Top right: north façade showing main entrance and Cooper's studio wing with skylight. Bottom and top left: south façade. Bottom right: southeast corner of façade showing end wall of Cooper's studio.

Figure 37. John Paul Cooper, 1913.
Cooper Family Archives.

began to widen. In 1910, the Berlin goldsmith Emil Lettré (1876–1954) requested some of Cooper's pieces to sell in his shop. A mutual friend relayed the request: 'Mr. Lettré thinks a good deal of your work and also thinks he can make it sell here in Berlin, so wishes me to ask if you would care to send him a little gathering of articles from which he could select a number, more especially the gold and silver jewellery.'[155] During 1911, Cooper sent Lettré thirty-six pieces of jewellery and small metalwork, seventeen items of which the German kept.[156] At the 1912 Arts and Crafts Society exhibition, Cooper's sales reached a total of £131 17s, an amount he never surpassed at any other Society exhibition.[157]

As indicated earlier, Cooper's decision to move to Kent was linked to the location of Wilson's own residence and workshop in St Mary Platt. The two artists were once again in close communication with each other. They collaborated on the design and execution of a church's chancel, erected as part of the British section at the Ghent International Exhibition in 1913. Cooper modelled two figures of St Anne, which were positioned over the altar, and also portions of the altar screen.[158] While Wilson was in Ghent, helping to install the church interior, Cooper was making arrangements for its decoration to be completed in England and sent to the exhibition (Figure 37).[159] Likewise, while Wilson was working in Venice during 1914, he asked Cooper to take charge of one of his workmen, Sidney Wiseman.[160] Cooper agreed, employing Wiseman to execute enamel work seen for the first time on his pieces dating between 1914 and 1915.

In 1916 Wilson became president of the Arts and Crafts Exhibition Society and the undisputed leader of the Arts and Crafts Movement until his permanent move to France in 1922. In his capacity as leader of the Society, Wilson asked Cooper to design and coordinate the execution of the Nursery Room, one of the 'interior environment' exhibits at the 1916 Arts and Crafts Society exhibition held at the Royal Academy (Plate 9).[161] This idea for collaboration between the Society's artists to produce a collective work of art, such as a church or domestic interior, seems to have stemmed from a proposal submitted by Cooper in January 1913.[162] Cooper suggested that the Society could have a greater impact on public taste, and would be able to secure for its members large public commissions, if it exhibited whole interiors such as a church apse (undertaken at the Ghent exhibition), a dining-room, or even a nursery executed collectively by a group of its artists:

> The new aim, the new ideal we would propose is that of Co-operation. This might be accomplished by forming groups amongst ourselves who would combine to produce large and important pieces of work. . . . Such an exhibition might take the form for instance of . . . a Nursery with a collection of children's toys, cots, chairs etc. (Children are at present rather neglected by artists. Our President [Walter Crane] is one of the very few who have done anything for them, and yet no one would deny the importance of influencing their taste at an early age, and it is somewhat shortsighted not to do what one can to teach the future generation at its most impressionable age).[163]

It is a matter of conjecture where Cooper got the inspiration for these 'cooperative interior environments.' This certainly was not a novel idea, having already been tried by artists who created the German and Viennese sections at the Paris International Exposition of 1900.

Perhaps the most significant event for the Arts and Crafts Exhibition Society which occurred in the pre-war years was the Exposition des l'Art Décoratifs de la Bretagne et d'Irlande held at the Louvre's Marsan Pavillon, the Musée des Arts Décoratifs.[164] Apparently, the impetus for this large French exhibition of British decorative arts came from the officials of the Union Centrale des Arts Décoratifs. Having seen the Arts

Figure 38. Pair of lamp stands in silver, H 45.7, 1918. Archive Department, The Cheltenham Ladies' College.

Figure 39. Charcoal self-portrait,
1920s. Cooper Family Archives.

and Crafts display at the 1913 Ghent exposition, they requested that a similar exhibition be staged in Paris. This was the largest and most comprehensive show of British Arts and Crafts ever held abroad. Cooper contributed eighty-four pieces to the exhibition, recording in his diary on 2 May 1914: 'Heard Mons. J. Reubell of 23 Rue de Marignan one of the greatest connoisseurs & collectors of old work in Paris had spent an hour looking at my silverwork which much pleased him, he bought some pieces, & as result of his admiration 2 of the Louvre Conservatoires had also bought.'[165] Likewise, Cooper's exhibited silver received favourable mention and was illustrated in *Art et décoration*.[166] The esteem in which

Cooper's work was held at this exhibition was further exemplified by the fact that Paul Alfassa, one of the French organizers of the British display, was presented in appreciation of his work with a silver cup executed by Cooper. Alfassa, an official of the Union Centrale des Arts Décoratifs, was greatly honoured by the gift and already owned several other examples of Cooper's work: 'La coupe que vous m'avez envoyée me sera précieuse par les souvenirs qu'elle me rapellera; elle me l'est aussi par sa beauté. Il y a longtemps que j'aime les oeuvres de M. Paul Cooper, dont je possède déja deux ou trois . . . lui [Cooper] dire combien il m'est agréable d'avoir cette piece d'orfèvrerie d'un si noble dessin et d'un si parfaite exécution.'[167]

With the escalation of the First World War between 1916 and 1918, Cooper lost all his workmen to war service, either to active duty or munitions manufacture. Naturally, the volume of Cooper's artistic work was greatly reduced. The pieces that had to be executed during this time at Betsom's Hill, such as the liturgical plate for St Paul's, Four Elms, and the electric lamps for the Cheltenham Ladies' College, were largely the handiwork of Cooper himself; he was no longer able to rely on his workmen to execute the preliminary stages of the designs (Plate 10, Figure 38).

In 1918, Cooper also began active war work at W.A.S. Benson's (1854–1924) metalworks in St Peter's Square, Hammersmith, London, under R.L.B. Rathbone (1864–1939). Here he was occupied with sorting steel rods, stamping brass labels, making jigs and a glass gauge for aneroid barometers, and executing a brass model for torpedo sights.[168] This kind of mechanical factory work seems to have influenced Cooper. During the 1920s a new impersonality characterized by geometric hardness and streamlined repetition appeared in his work.

'Mr. Cooper has the most perfect taste in design. Nobody in England is handling silver with greater felicity.'

KENT: 1920–33

Following the war, Cooper's artistic reputation was consolidated (Figure 39). The focus of his metalwork now turned towards important public commissions, mainly liturgical, which were the result of a popularly acknowledged respect for his artistic skill: 'With the keenest appreciation of the intrinsic qualities for his materials Mr. Cooper has the most perfect taste in design. Nobody in England is handling silver with greater felicity. Without any effort, but by concentrating upon the object of the piece, he avoids both the "period" and the consciously "modern" effect.'[169]

In 1919, Cooper was commissioned to execute a sword of honour for presentation to Field-Marshal Sir Douglas Haig (Figure 40). During the 1920s and early 1930s Cooper executed liturgical plate for Edinburgh Cathedral, Canterbury Cathedral, Eton College Chapel, Oakham School chapel (Plate 11), St Andrew's Church in Limpsfield Chart, St James's Church Muswell Hill in London, and for St James's and St Basil's Church, Fenham, Newcastle. He was also asked to design a First World War Memorial in St Mary's Church Tatsfield, the King's Royal Rifle Corps Memorial in Winchester Cathedral (Plate 12), a memorial for the crash victims of Airship *R38* (Figure 41), a niche in St Paul's Church Covent Garden for Ellen Terry's ash casket (Plate 8), previously executed by Cooper, and a reliquary for George Bernard Shaw (Plate 13).[170]

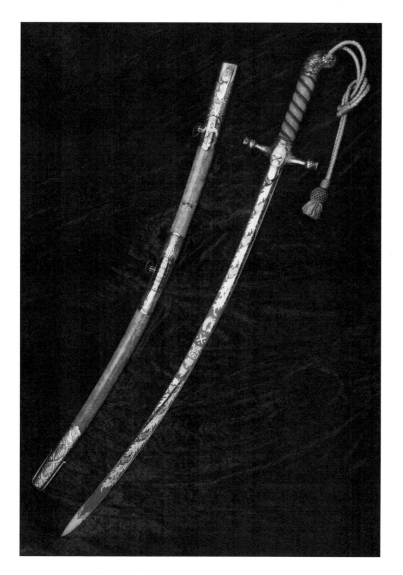

Figure 40. Sword of Honour presented by the Association of Lowland Scots to Field Marshal Sir Douglas Haig in tribute for his mililtary service during the First World War. Executed in silver, shagreen and enamel, L 97.5, 1919. Earl Haig (1861–1928) was commander-in-chief of the British Army during the last three years of the First World War. The inscription on the sheath also mentions his active duty in the Nile campaign of 1897–8 and the Boer War of 1899–1902. Edinburgh City Museums.

In 1925, Cooper received a silver medal for his metalwork shown at the Paris Exposition Internationale des Arts Décoratifs et Industriels Modernes.[171] Simultaneously, a French magazine published a commendatory appraisal of Cooper's work on view at the Liverpool Walker Art Gallery: 'D'un style excessivement élevé et d'une exécution parachevée, les objets en orfèvrerie . . . par Paul Cooper. . . . Tous les objets sortant de ses mains sont d'une élégance rare. C'est pourquoi ils occupent une situation en vedette, dans le domaine de l'art appliqué.'[172]

In 1926, Cooper received a direct invitation from the Goldsmiths' Company to submit designs for the Ascot Cup competition.[173] The design competition, held by the Goldsmiths' Company, was for three cups which the King was to award during the 1927 Ascot races: the Ascot Cup, the King's Gold Vase, and the Silver Hunt Cup. The competition hoped to attract public attention to contemporary silverwork and encourage originality in design, purging the perceived commercial and creative stagnation in the gold and silver trade. Cooper submitted designs for both the King's Gold Vase and Ascot Cup. Only his design for the gold Ascot Cup was selected, and he received a cash prize of £100. Unfortunately, the King turned down all the winning designs. Nevertheless, the Goldsmiths' Company paid for the winning designs to be executed. Cooper's design was executed in silver and exhibited at the British Industries Fair in 1927 where it was personally examined by the King (Figure 42).[174]

On 13 February 1929, Cooper was granted the freedom of the Goldsmiths' Company by special invitation: 'The Court feels that at the present juncture when so much thought is being given to the improvement of modern silverwork it is fitting that certain members of the silversmith's craft and industry who are greatly interested or have shown marked ability as craftsmen should be asked to join the Company with a view to co-operating in their efforts . . . such membership does not involve either entrance fee or subscription.'[175]

After his admission to the Goldsmiths' Company, Cooper was automatically eligible to receive the freedom of the City of London upon the presentation of his birth certificate to verify his British citizenship. Since Cooper's birth certificate indicated his illegitimate birth, he declined to apply.

In addition to the above activities, Cooper also held four one-man exhibitions at the Three Shields Gallery, London, in 1924, 1927, 1929 and 1932.[176] This Kensington gallery, opened in 1922, was owned and managed by Dorothy Hutton (b. 1889). Trained as a calligrapher and painter, she was a shrewd, well-connected businesswoman. Fashionable society frequented her gallery and directly applied to her for the execution of specific commissions, making it an ideal commercial outlet for Cooper's work. It continued as the primary retail agency for Cooper's work even after his death. Besides sponsoring his one-man exhibitions, the gallery continually kept his work in stock and arranged for Cooper to carry out specific commissions for its wealthy clientele. At the gallery, Cooper's shagreen pieces sold the best. The commissions that Cooper received from Hutton's clients also tended to be for shagreen items, such as a spectacle case for the 9th Earl of Sandwich (1874–1962) and a toilet set for Miss Alys Kingsley of Paris.[177]

In 1931, Walker's Galleries in Bond Street held a major retrospective of Cooper's work, including eighty pieces of metalwork and shagreen and fifty-eight watercolours (Plate 14).[178] The inclusion of so many watercolour renderings of visited geographic sites was a novelty. Cooper had in the late 1920s exhibited a few of them at various small, local exhibitions, but never in such large number in London. Increasingly, during the late 1920s and early 1930s, watercolours began absorbing his creative energies. Since entering Sedding's office, Cooper had continually made sketches of places he visited, but the more finished of these earlier renderings tended to be in pastel (Plate 15). The published reviews of the exhibition found the watercolours pleasing but commented that his shagreen and metalwork was clearly of a higher artistic quality.[179] Gordon Craig tried to describe the charm of Cooper's watercolours:

He does it as might an architect who for many a year has mislaid his ruler . . . he is, as it were, writing one a letter in watercolour. And in these letters – these letters about places – he is as careful of the calligraphy as possible, and careful, too, to write us particulars of each tree, column, wall or lane – not dashing off these things in any Cooperesque manner. There is no Cooperesque manner, and it seems to me that this is the best thing that any work can have said of it.[180]

Figure 41. Airship R38 Memorial in copper with enamel, H 174, 1925. Having been sold to the US, this rigid dirigible crashed during a test flight in 1921 over the Humber River, killing most of its crew of Royal Air Force and United States Navy men whose names appear on the tablet. Royal Aeronautical Society, London.

Figure 42. Ascot Gold cup in silver, H 34.3, 1927. The Worshipful Company of Goldsmiths.

Queen Mary visited the retrospective and bought four pieces of Cooper's work, remarking that she was already familiar with his work (Figure 43).[181]

Throughout the 1920s, Cooper also continued to exhibit regularly with the Arts and Crafts Exhibition Society, though gradually reducing the number of pieces he contributed. From 1917 to 1929 he was a member of the Society's council, which managed the actual affairs of the organization.[182] In 1932, Cooper resigned from the Society immediately following its Fifteenth Exhibition in 1931.[183] The resignation was caused by the changing policies and outlook of the Society. All the members' work in 1931 had to be approved by a selections committee before being allowed on exhibition. Three of what Cooper considered his best works were rejected by the committee, including the candlesticks he had executed for Edwin Lutyens's (1869–1944) music chapel at Tyringham Hall, Bletchley, Buckinghamshire (Figure 44).[184] Cooper considered that the work which was accepted – twelve neckchains and two shagreen boxes – was very commercial and not as good as the pieces that were rejected. Harry G. Murphy (1884–1939), who had started out as an errand boy in Wilson's Vicarage Gate studio and whom Cooper had sponsored as a new member in the Arts and Crafts Exhibition Society, was on the 1931 selection committee. He was responsible for the rejection of some of Cooper's pieces. Cooper pouted: 'I had proposed Harry Murphy for membership as being a good craftsman, not designer.'[185] Similar rejections and acceptances happened to many of the older members of the Society including Edward Spencer (1872–1938) and May Morris (1862–1938), the daughter of William Morris, who, as a result, also resigned from the Society.[186]

On 3 May 1933, Cooper boarded a bus from Westerham to London, intending to buy watercolour paints and attend the theatre (Figure 45).[187] Shortly after getting on the bus, he had a heart attack; he was

Figure 43. Casket in shagreen and silver purchased in 1931 by Queen Mary at a Cooper retrospective exhibition, 1928. Photograph in the Cooper Family Archives.

Figure 44. Pair of candlesticks for Lutyens's Temple of Music, Tyringham Hall, in silver, 1929. In keeping with the musical theme of their surroundings, the angels on the candlesticks' bases play wind instruments while the mermaids above them sing. Hancocks, London.

taken to a nearby cottage where he died (Figure 46).[188] Seventeen of his shagreen and metalwork pieces were shown posthumously at Dorland Hall in the Exhibition of British Industrial Art in Relation to the Home in the summer of 1933.[189] In October the same year, a memorial exhibition of his work was held at the Rembrandt Gallery, Vigo Street, London. As a general survey of his career, the exhibition included 236 pieces of Cooper's jewellery, metalwork, shagreen, gesso work and watercolours.[190]

CHAPTER TWO

STYLISTIC DEVELOPMENT

In the work of Paul Cooper one feels the intimacy with the great world of art, with poetry, the plastic arts, architecture and music, and if we look thoughtfully at these works and handle them, they will delight us and convey their own message in their own language, lucidly and truthfully.

F. Ernest Jackson[1]

INTRODUCTION

The following chapter examines Cooper's executed work in four specific media: gesso, mother-of-pearl, shagreen, and metal. The examples selected for discussion in each section demonstrate the salient characteristics of Cooper's work in each medium. A discernible progression of style is most evident in Cooper's shagreen work, which, as a result, can be readily organized into definable chronological periods displaying distinct stylistic traits. Cooper's early experimental shagreen done between 1899 and 1902 was followed by a second, more mature stylistic phase between 1903 and 1907, characterized by larger, more monumental pieces often associated with his client Arthur Samuel (1872–1942). Between 1908 and 1915 Cooper began fully to exploit the commercial potential of his shagreen, standardizing its design and thereby substantially increasing the speed of production and the quantity that could be executed. In the 1920s, standardization continued, the design of the objects and in particular of their mounts evolving towards greater sleekness and geometric abstraction, a trend which intensified after 1925.

Cooper's jewellery and metalwork are less easily organized into stylistic categories. The experimental nature and variety of much of this work make it extremely difficult to classify. Nevertheless, an attempt has also been made to organize Cooper's jewellery and metalwork into specific stylistic periods that share broad, common characteristics. While he was in Birmingham between 1902 and 1906, Cooper's jewellery was dominated by representational imagery, characterized by an expressive, sculptural rendering. His Birmingham metalwork was limited, mainly composed of simple domestic plate. At his studio at Hunton in Kent between 1907 and

1910 Cooper's jewellery began moving away from representational imagery towards a greater interest in stones, compositional delicacy and refinement. Contemporary metalwork pieces became more numerous and confident, with a greater display of chased ornament. During the 1910s, the stylistic changes adopted by Cooper's Hunton studio intensified. His pre-war metalwork in particular exhibited a tight aesthetic integration of numerous decorative elements to produce some of his most opulent and elegant works. Finally, during the 1920s and early 1930s, Cooper's style displayed a new hard-edged simplification and detachment, which intensified toward the end of his life.

Cooper preferred line and surface to mass and volume, ... and restraint and grace to exuberance and lavishness.

Cooper's gesso and mother-of-pearl work resists all stylistic grouping. Instead of organizing the objects into stylistic periods, the analyses of these two sections of his output concentrate on Cooper's sensitivity to the natural properties of each material. This sympathy extends beyond the mere physical properties of the materials to the symbolic significance that the materials and the images they render impart to the viewer and to the object they decorate.

Cooper's work in all four media does, however, exhibit a few common, general tendencies. He usually drew his artistic inspiration directly from nature, most frequently from the vegetal world. Marine imagery also seems to have stirred his imagination strongly. His historic inspirations usually came from pre-sixteenth-century sources, often associated with architecture. Cooper preferred line and surface to mass and volume (i.e., linear flatness to three-dimensional roundness), and restraint and grace to exuberance and lavishness. The physical characteristics of his materials dictated their combinations and treatment, while hand execution determined the external finish of his pieces. Such stylistic tendencies reverberate like a 'Ruskin litany' of traits essential for a successful work of art. These traits were adopted, to some degree, by all the Arts and Crafts artists, including William Morris, Walter Crane (1845–1915) and Henry Wilson.

GESSO

As stated in the previous chapter, the first artwork Cooper ever exhibited was a gesso box, which was shown at the 1893 Arts and Crafts Society exhibition. During the 1890s, aside from his architectural work, gesso-decorated objects dominated Cooper's artistic output. Between 1893 and 1904 he completed twenty-two such boxes and frames.[2] The majority of these were made at the turn of the century (i.e., 1899–1903) when his future wife, May, began working in his studio: Cooper provided the designs, an outside craftsman constructed the wooden carcasses, and May executed the gesso decoration.[3] Cooper's costing books, which break down the costs of labour and materials in making specific pieces, often give the exact amount of hours May spent working on them.[4] According to their son Francis, May was a careful, patient worker unlike Cooper, who tended to be fiery. Such qualities made May an ideal craftsperson to work at the extremely time-consuming and tedious techniques of gesso work. Little else is known about her gesso collaborations with Cooper but

Figure 45. John Paul Cooper,
c. 1930. Cooper Family Archives.

no doubt, as May became more proficient at gesso modelling, she also
contributed ideas towards designs.

Cooper's preoccupation with gesso work was a logical development of his
early artistic interests in London. As mentioned earlier, in the autumn of 1889
Cooper began attending evening classes at the Royal Architectural Museum
in Westminster. There he began his studies by modelling in clay from plaster
casts. In Sedding's office, especially after it was taken over by the more

Figure 46. Tombstone designed by son Francis for John Paul Cooper's grave at the Church of St Peter and St Paul, Cudham, Kent. Photograph in Cooper Family Archives.

'decorative-minded' Wilson, Cooper was primarily involved with the interior plaster work decorations for various architectural commissions. Cooper's remarkable skill in plaster modelling, a technique closely related to gesso work, was commended by professional plasterers and Henry Wilson.[5] Similarly, Cooper's plasterwork style, as seen in the few known interior decorations he executed, also corresponded to his gesso work (Figures 25, 26, 27, 28, Plate 2): his plasterwork is done in low relief and represents floral and animal motifs in a decorative manner similar to his ornamental modelling of gesso (Figures 19, 47, 49, Plates 18, 19, 20).

Cooper's gesso work was also part of a broader revival of interest in this medium among many Arts and Crafts artists at the end of the nineteenth century. Walter Crane's own experiments with various grounds and media – in particular with perfecting the egg tempera medium that he employed to portray figurative allegorical compositions during the 1880s – made a substantial contribution to this revival.[6] As early as 1889 the Arts and Crafts Exhibition Society proclaimed the ethical suitability of the gesso medium for the craft worker. In contrast to fired clay, marble and bronze, stucco and gesso were the only plastic processes 'by which the artist is enabled to finish, and render durable and vendible, his work, without having to part with it or pay for another's aid'.[7] In other words, the artist could solely execute and render permanent by himself a sculpture in gesso.

In 1893, for interested amateurs, Walter Crane published a seminal article on gesso in *The Studio*; it lucidly explained the 'nuts and bolts' of the gesso technique as practised by himself and by other Arts and Crafts artists at the time.[8] Crane's own gesso work, usually destined for wall decoration, tended to be figurative and large scale. Among Cooper's papers there exist notes that carefully outline three different recipes used by Crane to make gesso. All three recipes describe a mixture of resin, linseed oil, and glue to which either whiting (powdered chalk) or plaster of Paris was added. Surviving correspondence also indicates that Cooper's election into the Arts and Crafts Exhibition Society was partially based on Crane's admiration of his gesso boxes. In fact, Crane seconded Cooper's nomination to the Society.[9] After Crane's article appeared in *The Studio* another on gesso was written by painter Matthew Webb (*c.* 1851–1924).[10] Here, Webb discussed in greater detail the various techniques used to colour the medium.

Of the first gesso box Cooper sent to the 1893 Arts and Crafts Society exhibition, only two rough designs and a published drawing in *The Studio* remain (Figures 19, 47). *The Studio* critic declared that Cooper's box 'must not be overlooked'.[11] The surviving designs and published drawing

Figure 47. Design for Cooper's earliest executed gesso box, dated 1893. Cooper Family Archives.

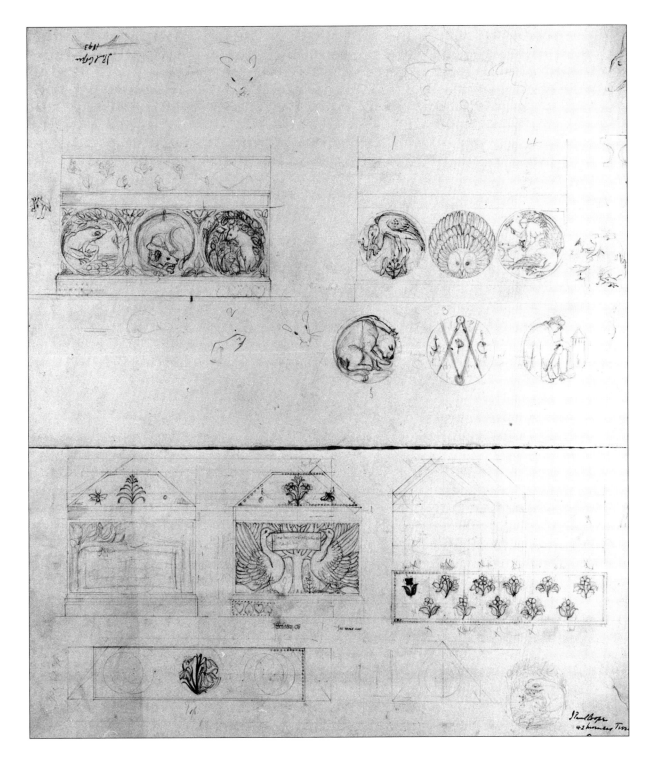

indicate a casket-shaped box (i.e. a box with a raised lid) decorated with stylized flowers and animal motifs, closely linked to the subject matter of Cooper's contemporary plasterwork. Its subject matter also recalls Cooper's boyhood interest in rural country flora and fauna. Its wooden carcass was probably made by Augustus H. Mason who, until the First World War, made all the wooden articles Cooper used in his work.[12] The gesso decoration was modelled by Cooper himself.

The shape of the box seems to derive from a medieval ivory casket Cooper quickly sketched at the Victoria and Albert Museum (Figure 48).[13] This casket (acc. no. 369–1871), constructed of wood with ivory plaques and gilt-metal mounts, is of Siculo-Arabic origin, dating from the twelfth to thirteenth centuries, with later French decoration. This is one of the rare instances in Cooper's surviving sketchbooks where a direct museum prototype can be linked to an executed work. The museum also owns another Siculo-Arabic casket (acc. no. 700–1884), whose placement of animals in roundels seems to be even more closely related to Cooper's gesso decoration on the 1893 box. Interestingly, Cooper's sketchbooks contain few drawings of actual museum objects and are mainly filled with architectural sketches. Rather than sketching regularly, Cooper went to the Victoria and Albert Museum and the British Museum to view specific historic objects that might provide solutions for particular design problems he encountered.

The experimental nature of his 1893 box, particularly with regard to its colouring and gilding, and the remarkable sense of dilettante camaraderie which characterized Cooper's incursions into the decorative arts at this time was documented by Wilson in a letter sent to Cooper, who had left for Italy with Powell before the opening of the exhibition:

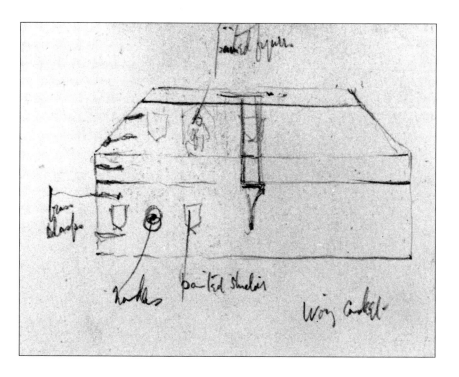

Figure 48. Pencil sketch of Siculo-Arabic ivory casket in the Victoria and Albert Museum (acc. no. 369-1871), dated 1892. Cooper Family Archives.

Your box is in the Exhibition but does not look as well as it might because Ellis made a sad muddle of the gilding but as he only got it done a short time before it was to be sent in, little alteration was possible. Still I [Wilson] did what I could to improve it and that little, I think helped it. The trouble was that instead of having the gold parts smooth and glistening they were gritty and dull and he had altered the former rose colour on the top because that which you placed there would not dry. However people liked it and that's the chief thing.[14]

The box, in fact, was so admired that there were two inquiries concerning its price.[15]

The next gesso box Cooper executed, decorated with a frieze of female musicians, was exhibited at the 1896 Arts and Crafts Society exhibition (Figure 49)[16] This was the first gesso box Cooper recorded in his stock and costing books, specifically noting that its decoration was executed in 'Denoline',[17] a commercial brand name of a premixed powdered gesso which was converted into paste by the addition of water.[18] Cooper's journals make several references to the execution of this 1896 workbox. In June 1896, Cooper wrote: ' . . . have been working at Gesso workbox particularly the frieze of figures on the front for which I have had Alice Arter to sit to me. She sits to Burne Jones, Sergeant [sic], Abbey and Waterhouse.'[19] In August Cooper noted: 'Started Colouring Denoline box.'[20] The inclusion of human figures in its decoration stemmed from Cooper's related studies at Heatherleys art school where he was attending life classes, drawing nudes, and working in watercolours from draped models.[21] The costume and elongation of the figures on the 1896 box bears a striking resemblance to the female figures of Edward Burne-Jones. Cooper's use of a model who also sat for Burne-Jones and his simultaneous study at Heatherleys school, where Burne-Jones had worked, must have influenced the decoration on the box. Among Cooper's papers are several clipped articles on the artist, whom he obviously greatly admired, though no factual evidence exists that Cooper ever had any direct contact with him or with any of the other Pre-Raphaelites. Cooper's journal entries for the second half of the 1890s record numerous female models posing for him, including Muriel Kohler, one of James McNeill Whistler's (1834–1903) favourite models.[22]

The gesso swallows, identified by their split tail feathers, and the stylized trees depicted in the friezes on the back and sides of the 1896 box recall Cooper's contemporary plasterwork. Specifically, they are related to plasterwork he executed during April and November of the same year at St Martin's Church, Marple, Cheshire (Figure 28).[23] The inspiration for decorating the front of the box with a frieze of musicians set against a blue-green background and the lid with a repeating pattern derived from an Italian gesso box Cooper had again sketched at the Victoria and Albert Museum (Figure 50).[24] This gesso box (acc. no. 110–1887), dates from about 1500; its left side is decorated with a processional group of musicians and its lid with a repeating scalloped pattern. Crane, in his *Studio* article, had stated that good examples of gesso work could be seen at the Victoria and Albert Museum, particularly those executed by Italian Renaissance artists, the Italians being the originators and the most successful manipulators of this medium.

*Figure 49. Workbox in Denoline,
H 15.5 × L 45.1 × W 21.6, 1896.
Private Collection.*

The damaged portions of the 1896 workbox disclose the technique Cooper used to execute his gesso decoration. The wood carcass was covered by a linen cloth to enable better adhesion of the gesso. To this cloth ground, gesso was then applied in thin coats with the relief portions of the decoration being directly modelled on the box with a gesso-soaked brush. In his *Studio* article, Walter Crane had particularly stressed the spontaneous, unlaboured, painterly effect that could be achieved by applying the gesso directly to a ground with a watercolour-type brush and then allowing it to dry without subsequent alteration, a technique Crane thought best suited to exposing the inherent qualities of the gesso material.[25] According to Crane, brush-applied gesso was particularly suited to model 'delicate branch and leaf and scroll work, for instance, and dotted and linear borderings, lines of hair and drapery arranged in pattern. . . . Such forms as these the brush charged with gesso almost naturally falls into, and, indeed, leaf shapes may be considered almost as the reflection of the form of the brush itself.'[26]

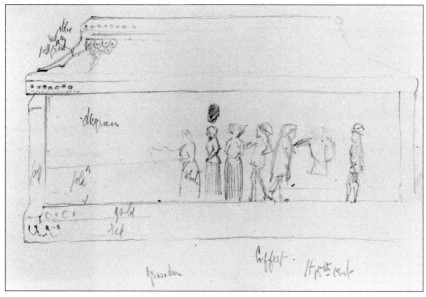

Figure 50. Pencil sketch of Italian gesso box in the Victoria and Albert Museum (acc. no. 110-1887), dated 1892. Cooper Family Archives.

Figure 51. Box for Alice Radcliffe in ebony with mother-of-pearl, gesso, beetle wings and bronze, H 20.3 × L 19 × W 14, 1897–8. Photograph in Cooper Family Archives.

Correspondingly, Cooper's decoration on the 1896 workbox fully satisfied the Arts and Crafts maxim that a design and its treatment should derive and reflect both the material and tools used by the craftsman to execute it. The modelling of Cooper's figures is kept simple, direct and in low relief. The representational imagery is stylized and the spatial relationships are flattened to emphasize the ornamental aspect of the decoration. As suggested by Crane, Cooper modelled the main masses of his forms in isolation from each other with successive applications of wet-on-wet gesso, similarly to the *pâte-sur-pâte* technique – that naturally blended and softened their contours as the gesso dried.[27]

Cooper's colouring of the modelled gesso forms on the workbox also stresses the spontaneity and fluency inherent in brush-applied gesso. Instead of strong, dominating, opaque colours which would conceal the gesso surface, Cooper uses semi-transparent pigments whose ephemeral colour effects expose the gesso brush work underneath. Cooper had requested samples of French lacquer colours from a fellow artist.[28] Matthew Webb's article had also stressed the use of semi-transparent lacquer pigments to colour gesso work: '. . . as gesso is properly but a slight modelling so the spontaneous, unlaboured, easy look which lacquer possesses, suits gesso exceedingly well, especially for the light ornamental themes which fluent gesso is best suited to express.'[29] These lacquer colours had pigments suspended in a gum spirit varnish (i.e. an alcohol-based solution), which, in addition to colouring the relief, also hardened and protected the gesso surface from damage. Webb also recommended the practice of incessant glazing of one transparent colour over another to achieve the best colour effects. Moreover, Webb was in favour of using gold to colour gesso reliefs: 'Metal is always valuable in colouring a relief, because it forces you to avoid realistic treatment. It should be used as a colour rather than as representing metallic objects.'[30] It is significant to note that in executing the 1896 box, the gold decoration was painted rather than done by the more technically accomplished method of gold leaf. In his *Studio* article, Webb discussed the mixing of metallic powders to produce various gold paints, but he clearly preferred the greater brilliance and overall aesthetic effect of gold leaf. It is interesting to speculate why Cooper was reluctant to employ gold leaf on the 1896 box since on the 1893 box he had already done so. Perhaps he was worried that he might encounter similar gilding problems to those of the 1893 box. Cooper concurred with Webb's insistence that the gold surface on a gesso relief should be smooth and textureless.[31]

The next important stylistic development in Cooper's gesso work occurred with the completion in 1897–8 of a box for Alice Radcliffe, a Cooper acquaintance and occasional model (Figure 51).[32] The box itself was not primarily made of gesso, but rather of ebony inlaid with ivory and mother-of-pearl, supported on four bronze feet. The use of these materials together seems to stem from similar material combinations Cooper observed on Japanese objects.[33] Its physical size, however, greatly influenced the proportions of Cooper's subsequent gesso boxes. In a letter to Cooper, Alice Radcliffe noted this dimensional change: 'It was very kind of you to say that I had anything to do with altering the size [of gesso boxes Cooper exhibited at the 1899 Arts and Crafts Society exhibition], but I really can't take any credit to myself in the matter! – I wanted the one you made for me to be

Figure 52. Pencil drawings of thistle, on right, and chestnut, on left, c. 1900. Cooper Family Archives.

Figure 53. Watercolour and pencil sketches of birds. Cooper Family Archives.

smaller than the one you showed at the last Exhibition of the Arts and Crafts [in 1896].'[34] The 1896 workbox had measured an ungainly H 15.5 × L 45.1 × W 21.6, making it rather cumbersome and heavy. The Radcliffe box measured H 20.3 × L 19 × W 14. The new compact size made it easily manoeuvrable and helped to unify its decorative composition. This pivotal box was included in the April 1899 exhibition of the International Society of Sculptors, Painters and Gravers held in London.[35] A couple of years later, it was also illustrated in the *Builder's Journal and Architectural Record*.[36]

As indicated by Radcliffe's letter, the smaller size of her box was immediately adopted by Cooper for his subsequent gesso boxes, particularly those exhibited at the 1899 Arts and Crafts Society show. The first Cooper gesso box to adopt the dimensions and general shape of the Radcliffe box was the 'Seasons' workbox executed in 1898–9 and decorated in Denoline (Plate 16).[37] Its size of H 22.9 × L 20 × W 14.3 and general form immediately recall the Radcliffe one. Its figurative decoration, allegorically representing the four seasons, was modelled directly on the box's surface, the strokes of the gesso-saturated brush being visible under the semi-transparent colouring. The foliage decoration on the lid likewise exemplifies Crane's earlier statement that leaf forms suitably reflect the shape of the brush used to apply the gesso.

Though the figures in the gesso panels are competently modelled, their rendering lacks self-assurance. Despite his frequent sketching of models during the 1890s, Cooper never fully mastered the human form. In particular, he had trouble rendering hands and feet. As a result, the most successful of his gesso decorations are those that abandon the human form altogether or merely incorporate it as a stylized, subsidiary element. Cooper's artistic talent is best expressed in his renderings of animals, plants, and flowers (Figures 52, 53). His early interest in nature, traced back to his student days at Old Hall School in Shropshire, made him a keen and sensitive observer. His fascination with the natural world must have also been strongly encouraged by Sedding, who placed a high value on the observation and rendering of nature.

The gold decoration on the 'Seasons' box was executed in gold leaf. All the gold decoration on subsequent gesso boxes was also done in gold leaf rather than gold paint. With each successive box, the application of the gold leaf became more skilful and visually satisfying.

Another important feature of these early gesso boxes was the matching keys Cooper designed for their respective locks. The gilded key for the 1896 box was, in fact, one of the earliest pieces of metalwork Cooper ever executed (Figure 54). Its shape and design seem to suggest a possible link to the 'heart tree' motif on a door plate Cooper made in 1896 and described as a beginning of his metalwork.

One of the gesso pieces that Cooper exhibited at the 1899 Arts and Crafts Society exhibition was a jewel box again decorated in Denoline (Plate 17).[38] The box featured fourteen oval reliefs that were meant to represent various gem stones. Above each panel appeared the name of a particular stone. In 1902, with minor altera-tions, the box was reproduced in silver (Figure 55).[39] Eventually, the oval chased panels were removed and the remaining metal casket melted down. These oval plaques have survived and indicate the compositions of the original gesso reliefs (Figures 56, 57).[40] Cooper based the iconography of these compositions on descriptive passages about jewel stones in Pliny the Elder's *Naturalis historia*, written during the first century AD.[41] Cooper owned a seventeenth-century edition of this work; it still remains among his personal effects and contains his handwritten notations.[42] The Pliny-inspired plaques illustrated in Figure 56 were all mounted on the front of the jewel box. The opal panel, depicting a woman among flames, derives from Pliny's statement that in an opal one could see the 'flaming fire of brimstone' and the 'bright blaze of burning oile.'[43] In antiquity, amethysts were thought to ward off drunkenness, and Pliny wrote that they approached the colour of wine; this inspired Cooper to portray an infant Bacchus holding grapes. The figure surrounded by serpents illustrates Pliny's assertion that 'the diamant hath a property to frustrathe malicious effects of poyson; to drive away those imaginations that set folke besides themselves; & to expell vaine feares that trouble and possesse the mind.'[44] The mental and physical poisons described by Pliny are symbolized by the serpents. In another, even more literal adaptation of Pliny, Cooper uses a leek plant to represent a chrysoprase (Figure 57). Describing the stone, Pliny wrote 'it resembleth the green juice of a Leek'.[45]

Cooper reused this leek plant design as the central image on a belt buckle now in the Cheltenham Art Gallery and Museum (acc. no.

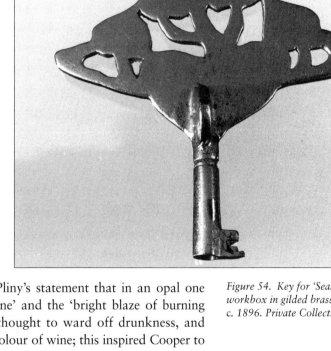

Figure 54. Key for 'Seasons' workbox in gilded brass, L 4.9, c. 1896. Private Collection.

1982.1196). He often recycled isolated decorative motifs and also reused the clever application of a symbolic image derived from literary sources, rather than working with the actual stone, to decorate a piece of jewellery.

The central oval in Figure 57 represents the semiprecious stone taos, whose appearance Pliny likened to a peacock. The remaining plaque in Figure 57, depicting poplar trees, represents amber. In his book, Pliny recounted the Greek myth of how the Heliades, the daughters of the Sun god Helios, incessantly wept over the death of their brother Phaethon; they were turned into poplar trees along the River Eridanus and their tears became amber beads.[46]

Being well read and having studied classics at Bradfield College, Cooper typically turned to such obscure passages in historic texts for his visual imagery. This was also typical of other Arts and Crafts artists, such as Lethaby and Wilson, who were equally interested in giving fresh symbolic and moral significance to their imagery which they believed would enhance the aesthetic appeal of their work. Cooper's keen interest in the function and purpose of symbolism and allegory led to his publication of an article on the subject in an issue of *The Architects' Journal*.[47] According to Cooper's article, symbolism provided links between seemingly disparate and unrelated elements. The ability of symbolism to bind these elements together supported Cooper's belief in the existence of an ultimate universal unity where all mental and physical imagery was interconnected: 'Symbolism is universal. . . . Directly one looks upon the universe as a whole connected in all its parts everything becomes symbolic by superordination, subordination, and correspondence. . . . The more universal the symbol the higher it is, and the nearer it approaches the idea of unity. . . . Any symbol, indeed, may have an ascending scale of significance, each higher, more interior, and more universal than the preceding.'[48]

The belief in the inevitable interrelationship of all seemingly disparate visual and mental elements was very popular at the turn of the century. Henry Wilson's letters to Cooper indicate similar ideas. W.R. Lethaby, a close friend of both Wilson and Cooper, devoted an entire book, *Architecture, Mysticism and Myth* (1891) to discussing the symbolism and myths of various cultures and historic periods, and to exposing the essential interrelationship between those symbols and myths through their visual expression in architecture, particularly in sacred buildings, which Lethaby considered microcosms of man's perception of the universe. In the book, Lethaby organized myriad myths and symbols into a few basic iconographical categories as further proof of their essential interconnection and interdependence.

The aim of Cooper's imagery, therefore, was not merely to satisfy the aesthetic requirements of a design. He believed that an artist's task was to discover 'the inner properties in things – the ideas underlying them' and pass that knowledge on to his viewer.[49] These 'inner properties' could only be expressed through symbolism, which in turn revealed their cosmic relevance. Accordingly, Cooper's compositional elements always carry symbolic meanings related to the material, function or intended recipient of the object.

'Directly one looks upon the universe as a whole connected in all its parts everything becomes symbolic by superordination, subordination, and correspondence. . . . The more universal the symbol the higher it is, and the nearer it approaches the idea of unity. . . .'

Figure 55. Jewel box in silver after Denoline box in Plate 17, H 21.6 × L 20.3 × W 15.2, 1902. Photograph in Cooper Family Archives.

An ebony box made for Miss Cochran, a Cooper family friend, provides an intriguing example of symbolic imagery designed for a specific client (Figure 58).[50] Though no factual information concerning Miss Cochran exists, Cooper's designs make it quite clear that its decoration was specifically designed for a woman for whom it had some special significance. A gesso panel on the box's lid depicts Griselda, a character in Boccaccio's *Decameron* (*c.* 1353) and the clerk's tale in Chaucer's *Canterbury Tales* (*c.* 1387–1400).[51] These narratives recount how Griselda was put through three severe trials by her husband. With dutiful humility, she submitted and passed the trials, becoming a model of enduring patience and marital obedience. It is interesting to speculate how this tale related to Miss Cochran: had she suffered similarly to Griselda or was Cooper conveying prenuptial advice?

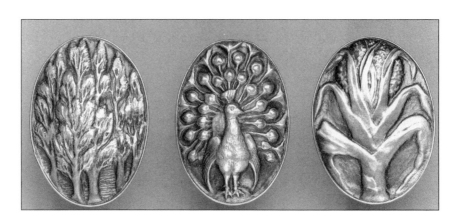

Figure 56. Left to right: opal, amethyst and diamond plaques in silver removed from jewel box in Figure 55, approx. L 6.3, 1902. The Mitchell Wolfson Jr Collection, The Wolfsonian-Florida International University, Miami Beach, Florida.

Cooper's fully developed, mature gesso style is illustrated by the 'Flowers' box completed in September 1901 (Plate 18).[52] The execution of the gesso work here was done by his wife, May, who is recorded as working 289 hours on the box.[53] Both the design and workmanship of the box fully exploit the decorative possibilities of the gesso medium. Its floral designs and colour tones are carefully limited to create a focused aesthetic impact. The octagonal shape furnishes a central compositional axis that further contributes to the unity of the design. Particularly effective is the gilded beading along the edges; it forms a dotted border which Walter Crane considered especially well suited for modelling in gesso.[54] The flowers depicted on the box, aside from their aesthetic appeal, also carry symbolic significance. Among them is the Honesty plant whose transparent seed pouches visually symbolize the moral qualities of openness and frankness: Cooper had concluded that 'all human passions and types of character are symbolized by plants and animals'.[55]

The interior of the 'Flowers' box, which visually confirms the careful attention Cooper gave to all the craft aspects of his objects, is made of cedar wood. In general, the wooden carcasses of boxes used by Cooper for his gesso and shagreen work were made of either cedar wood or walnut. The 'Flowers' box carcass, probably executed by Augustus Mason, is composed of alternating cubic and rectangular pieces of wood whose

Figure 57. Left to right: amber, taos and chrysoprase plaques in silver removed from jewel box in Figure 55, approx. L 6.3, 1902. The Mitchell Wolfson Jr Collection, The Wolfsonian-Florida International University, Miami Beach, Florida.

divergent grain produces an interesting checkered pattern on the interior of the box. As a result, the box becomes visually stimulating on both the interior and exterior.

Cooper's subsequent recorded gesso work, between during 1902 and 1904, falls into two general stylistic categories. The first grouping is characterized by the practice of leaving the modelled gesso relief uncoloured, tinted only by a thin coat of shellac or varnish, which sealed and protected the surface. Cooper framed such uncoloured gesso reliefs with gilded borders whose warm colour tone effectively complemented the glazed gesso surface. Cooper's works in this style postdate an uncoloured gesso relief panel entitled *The Battle of the Kings*, exhibited by Arthur Gaskin (1862–1928) at the 1899 Arts and Crafts Society exhibition.[56] During the 1890s, Arthur Gaskin began working in tempera as part of a revival of this medium by a group of Birmingham artists, including Joseph Southall (1861–1944) and Charles Gere (1869–1957), both of whom Cooper had met in April 1896 while visiting France.[57] Cooper did not meet Gaskin until he began teaching at the Central School in Birmingham in 1901 where Gaskin was already employed. The association of gesso with tempera probably inspired Gaskin to model an entire composition in this material. Gaskin's panel received critical acclaim at the exhibition where, no doubt, Cooper must have seen it.

Of the several pieces Cooper executed in this uncoloured gesso technique, his box entitled *Porta Vitae* is the most ambitious and successful (Plate 19).[58] The gesso scene on the lid of the box, left uncoloured except for a tinted glaze, was entirely modelled by Cooper himself.[59] The skilful execution of the relief supports the complimentary statement made by the Maybury plasterer in 1894 concerning Cooper's modelling dexterity. While the scene is rendered in extremely low relief, the composition maintains a strong sense of deep spatial recession similar to Gaskin's 1899 panel. The surface glaze, effectively lodged in the cavities of the gesso design, emphasizes the gesso brush work, contributing to the spontaneity and directness of the entire composition. The title of the scene, 'portal of life', again indicates Cooper's interest in symbolic, quasi-mystical imagery with superimposed layers of associations and meanings.

The exact source for the title of this box is not known but the broad allegorical implications of such a name open a 'flood gate' of possible interpretations for this scene, much to the probable delight of Cooper himself, who enjoyed such multi-referential imagery. Does this scene depict a child's passage into adulthood? Is the represented walled city heavenly Jerusalem, suggesting a gateway to eternal life? Is the presence of a boat, water, and city meant to portray a harbour and therefore a word play on the meaning of 'porta'? It is probable that Cooper had all three interpretations in mind when he designed the composition. According to Cooper's thinking, such a complex strata of meanings and associations brought one closer to understanding the unified cosmic order.

The second stylistic grouping of Cooper's 1902–4 gesso work is exemplified by the frame entitled *Venus Mirror*, completed in January 1904 and depicting the flowers love-in-a-mist and Venus's looking glass (Plate 20).[60] The mirror's entire modelled gesso surface has been gilded with the raised flower reliefs being coloured over by semi-transparent

GRISELDA BEFORE SHE MET THE MARQUIS.

Figure 58. Design for gesso decoration on workbox commissioned by Miss Cochran, 1899–1900. Cooper Family Archives.

pigments. The 1899 Arts and Crafts Society exhibition had featured a mirror decorated with modelled gesso, entirely gilded and inset with six small tempera panels. The mirror was designed by Joseph Southall and executed by several members of The Birmingham Group. Cooper must have seen this object at the exhibition and perhaps its overall gilding inspired him to try a similar technique in his own gesso work.

The general aesthetic effect of Cooper's mirror, however, is not successful. The metallic glow of the surface overpowers any suggestion of colour or of the gesso surface underneath. Matthew Webb, in his *Studio* article, had cautioned against such dominant use of gold, advising a moderate use of gilding to give jewel-like, decorative accents to a gesso design.[61] The overall gilding of Cooper's frame, and of his other pieces which fall into this stylistic category, completely camouflages the natural properties of the gesso surface, negating the 'truth to materials' dictum of the Arts and Crafts Movement and inadvertently proving the essential soundness of this principle.

In addition to the above twenty-two gesso objects Cooper completed between 1893 and 1904, there exist at least three other gesso boxes that were never recorded by Cooper in either his stock or costing books. All three boxes appeared for sale at the 1923 Arts and Crafts Society exhibition. In his Exhibition/Approval Book II Cooper listed them as follows: 'Gesso & tempera casket' (now in the Cecil Higgins Art Gallery, Bedford and one of the rare examples of Cooper's use of tempera to colour his gesso work); 'Bird Casket' (now in a private collection); and 'Atlantis Casket' (now in the Leicester Museum and Art Gallery).[62] Since Cooper's stockbooks indicate that he practically gave up gesso work after 1904, it is interesting to speculate why at such a late date he decided to exhibit so many boxes decorated with the medium. Perhaps the impetus came from seeing gesso boxes for sale in a tea shop in Monreale during a trip to Sicily in April 1922.[63]

It has traditionally been assumed that all three boxes must date from about 1902 because of their similarity to other Cooper gesso work of that date.[64] However, considering how meticulous Cooper was about recording all his executed pieces in his stockbooks and that the last stockbook entry for his gesso work is dated August 1904, the three boxes must have been executed after this date. Stylistically, all three boxes typify his mature work. An entry in Cooper's journal for 10 February 1908 indicates that even at this late date he was still occupied with some gesso work.[65]

Figure 59. 'Atlantis' box in gesso with gilding, H 11.4 × D 14.6, c. 1908. Leicester City Museums Service.

Of these three boxes, only the 'Atlantis' casket can be dated with some certainty based on the subject matter of its decoration (Figure 59). The name of the box and the images depicted on can be traced to sketches Cooper made of visions he was having in November and December 1907.[66] These visions were the result of mental exercises inspired by occult lectures given by a psychic named Martha Craig, whose sessions Cooper attended during the second half of 1907.[67] These lectures discussed ways in which an individual could achieve cosmic consciousness and prescribed mental exercises to facilitate this. The exercises consisted of concentrating on given coloured symbols and recording the images (i.e., visions) that resulted from this concentration. During these visions, one achieved cosmic consciousness.

As pointed out in Chapter 1, Cooper increasingly became fascinated with mysticism and the occult. In his first lecture to the Art-Workers' Guild in 1907, entitled 'Sources for Inspiration in Modern Art', Cooper

Figure 60. Watercolours of visions Cooper experienced while concentrating on the 'Atlantis' symbol, three of which are reproduced on the body of the box in Figure 59, 1907. Cooper Family Archives.

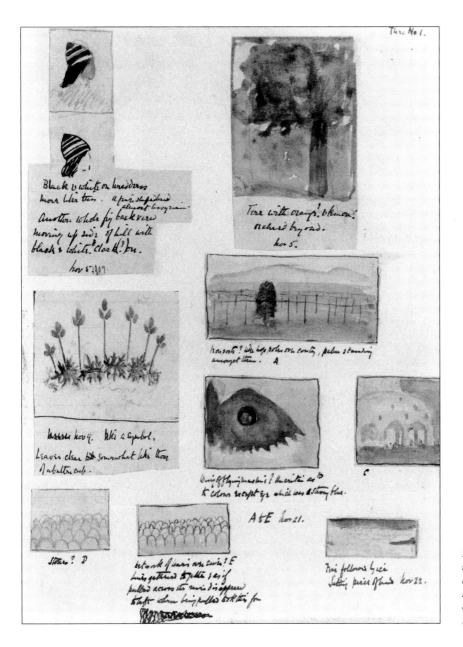

Figure 61. Watercolours of visions Cooper experienced while concentrating on the 'Atlantis' symbol, one of which is reproduced on the body of the box in Figure 59, 1907. Cooper Family Archives.

stated his belief that all artistic inspiration came from 'latent memory', a vast reserve of recollections and experiences accumulated by an individual in his past lives. The symbols supplied by Miss Craig triggered visions of events a person had experienced in his past incarnations. Consequently, achieving cosmic consciousness also meant actively coming into contact with one's latent memory, a direct siphon for artistic inspiration.

The visions represented on the 'Atlantis' gesso casket came to Cooper while he was concentrating on a symbol given by Craig as representing the mythical city. This Atlantis symbol, which depicted a lotus with rising blue smoke, is included on the lid of Cooper's box (Figure 59). The relief panels along the body of the box depict other visions Cooper experienced while concentrating on the Atlantis symbol (Figures 60, 61). Based on this evidence, the casket must date from about 1908, the period immediately following Cooper's visions.

The dating of this box exemplifies the longevity of Cooper's interest in sculptural modelling. This interest, first expressed by the plasterwork he executed for Henry Wilson's architectural commissions, was quickly channelled into gesso. Even after 1901, when shagreen and metalwork began to dominate his output, Cooper remained faithful to the medium in which he had executed his first exhibited artwork.

MOTHER-OF-PEARL

Cooper's non-metal, mother-of-pearl pieces were conceptually related to his work in gesso, both media being concerned with the exterior decoration of wooden objects, mainly boxes and frames.[68] On a few occasions, Cooper even combined gesso and mother-of-pearl in the decoration of a single object (Plate 22). In the case of his ebony cardboxes, executed in 1901 with either gesso or mother-of-pearl decoration, the shapes of the boxes and placement of the decoration were identical in both the mother-of-pearl and gesso ornamented examples (Plate 21).[69] The mother-of-pearl cardbox in Plate 21 also shows Cooper's keen sensitivity for matching the graining of the green mother-of-pearl to that of the ebony – Cooper's most frequent choice of wood for mother-of-pearl inlay.

As with the gesso work, the mother-of-pearl decorations were the sole collaboration of Cooper and his wife: Cooper provided the designs and May usually executed the shell inlay.[70] For example, it is recorded that May spent fifty hours fitting the mother-of-pearl on to the box in Plate 21. In fact, Cooper did not complete any of his stockbook-recorded mother-of-pearl pieces before May joined his studio in 1899. The wood carcasses for his mother-of-pearl objects, like those for his gesso work, were made by Augustus Mason.

Cooper only worked in this medium between 1901 and 1905 when he executed a recorded total of fifteen mother-of-pearl objects, including boxes, candlesticks, and a frame.[71] The majority of these pieces were made in 1901 and were exhibited only once at the Arts and Crafts Society exhibitions.[72] The earliest of these mother-of-pearl pieces, exhibited at the 1903 Arts and Crafts Society exhibition, was a jewel box completed in 1900 and now located at the Cecil Higgins Art Gallery in Bedford (Figure 62).[73] The shape and size of this box again recall the influential Radcliffe workbox Cooper completed in 1898 (Figure 51). The Bedford box is also constructed of ebony with mother-of-pearl panels depicting flowers. But unlike the Radcliffe box, the shell decoration on the Bedford casket is primary and dominant. Also unlike the Radcliffe box, where the mother-of-pearl pieces have been ground flat to conform to the surface of the box, some of the shell pieces on the Bedford casket retain their natural curvature.

According to Cooper, inlay that employed naturally curved shell pieces was the oldest and most aesthetically effective mother-of-pearl technique.[74] Unfortunately, the curvature enormously increased the time needed to fit the pieces together and was therefore abandoned in favour of flat pieces in most contemporary work. Cooper's mother-of-pearl work often combines

Figure 62. *Jewel box in ebony with mother-of-pearl, H 29.2 × L 24.8 × W 17.1, 1900. Trustees of the Cecil Higgins Art Gallery, Bedford.*

the two techniques, as seen on the cardbox in Plate 21, simultaneously exploiting the natural properties and technical possibilities of the medium. For colouring his mother-of-pearl work, Cooper avoided using artificially stained shell pieces and restricted his palette to the natural pigmentation of the mollusc shells: white, green, black, and occasionally red.

The poor condition of the Bedford jewel box illustrates the difficulties Cooper encountered in working with this medium and also shows the best way of avoiding them: 'One of the difficulties with . . . working in M of P is that the pieces are liable to come detached, but if it [an object with mother-of-pearl work] is kept in a dry atmosphere there is not much risk if it is properly fixed.'[75] To properly fix the shell pieces, Cooper stated:

. . . use the best glue rather thin & mix it on a hot iron plate, with whitening [whiting] that has been well dried and warmed, to the consistency of thick cream, the shell itself & the article to which it is attached should also be warmed. The Mother-of-Pearl having had its back roughened to give a hold to the glue & whitening, you apply the mixture & then fix the pieces down with clamps. If the wood to which the M of P is to be attached is of a greasy nature like ebony, it is necessary to scratch the surface of that also.[76]

According to the above explanation, the grout-like material seen under the missing mother-of-pearl pieces on the Bedford box is composed of a mixture of glue and whiting, the same ingredients used to make gesso. The deteriorating condition of this box is probably due to the combined effects of too much humidity and of the shell work not having been properly fixed.

The next recorded mother-of-pearl piece Cooper executed was a stampbox whose decoration included beetle wings embedded in gesso.[77] The use of gesso-embedded beetle wings, a symbolic allusion to the derivation of Cooper's name (see pp. 19–20), also pays homage to the

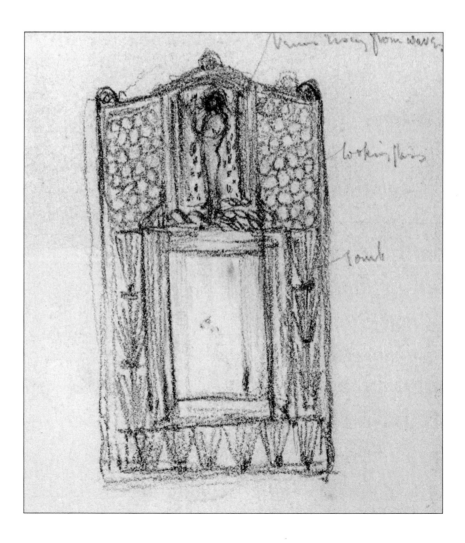

Figure 63. Preliminary design for mirror in Plate 22. Cooper Family Archives.

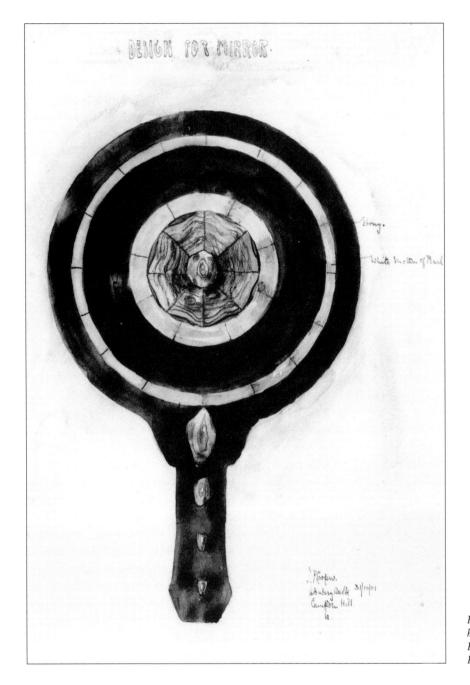

DESIGN FOR MIRROR.

Ebony.

White Mother of Pearl

Figure 64. Watercolour design of hand mirror for a Montague Fordham client, 1901. Cooper Family Archives.

Radcliffe box, which featured a similar decoration on its lid, and again suggests the Radcliffe casket as the stylistic point of departure for Cooper's subsequent mother-of-pearl work. However, the aesthetic success of the stampbox was largely based on the abandonment of all representational imagery in its decoration, relying instead on the colour, texture and patterning of its materials to create an abstract design.

It took 113 hours to decorate this stampbox, making Cooper's mother-of-pearl work as labour intensive as his gesso.[78] The amount of labour required to execute such pieces was responsible for their relatively high sale price (e.g. the Bedford box cost £28 10*s* 8*d* to make and was priced over £50). To the general public, such prices did not reflect the intrinsic value of the materials used and the pieces remained unsold during Cooper's lifetime.

The combination of gilding and shell work used in the stampbox was only repeated once by Cooper in the decoration of a mirror frame now also in Bedford (Plate 22).[79] The practice of combining mother-of-pearl and gilded gesso was not exclusive to Cooper. A noted practitioner of this technique at the turn of the century was the London artist Frederick Marriott (1860–1941).[80] Unlike Cooper, Marriott primarily used mother-of-pearl and gesso to render representational imagery, usually romanticized medieval subjects. The colouring of his images was frequently obtained by staining the shell pieces in order to expand the limited range of colour found in natural sea shells.[81] Such chemical manipulation of materials was not ethically acceptable to Cooper who rejected it on the grounds that it artificially altered too much the natural properties of the material. Likewise, Cooper rejected art work in which the characteristics of the shell material were subordinated to the imagery they were used to portray: 'M of P on account of its colour & the possibility of filing and cutting the surface without damaging its colour & on account of its being capable of being cut into very small pieces runs the danger of being used for making pictures, & in picture making with such a brilliant material the danger is of the worker forcing his material & working his subject in such a high key that it shrieks.'[82]

Cooper's interest in the decorative and symbolic appropriateness of a design and its materials to the function of an object is superbly exemplified by the Bedford mirror. A mirror related the grooming habits and appearance of a woman: Venus was the archetypal female beauty whose legendary birth from sea foam evoked numerous marine associations. Consequently, Cooper chose to decorate the mirror with mother-of-pearl, a material supplied by the sea, depicting a plant commonly called Venus's comb, the comb being yet another article associated with a woman's toilet. It is interesting to note that in a preliminary sketch for this mirror, Cooper had planned to include the figure of Venus in the central section above the glass (Figure 63). Perhaps heeding his own theories concerning the rendering of pictorial imagery with mother-of-pearl, Cooper abandoned this idea and replaced the goddess with the Venus's comb plant. On the mirror, this plant is cleverly abstracted to the point of resembling underwater vegetation, invoking many further associations between the shell material, its place of origin and various aquatic legends.

The selection of mother-of-pearl to decorate the mirror was further enhanced by Cooper's belief in the essentially feminine nature of this material. Explaining how the mother-of-pearl material reflected the spirit of its underwater origin, Cooper described it as possessing 'the dreaming shining peaceful atmosphere one associates & connects with the depths of the sea', qualities Cooper himself associated with femininity.[83] Cooper again employed mother-of-pearl to decorate pieces of a lady's toilet set which he designed and executed as a commission for one of Montague Fordham's clients (Figures 64, 65).[84] The set consisted of a hand mirror, a pair of hair brushes, and a pair of clothes brushes made of ebony and inlaid with white and green mother-of-pearl.[85] This toilet set was one of only two commissions Cooper executed for a specific Fordham client. The other commission was for a dispatch box made of oak and gesso for the great Italian actress Eleanora Duse (1859–1924). Cooper received both of these commissions before 1903 when Fordham acquired the Artificers' Guild, which must have subsequently executed such commissions for his clients.

Because of its associations with the sea which in turn provoked broader reflections concerning the physical fabric and creation of the universe, mother-of-pearl particularly appealed to Cooper's imagination. In his book *Architecture, Mysticism and Myth*, W.R. Lethaby explained the role and significance of water in the conceptual theories of the universe.[86] He stressed myths that described water as a primordial element in the formation of the universe. The inherent iridescence of mother-of-pearl effectively conveyed the restlessness, elusiveness and ultimate mystery of water, characteristics Cooper most successfully expressed in the shell decoration of his stampboxes, which avoided all literal representation and relied on abstracted design to achieve their aesthetic effect (Figures 66, 67, Plate 23).

The lids of all these stampboxes are outlined with scallop-shaped pieces of mother-of-pearl that provide a conceptual 'wave' perimeter for the central decoration. The central lid decoration of the stampbox design in Figure 66, from which an actual stampbox was executed, could be interpreted as a murky pool of water in which ambiguous oval shapes suggesting fish or rocks appear.[87] Cooper used such an interpretation to describe shagreen's resemblance to mother-of-pearl.[88]

An even more literal representation of water occurs on the stampbox lid design in Figure 67.[89] Here the central wave image is closely related to a sketch of a marble mosaic floor known to represent water that Cooper made in 1899 at the Florence Baptistry (Figure 68).[90] Because of the mosaic's inlay technique and conceptual rendering, Cooper easily adapted the abstract design for his mother-of-pearl work. In *Architecture, Mysticism and Myth*, Lethaby had included a similar rendering of the Florence Baptistry floor.[91] This illustration formed part of an entire chapter entitled 'Pavements Like the Sea' that discussed the representation of water on earthly temple and palace pavements and their symbolic significance.

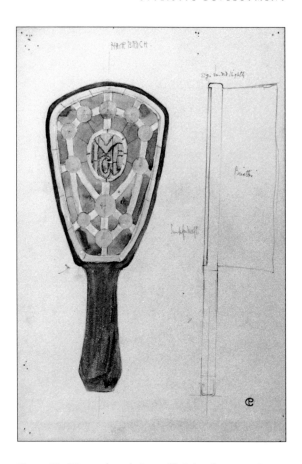

Figure 65. Watercolour designs of hair brush, top, and clothes brush, bottom, for a Montague Fordham client, 1901. Cooper Family Archives.

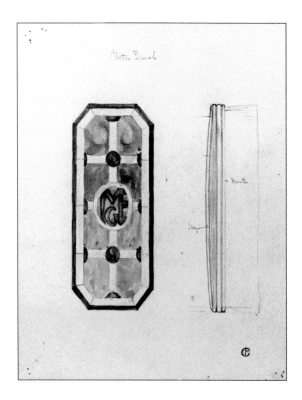

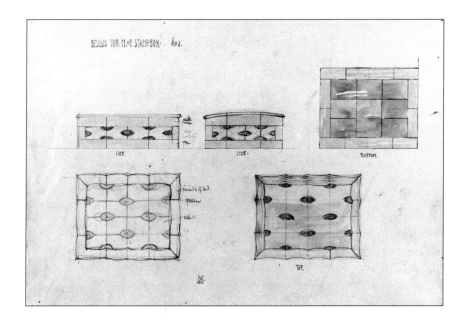

Figure 66. Watercolour design for stampbox in mother-of-pearl, c. 1900. Cooper Family Archives.

The lid of the mother-of-pearl stampbox in Plate 23, executed in 1904, is decorated with a standard marble floor pattern.[92] This decoration is again surrounded by wave-shaped green shell work, implying a symbolic connection between pavement and water. Such an association was proposed by Lethaby in *Architecture, Mysticism and Myth* where he described how water was often thought to form floors in heavenly or otherworldly structures.[93] These heavenly floors were formed by the 'oversea', a body of water which according to numerous legends existed above the firmament: 'There is an abundance of evidence besides what has been given, that the celestial sea forms the floor of the over-world; our

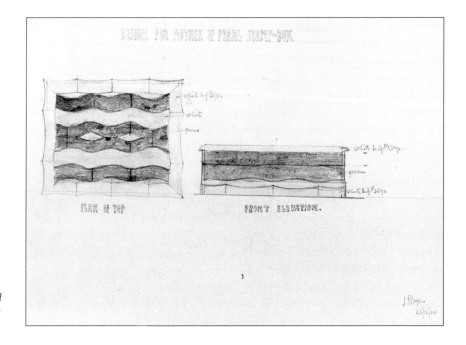

Figure 67. Watercolour design for stampbox in mother-of-pearl, dated 26 December 1900. Cooper Family Archives.

dome [the earthly sky] being the under side of the pavement.'[94] Accordingly, the decoration on Cooper's stampbox lid suggests such a 'sea pavement'.

Rather than revolutionizing Cooper's thinking, Lethaby's book systematized and expanded ideas that were already prevalent at the end of the nineteenth century and that well-read contemporary artists, such as Cooper, were already contemplating and debating. A copy of Lethaby's book was given to Cooper by Wilson with the inscription: 'To J.P. Cooper with regrets H. Wilson'. This inscription, typical of Wilson's wit, suggests that Lethaby's attempt at organizing these ideas was not considered a great success by his friends.

Cooper's mother-of-pearl stampboxes rank as some of his most successful objects and are unique among the extant work of the Arts and Crafts Movement. Their decorations exemplify just how profoundly mother-of-pearl stirred Cooper's imagination and provided him with artistic inspiration. The pleasing aesthetic effect of their decoration alone justifies their artistic success. But when this aesthetic achievement is coupled with the ability of the materials and designs to evoke symbolic and multi-layered associations, Cooper's mother-of-pearl objects truly become artistic masterpieces.

SHAGREEN

Shagreen is perhaps the medium with which Cooper's name is most frequently associated today. His work also won a profusion of accolades from contemporary critics, particularly after 1920 when shagreen-decorated objects became fashionably popular. A London *Times* critic succinctly summarized the praise which Cooper received: 'Mr. Cooper's work in shagreen – or shark skin – mounted in silver and made into boxes and caskets, is now generally accepted as perfect of its kind.'[95]

As this critic pointed out, shagreen is a type of fish skin. Aside from small tropical sharks, it is also obtained from the skins of rays and dog fish (Figure 69). In his various writings, Cooper distinguished between ray fish shagreen, which has a coarse texture, and that of dog fish which has very fine nodules.[96] Explaining further, Cooper wrote: '. . . the integument of sharks, rays, &c., does not possess scales like those of ordinary fish, but very commonly it is developed into papillae which become calcified and give rise to tooth-like structures [nodules], and these when they are very small and close-set constitute what is called shagreen.'[97] In other words, fish skins that are composed of nodules rather than scales, whether left in their natural rough state or prepared by having their nodules filed down to expose a cellular-like pattern of graduated circles, are known as shagreen (Plate 24). The material is extremely durable and scratch resistant. From at least 1907 on, Cooper purchased his supply from a London importing company, W.R. Loxley, which procured the skins in China. The material Cooper used, judging from its texture and size, mainly came from ray fish, which Cooper thought inhabited the Red Sea and the Indian Ocean.

According to Cooper, the name shagreen probably derived from the Turkish and Persian word 'saghi', meaning the back of the horse and

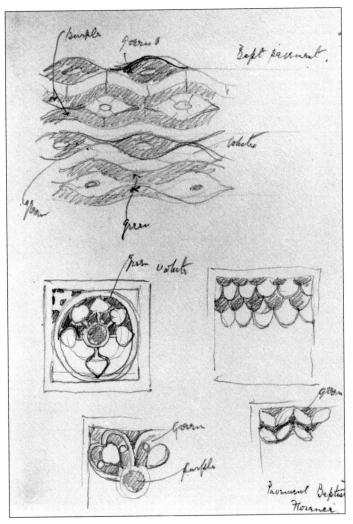

Figure 68. Pencil sketches of pavement in Florence Baptistry, 1899. Cooper Family Archives.

referring to the leather made from that part of the animal. In the preparation of this leather, the wet skins were embedded with seeds that imparted a pitted texture to the leather as it dried, giving it a nodule-like appearance.[98] Fish skin shagreen was first introduced into Europe from China and Japan. In Japan, it was most frequently used in its rough state to cover sword hilts because of its durability and the grip it afforded. Cooper cited several examples of such swords in private collections and in the Victoria and Albert Museum.[99] It is not known how long shagreen in its rough state had been used in Europe but during Cooper's day it was still employed by cabinet makers for smoothing wood, in a similar way to sandpaper.

Shagreen in its smooth, prepared state first appeared in France during the seventeenth century and shortly afterwards was introduced into England. By the second half of the eighteenth century it had become extremely fashionable and common. Because of its attractiveness and durability, it was used to cover spectacle cases, étuis (small cases for female personal articles), instrument cases for doctors and architects, telescopes and watch cases (Figure 70). Its use gradually declined and by the middle of the nineteenth century the very process of preparing and dyeing shagreen was forgotten. According to Cooper, in spite of this technical loss:

the trade in it was continued to about 15 years ago [*c.* 1899], long after the way of working it was practically lost, because certain firms bought up the old instrument cases, telescopes & boxes that were in a poor condition, stripped them & used the skins for mounting on new boxes etc. This went on till no more telescopes could be picked up except at a prohibitive price for people had begun to look upon shagreen as a rareity [*sic*] & curiosity & starting collecting it. It was at this time I became interested in it through Andrew Tuer, the publisher.[100]

As stated in the previous chapter, Cooper recorded a visit to the Tuer household for the first time in February 1898. Cooper recalled that at about this point Tuer:

had made a collection of shagreen & thought that he would like to find out the way it was worked. He soon found out that nobody knew & that it was considered one of the lost arts. This seemed to increase his

enthusiasm. He had recently invented, shall I say, stickphast paste & put it on the market & hoped to do with shagreen what he had done with the stickphast, make a commercial success of it. . . . With regard to the [shagreen] skins it was agreed that we should experiment with them separately. We both started at opposite lines. I started to file mine down & he sent his to a billiard table makers. The first result was that he got his skins nice & thin, too thin in fact, but with the nodules cracked & I got mine with the nodules intact but with a terribly uneven surface. As to colour he bought a lot of photographic dishes & no end of chemicals and a large stock of aniline & other dyes & after dinner & a long day's work at his office he would retire to his study & with the help of his coachman work there till the early hours of the morning. . . . His chief aim was to get what he called the old English green. I don't yet know what that was for when he at last got it and shewed it to me on a fine skin he had got from the East though it was a good colour it was like nothing I have ever seen in old pieces of shagreen. After his death [24 February 1900] I bought up his collection of skins.[101]

Cooper's 'Arts and Crafts' insistence that the skins be prepared by hand is underlined by his statement that the 'finer specimens can only be prepared by hand as the machine in filing down the nodules cracks them'.[102] After explaining the various ways of filing the nodules, Cooper admitted that the process was very lengthy, tedious and required a lot of

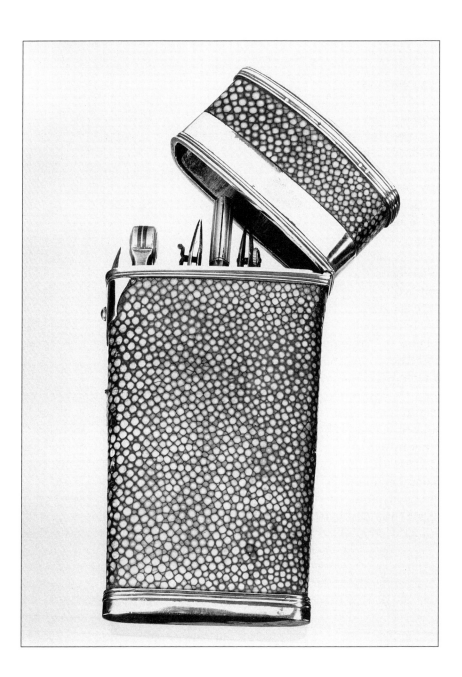

Figure 70. Architect's instrument case in shagreen with silver owned by Cooper, H 12.7, nineteenth century. Private Collection.

skill. The majority of skins he bought, particularly those acquired from Loxley, were already filed, the work having been executed by Chinese workmen. Cooper's contribution to the preparation of the skins usually only consisted of staining, polishing and mounting them.

Unfortunately, Cooper did not leave a detailed account of his own experiments with staining the shagreen skins. It seems that, like Tuer, he first tried to achieve the green colour typically found on most eighteenth-century shagreen pieces. By 1900, Cooper had also mastered yellow, violet, purple, blue and red stains, which he used to dye shagreen skins seen on his contemporary stampboxes.[103] In his notebooks, Cooper gives various recipes for staining the material.[104] The natural colour of shagreen, with its nodules intact, is brown. When the nodules are filed, the natural colour changes to a pearly white (Plate 24). One of Cooper's favourites was stain 'No. 6' which produced a green colour. Its ingredients included two ounces of acetate of copper, a half ounce of cream of tartar, a half ounce of glacial acetic acid and one pint of water. To dissolve, these ingredients were kept in a shaking bottle for about a fortnight and the shagreen skin was then soaked in the mixture for several days. Cooper's daughter Ursula remembered the awful smell of the various stain solutions and the constant experimentation and variation of the recipes to attain new nuances of colour.

Once filed and stained, Cooper proceeded to fill in the interstices between the nodules with cobbler's wax, often mixed with oil colour to complement the colour of the skin. The wax was first rubbed on to the skin's surface and then pressed in with a hot tool. Superfluous wax was taken off with a rag and turpentine.[105] Finally, the whole skin was polished.

To mount the shagreen on to its wooden carcass, Cooper used Cox's Edinburgh Scotch Glue, the wooden surface first being coated with a weak solution of glue and water to stop absorption. Cooper wrote the following instructions concerning the actual mounting: 'Cut skins slightly under what is required as skins stretch when wet. Soak them till soft. Glue box and skins thinly in warm atmosphere over 70 deg. best & iron them with hot iron to squeeze out glue & put under pressure.'[106] A veneering tool could be used instead of an iron, avoiding the necessity for clamps. On round surfaces, wet strips of paper were applied to the newly mounted shagreen; as they dried, they contracted and thereby exerted pressure similar to clamps. In fitting the shagreen to its wooden carcass, Cooper was extremely careful about the placement of the skin's variously-sized nodules. In order to maximize their decorative effect, the biggest nodules were placed

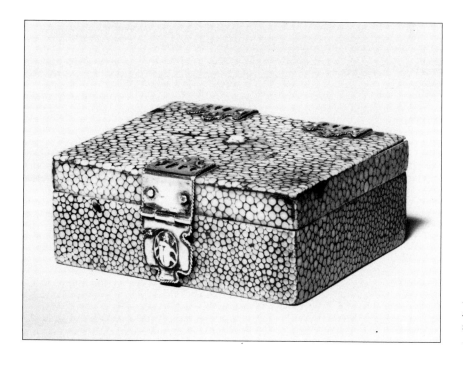

Figure 71. Stampbox with signature beetle clasp in shagreen with silver, H 2.7 × L 7 × W 6, 1899–1900. Private Collection.

Figure 72. Stampbox with butterfly clasp in shagreen with silver, H 2.7 × L 7 × W 6, 1900. Birmingham City Museum and Art Gallery.

Figure 73. Octagonal box in shagreen with silver illustrated in The Studio, 1899–1900. Clipping in Cooper Family Archives.

towards the centre of the surface they covered. Once mounted, the shagreen object received its decoration, which usually comprised a silver catch and mouldings that cleverly concealed the shagreen seams.

Cooper's earliest surviving design for an object decorated in shagreen is dated 30 January 1899 (Figure 30). Cooper seems to have exhibited his shagreen work for the first time in September 1899 at the Arts and Crafts Society's show. At this exhibition, Tuer also exhibited one of his shagreen pieces, a silver-mounted, ruby-glass box with a shagreen lid.[107] Tuer's premature death the following year put an end to his plans for commercially launching shagreen. Cooper was left as the sole pioneer of a revival that culminated during the last years of his life. Today, shagreen is again a lost art; artists are no longer familiar with its technical processes.

From 1899 onwards Cooper's stockbooks record an approximate total of 948 shagreen objects.[108] Over 700 of these were executed after 1910, of which approximately 460 were made between 1920 and 1933.

It is not surprising that Cooper should have been attracted to the decorative possibilities of shagreen work even before he developed his metalworking skills. Like gesso and his contemporary mother-of-pearl work, Cooper used shagreen to decorate the exterior of wooden objects, mainly boxes. However, although she contributed substantially to the gesso and mother-of-pearl, May Cooper did not actively participate in the execution of the shagreen work. A few of the early shagreen pieces were decorated with gesso which May executed but after 1902, Cooper's shagreen was no longer ornamented with gesso.[109] As usual, Cooper provided the designs and Augustus Mason, until 1916, made the wooden carcasses for the objects. Following Cooper's initial experimentation with filing, staining and mounting shagreen, the work of applying the material was increasingly done by his workmen. An examination of Cooper's costing books quickly discloses that all of Cooper's employees, including Lorenzo Colarossi (recorded working on shagreen pieces as early as October 1900), George Romer, William Hazlewood, George Middleton and Bernard Instone, were involved with shagreen work.[110] The work included mounting and polishing the material, as well as making and applying the mouldings. Only if some aspect of the work demanded extra special attention – such as repoussé or chasing – did Cooper become involved with the execution. Normally, he merely monitored the quality of the work. Occasionally, Mason and later Laurence Turner would mount the shagreen on the wooden carcasses they made for Cooper. Mason also often mounted the hinges and locks.

Cooper's earliest recorded executed shagreen design was for a stampbox exhibited at the 1899 Arts and Crafts Society exhibition (Figure 30).[111] Measuring H 2.7 × L 5.8 × W 5.4 and covered in green shagreen, the box had a pyramidal lid surmounted by a beetle. Aside from two exterior silver hinges, the stampbox also had a silver, hinged snap catch (i.e. a protruding pin from the back of the catch plate snapped into a drilled hole on the body of the box). The box had none of the silver mouldings that became such a distinctive feature of Cooper's later shagreen work.

By the end of 1899, the pyramidal lid was replaced on subsequent stampboxes with a flat one. Executed in 1900, the two stampboxes in Figures 71 and 72 exemplify Cooper's standard stampbox design between 1900 and 1902: dimensions of approximately H 3 × L 6 × W 6; a flat lid; silver hinges, either decorative exterior ones or interior ones running the full length of the box's back; a silver, hinged snap catch outlined with rope moulding and decorated with a simple repoussé and chased design; and no silver mouldings.[112] Such stampboxes were the most numerous objects among Cooper's pre-1903 shagreen work and sold particularly well through Montague Fordham's gallery. In fact, most of Cooper's shagreen boxes executed between 1900 and 1902 found eager customers in Fordham's shop.[113] Though they were fairly crude in execution, the novelty of their material assured their success. Cooper's shagreen work at Fordham's Gallery was even singled out for special praise by *The Studio*: '. . . in Maddox Street, Regent Street, Mr J. Paul Cooper has recently been showing some refined work in shagreen and silver. . . . The varied qualities of delicate colour obtained by Mr. Cooper are very pleasing and it is to be hoped that he will succeed in his effort to make popular once more an exquisite material which has been too long neglected here in England.'[114]

Following the stampbox, the next shagreen-covered shape Cooper introduced was the oblong box (February 1899).[115] Approximately three times the size of the stampboxes, these rectangular boxes also relied for their decorative effect primarily on the colour and graining of the shagreen, the nodules of which were often left in relief on the top centre of the lid and on the chased decoration of their snap catches.

In April and May 1899 respectively, Cooper also introduced octagonal and circular shagreen covered boxes. (Figures 73, 74).[116] Both these shapes were now mounted with silver mouldings that cleverly concealed and secured the shagreen seams. However, unlike Cooper's later mouldings, these were relatively simple, composed of either plain wide flat bands or bands with very simple relief profiles and no twisted wires. The joints between the silver mouldings, as seen in Figure 73, were hidden beneath lumpy, silver disks.[117] By 1901, Cooper was also making card cases and match, necklace and ring boxes covered in shagreen.[118]

Following this creative outburst, which resulted in over fifty completed shagreen pieces between 1899 and 1901, Cooper suddenly turned his full attention towards metalwork. In the autumn of 1901, he assumed his metalwork post at Birmingham and was now obliged to develop and expand his silversmithing skills. Virtually no shagreen was executed in his studio during the first half of 1902. However, by the end of the year, shagreen work had once again resumed. The forced concentration on metalwork proved to have a beneficial influence on Cooper's shagreen. The earlier experimental awkwardness and naiveté of his shagreen silver mounts disappeared. The mounts gradually became more skilful and sophisticated with twisted wire and decorative headed pins being added to

Figure 74. Circular box in shagreen with silver, H 7.3 × D 10.8, 1899–1900. Private Collection.

Figure 75. Oblong box in shagreen with silver, H 7.9 × L 21.6 × W 9.8, 1906. Private Collection.

the mouldings. The press catch (i.e. a button-like mechanism which when pressed released the lid) began replacing the earlier hinged snap. Silver feet were added to the bases of the larger boxes, effectively redistributing their proportions and giving them a new sense of monumental presence and importance (Figure 75, Plate 25).[119]

In 1903, another important event occurred in the development of Cooper's shagreen work. On 28 March he met Arthur Michael Samuel.[120] Later known as Baron Mancroft, Samuel was a manufacturer who variously served as Mayor of Norwich, Member of Parliament and Minister for the Department of Overseas Trade. He also found time in 1910 to pen a monograph on the life of the famous Italian etcher Giovanni Battista Piranesi (1720–78). A collector of eighteenth-century French shagreen work, Samuel was very interested in the objects Cooper had exhibited at the 1903 Arts and Crafts Society exhibition.[121] Seeing great potential in Cooper's revival of this medium, Samuel commissioned him to execute several pieces 'of a much more ambitious kind than those exhibited', stressing that they should be 'bold and swashbuckling . . . a fine masterpiece'.[122]

Samuel's subsequent pressure on Cooper to make showy, grandiose shagreen pieces resulted in the production – between 1903 and 1907 – of some of Cooper's most ambitious and innovative objects. The surviving correspondence between Samuel and Cooper effectively illustrates how much Samuel's personal taste for the grace and elegance of the Louis XVI and Adam styles and his insistence that a shagreen piece should be remarkable for both its shagreen skin and silver mounts (e.g. 'I want these shagreen articles to be not only fine specimens of shagreen but also remarkable for the beauty of their silver decoration') affected Cooper's subsequent work. The designs Cooper sent to Samuel for his approval often came back with written comments and drawn alterations.

In fact, the period between 1903 and 1907, which forms the second stylistic phase of Cooper's shagreen work, could be labelled a 'golden age' of his shagreen designs. His shagreen output during these years was regularly punctuated with exceptionally large and expensive pieces which, after 1908, were rarely made except to satisfy specific commissions. Though not all the big, important shagreen pieces Cooper executed between 1903 and 1907 were commissioned by Samuel, he did buy most of them. During those years, Samuel purchased over twenty shagreen objects from Cooper, including vases, candlesticks, a mirror frame and numerous boxes.

In November 1903, Cooper completed a writing box for Samuel (Plate 26).[123] Measuring an impressive L 25.4 × W 19 and displaying a lavish set of silver mounts, this was Cooper's first important shagreen commission. The silver mounts, though still primarily composed of flat metal strips, were now enriched with twisted wire forming rope mouldings. The heads of the silver pins that held the mounts in place were transformed into decorative rosettes. The lock, as on the earliest shagreen boxes, still remained the focal point of the decoration. Executed by Cooper himself, the chased decoration on the lock plate depicts a laurel wreath and evokes the ancient belief that the laurel imparted the spirit of prophecy and poetry to its bearer.[124] As in his gesso and mother-of-pearl work, Cooper had carefully correlated the decoration to the function of the box.

Another large octagonal box, measuring H 22.9 × D 25.4 and completed in 1904, was purchased the same year by Samuel for over £37 (Figure 76).[125] Its monumental proportions required the use of five skins and 15½ oz of silver in its execution. This box's silver mounts immediately reveal a new sophistication and dexterity missing in Cooper's earlier octagonal boxes (Figure 73). The mounts have a new visual sharpness created by the inclusion of relief-decorated mouldings which accelerate the eye's movement around the box. The joints between the silver mouldings are now deftly concealed beneath clusters of rosette pins. In contrast to the flattened lid of the earlier octagonal boxes, the 1904 box is surmounted by a finial which visually unifies its decoration and balances its proportions, conferring a sense of dignity to the entire piece. According to Cooper's numerous designs and as further indication of the studious detail Cooper gave to his 'golden age' shagreen pieces, the finial represents the Temple of Vesta, an ancient circular building dedicated to the Roman hearth goddess which housed a constantly burning flame.[126]

The Temple of Vesta imagery occurs in at least two other shagreen designs by Cooper.[127] The exact reason for his interest in this building remains unknown: perhaps it was intended as an emblem of domestic virtue and chastity. The interior of the box in Figure 76 suggests that it was used as a sewing basket, implying a female owner for whom such symbolism would have been particularly appropriate.

A third impressive box Cooper completed during the 1903–1907 period (Figure 77) was purchased by Samuel for over £60 in 1908.[128] The care and effort that went into creating this box is evident from the amount of time and expense spent on its execution.[129] In addition to Colarossi

Figure 76. Octagonal box in shagreen with silver and Temple of Vesta finial, H 22.9 × D 25.4, 1904. Photograph in Cooper Family Archives.

spending over 300 hours, Middleton spent another 348 hours working on this object. Seventeen skins were used to cover it and over 40 oz of silver were used for its mounts. The total cost of execution exceeded £46. The box's interior contained an ebony tray inlaid with ivory, further attesting to the care and interest Cooper lavished on such early shagreen pieces. Rarely again did he make such an extravagant and expensive piece of shagreen.

Figure 77. Oblong casket in shagreen with silver, 1907. Photograph in Cooper Family Archives.

Figure 78. Scent bottle in shagreen with ivory by Richard Garbe, illustrated in The Art Journal, *1907. Clipping in Cooper Family Archives.*

It is interesting to note that Cooper's early lead in producing shagreen-decorated objects was quickly followed by the sculptor Louis Richard Garbe (1876–1957).[130] He was the son of a commercial ivory carver who ran G. Garbe & Sons at 11 D'Arblay Street, London W1; Cooper occasionally ordered ivory from this firm. After serving his apprenticeship in an ivory, tortoiseshell and mother-of-pearl workshop (presumably the family business), Garbe studied sculpture and eventually taught the subject at the Royal College of Art. He became one of the few artists of his time to employ ivory for serious sculptural work. According to Kanty Cooper, 'before it [shagreen] became fashionable in the 1920s and '30s there was only one man [besides Cooper] in England using the skins. He was the son of an ivory carver called Garbe who made articles on a commercial basis.'[131]

Garbe exhibited nine shagreen pieces at the 1906 Arts and Crafts Society exhibition, including a box and inkstand mounted in steel and brass, a scent bottle, and a clock case.[132] Most of these exhibited items were decorated with carved ivory plaques (Figure 78).[133] This combination of ivory and shagreen, as seen on the illustrated scent bottle, was extremely successful due to the sensitivity and skill with which the ivory was carved and related to the object it decorated. It is curious to note that Garbe's objects were never described as shagreen but always referred to as 'fish skin', both in the Arts and Crafts catalogues and in magazine illustrations, possibly because it was a more explicit term that a layman could understand. How Cooper viewed Garbe's shagreen work is not known. However, in his Technique Notebook 6 Cooper did write a note describing a solution Garbe used to stain shagreen. Interestingly, Cooper himself sent no shagreen work to the following Arts and Crafts Society exhibition in 1910, the only Society exhibition after 1906 not to feature his shagreen work.

On the very few occasions Cooper combined ivory with shagreen, as seen on his round boxes executed in 1913 and on his frames completed in 1920, the results were not aesthetically pleasing.[134] A critic for the *Morning Post* in 1924 noted: 'Mr. Cooper's sense of proportion and line is well shown in his shagreen and silver caskets, though his experiments in shagreen and ivory are not always so successful.'[135]

Aside from the inclusion of ivory, a further comparison between Garbe's 1906 pieces and contemporary objects by Cooper discloses an even more fundamental stylistic divergence (Figures 75, 79). Garbe's pieces have a strong medievalizing flavour. Cooper's, on the other hand, are much more elegant and refined, displaying an almost Edwardian modernity. This grace and elegance was to become even more pronounced in Cooper's subsequent shagreen work, reflecting Samuel's influential preference for the Louis XVI and Adam styles.

The years between 1908 and 1915 mark the third stylistic phase of Cooper's shagreen work. During this period, and particularly after 1910, Cooper began to exploit more fully the commercial success of his shagreen objects. His studio output of the material virtually doubled over that of the previous years.[136] Between 1903 and 1908, he produced approximately eighty shagreen pieces, mainly boxes. In 1914 alone, his studio produced over sixty pieces. Shagreen-covered frames mounted in silver were also now introduced. No longer indulging in the regular production of splendidly expensive pieces, Cooper's team now executed a steady stream of smallish boxes. Either oblong or round, these boxes were only distinguishable from each other by the colour of their shagreen, their press catches and minor variations in their silver

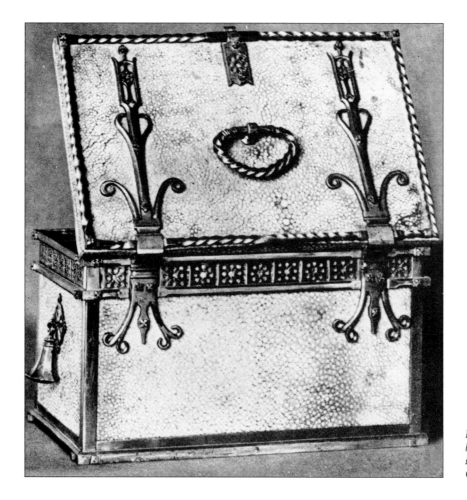

Figure 79. Casket in shagreen with brass and steel by Richard Garbe, illustrated in The Art Journal, *1907. Clipping in Cooper Family Archives.*

mouldings. A typical oblong box from this period cost about £5 to £6, had a domed lid, and was 8–10 centimetres long and three to four inches wide (Figure 80).[137] Its edges were outlined with silver mouldings composed of alternating plain and twisted bands. To make the mouldings, a narrow strip of silver was pulled through a die, the profile of which imparted a combination of plain and relief bands to the metal strip (Figure 81). The rope bands, made from separately twisted wire, were then soldered on top of this metal strip to complete the moulding. The earlier plain flat strip mouldings with their decorative pin heads gradually disappeared and were replaced by narrower and more delicate relief mouldings attached by plain, oval-head pins (Figure 82).[138] The profiles of the individual rope bands that composed these mouldings were now themselves varied, often being squared or flattened. Likewise, particularly on round boxes, the mouldings began to display tooled decoration, typically done in a scalloped or a 'purled' pattern, which featured a band of incised circles (Figure 87).

Figure 80. Oblong box in shagreen with silver, H 6.3 × L 16.5 × W 9.5, 1926. Private Collection.

The small round boxes introduced in 1908 became the most frequently made shagreen item in Cooper's studio (Figure 83). Their size – H 3.8–6.3 × D 7.6 – and their relatively simple mounts, made them quick and easy pieces to execute. Their relative cheapness, selling for under £2 before the First World War and for about £3 during the 1920s, made them a popular commodity with people eager to buy fashionable trinkets. As a result, both round and oblong boxes provided Cooper with a steady income and allowed him to devote more time to metalwork which, aside from public commissions, was rarely as profitable as the shagreen.

Between 1908 and 1915 the bulk of Cooper's shagreen work, especially the cheaper items, was sold through the Artificers' Guild, which had replaced Fordham's Gallery.[139] So fashionable had Cooper's shagreen become that in 1913 the Artificers' Guild ordered three small square shagreen boxes to contain 'Chinese puzzles', irregular pieces of mother-of-pearl that could be fitted together to form the interior lining of a box (Plate 27).[140] For Cooper, the marine affinity between the origins of

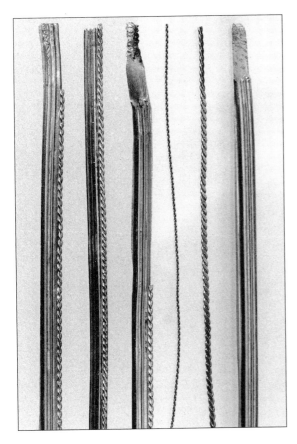

Figure 81. Silver mouldings in various stages of completion to be used as mounts for Cooper's shagreen work. Private Collection.

shagreen and mother-of-pearl dictated their use together. Likewise, the choice of shagreen for such expensive toys indicated the high artistic profile the material was acquiring, particularly when associated with Cooper's name. Not surprisingly, Queen Alexandra ordered an identical Cooper puzzle box for herself.[141]

The hinged snap on these boxes recalls a catch type Cooper used on his earliest shagreen stampboxes. Between 1903 and 1920 Cooper occasionally revived the silver decoration of his pre-1903 boxes, which had featured such hinged catches and decorative exterior hinges. Such mounts purposely gave a nostalgic, medievalizing quality to his objects.

The exposure his shagreen work was receiving between 1908 and 1915 at the Artificers' Guild shop, at the Arts and Crafts Society exhibitions and at various international exhibitions began to secure for Cooper an identifiable group of affluent clients who regularly acquired and commissioned his shagreen pieces.[142] Most prominent among them was the 5th Marquess of Lansdowne (1845–1927), one of the largest landowners in England and a trustee of the National Gallery. He bought three of Cooper's shagreen objects at the 1912 Arts and Crafts Society exhibition, including a large writing cabinet, the edges of which were outlined in ebony instead of the more usual silver mouldings (Figure 84).[143] The ebony cleverly emphasized the unbroken expanse of the shagreen surfaces. Subsequently, in 1913 Lansdowne commissioned a cigarette case, the first Cooper ever executed in shagreen, which became the catalyst for the production of several other smoking accessories.[144] Later that year, Lansdowne also commissioned an expensive cigarette box from Cooper (Figure 85).[145] Completed in November 1913, the style of this piece with its wide plain, flat mouldings and rosette pins recall Cooper's shagreen style of 1903–7. Between 1908 and 1915, when Cooper was called upon to make impressive, monumental boxes, his designs often recalled the ones he had made for Samuel.

Another frequent client was Lady Nina Corbet of Shrewsbury (d. 1921), later Mrs Reginald Astley. Between 1909 and 1911 she purchased six shagreen pieces from Cooper.[146] But perhaps the most artistically renowned of Cooper's shagreen clients was the Scottish architect Sir Robert Lorimer (1864–1929), known for the detailed craftsmanship of his buildings.[147] Aside from designing furniture, embroidery and stained glass, he, like Samuel, had a collection of old shagreen objects that Cooper repaired for him. He also had an extremely high regard for Cooper's own shagreen work, considering him 'the most eminent modern worker in shagreen'.[148] Lorimer purchased and commissioned numerous shagreen pieces from Cooper, even sending his own fish skins to be mounted.

Figure 82. Detail of shagreen box, 1912. Private Collection.

The expanding reputation of Cooper's shagreen work culminated in a commission from the Fishmongers' Company in 1917 for a Freedom Casket to be presented to Admiral Earl John Jellicoe (1859–1935), the First Sea Lord (Figure 86).[149] On hearing that Cooper had received the commission, Arthur Samuel imparted the following advice: 'The casket to my mind, should be very large, probably 16 ins. across, and very noble in proportion. It should have swankish silver dolphins for feet, with plenty of silver in them, and treated after the feeling of Paul Lamerie.'[150] Measuring H 15.2 × L 28.3 × W 15.2 and with silver-gilt dolphin feet, the freedom casket had a lavish display of silver-gilt mouldings and roundels with elaborately chased scenes, all executed by Cooper himself because of the wartime shortage of skilled labour. Cooper spent 528 hours working on the box. The wooden carcass for the casket was made by Laurence Turner. The casting of the feet and the engraving of the inscription were also done by outside workmen.[151]

Figure 83. Circular box in shagreen with silver, H 5.7 × D 8.9, c. 1928. Cheltenham Art Gallery and Museums.

Explaining the significance of the casket's material and decoration, Cooper wrote the following description:

The casket [is executed] in silver gilt and shagreen, as fish skin seems a most suitable material for a casket which is to be presented by the Fishmongers' Company to a seaman. The top is divided into panels with medallions in silver gilt. . . . On either side [of the central panel] are panels representing Venus and Neptune. Venus the sea borne in her car; Neptune with Britannia kneeling at his feet; for it is by the result of her long study at the feet of Neptune that Britannia holds her present

Figure 84. Writing cabinet in shagreen with silver and ebony, H 25.7 × L 31.1 × W 11.4, 1912. Photograph in Cooper Family Archives.

position. The two central panels on the back and front of the casket shew the two types of ship the sailing and the steamship, the protector and the protected. One symbolic of the Navy which Sir John Jellicoe represents, the other of the Fishmongers' Company.[152]

Figure 85. Cigarette box commissioned by the Marquess of Lansdowne in shagreen with silver, H 12.1 × L 22.9 × W 15.2, 1913. Photograph in Cooper Family Archives.

As in his gesso and mother-of-pearl work, Cooper had manipulated the materials and decoration of the casket to reflect its function and importance.

Following the war, which drastically curtailed Cooper's shagreen output, the 1920s and early 1930s saw an unprecedented explosion of shagreen work. During these years, Cooper's studio completed over 450 pieces.[153] A big impetus for this productivity came from the Three Shields Gallery and its owner Dorothy Hutton. The gallery's four Cooper exhibitions and its permanent in-house stock of Cooper's objects effectively disseminated his shagreen work through a fashionable cross section of affluent society. In fact, the Three Shields Gallery so effectively introduced Cooper to his subsequent clients that Hutton wanted a commission on the subsequent orders these clients placed with Cooper; he wisely refused such an arrangement.[154] By the mid-1920s, almost every shagreen piece, whether contemporarily made or unsold surplus from the 1910s, had an eager buyer.

The majority of shagreen pieces executed during the 1920s and 1930s copied the style of the oblong and round boxes made during 1908–15

Figure 86. Front and top views of presentation casket given by the Fishmongers' Company to Sir John Jellicoe in shagreen with silver-gilt, H 15.2 × L 28.3 × W 15.2, 1917. Photographs in Cooper Family Archives.

Figure 87. Oblong box in shagreen with silver, H 7 × L 16.8 × W 9.8, 1923. Private Collection.

period. However, now the silver mouldings became even slimmer, more refined and delicate, giving an almost aerodynamic sleekness to the objects they decorated (Figure 87).[155] The ornamental potential of the press catches was now exploited to its maximum, often becoming the most interesting aspect of the boxes and the only feature that distinguished one from another. Even on large, expensive pieces, the streamlined sleekness of the mounts was preserved, no attempt being made to evoke the wide, massive mounts on the large boxes made during 1903 and 1908 as had been the case during the 1910s (Figure 88).[156] Tall round boxes, meant either for string or cigarettes, measuring approximately H 10.2 × D 8.9, also now became common. Shagreen-handled knives and women's individual toilet articles, such as hand mirrors and powder boxes, were also introduced at this time.

Such specialized shagreen objects exemplified Cooper's attempt to target the consumer market and attract even more buyers. By the 1920s, his studio had become highly proficient in shagreen work, making it both time and cost effective. Though he only employed one full-time workman – Lorenzo Colarossi – in his studio during the 1920s and 1930s, Cooper was able to maintain a high output of shagreen by employing outside workmen such as E. Newton and Laurence Turner. They made the wooden carcasses for the boxes and sometimes also covered them in shagreen. The new sparseness and narrowness of the silver mounts also reduced the time necessary for their execution. The proceeds from Cooper's shagreen sales easily covered the basic expenses of his workmen and studio. The sales of his metalwork alone, aside from various public commissions, could never comfortably do that. The metalwork was much more labour intensive and did not sell as quickly or well as the shagreen. In addition, work on metal pieces could not be as easily or effectively subdivided among different workmen as on shagreen objects.

Figure 88. Casket in shagreen with silver, H 12.4 × L 27 × W 16.8, 1927. The Worshipful Company of Goldsmiths, London

In the second half of the 1920s, the silver mouldings on Cooper's shagreen work began frequently to display a machine-like, repetitive tooling (Figure 89).[157] Rough shagreen, the nodules of which were left intact and not filed, was now frequently used, particularly on round boxes where the protruding roundness of the nodules echoed the circular shape of the box. Tail-piece skins were now also mounted on Cooper's boxes (Plate 28).[158] The stark contrasts in the graining of these tail pieces and the resulting need for numerous vertical mouldings to hide their frequent seams gave boxes a stripped, geometrical surface. Such vertical mouldings were also introduced on tall round boxes that, by 1930, were often covered in contrasting colours of shagreen (Plate 29).[159] The contrasting colours further energized the geometric nature of the boxes' surfaces, producing a dynamic interplay between colour and shape.

One of the biggest and most successful shagreen commissions during the 1920s was a toilet service Cooper executed for Lady Armatrude Waechter de Grimston (d. *c.* 1982), who was known for repainting several damaged statues in York and Exeter Cathedrals following the Second World War (Plate 30).[160] Made in stages between 1925 and 1929 and costing over £90, the completed service was composed of six pieces: a hand mirror, button hook, shoe horn, pair of powder boxes and a standing mirror. Aside from the obvious elegance and grace of the service's design and the faultless workmanship, the aquatic subject matter of the chased decoration on its silver mounts is particularly poignant, recalling Cooper's description of shagreen as:

> a material possessing some of the qualities of both M of P [mother-of-pearl] & leather. Its little nodules of concentric rings give one, when the skin is particularly translucent, the feeling of looking deep down into a pool of seagreen water, there is a little mist at the bottom, so one never quite catches sight of what is there, if it would only clear a little one might get a glimpse of sea anemones, & seaweed waving in the wash of the tide or shells or fish or strange crawling beasts. One can't do much with a thing like that – put a silver bank round it, I mean a moulding, that is practically all.[161]

In fact, the chased decoration on the Waechter service is a visual translation of the above description, proving once again how strongly marine imagery

Figure 89. Detail of silver mouldings on shagreen box in Figure 80.

Figure 90. Pencil sketches of marine fauna done in Sheringham, Norfolk, 1927. Cooper Family Archives.

stirred Cooper's imagination. On its mounts are represented the inhabitants of the shagreen's murky depths – fish, lobsters, crabs, shells and seaweed – for which Cooper made preparatory studies during a 1927 summer family holiday in Sheringham, Norfolk (Figures 90, 91).[162]

In addition to such natural flora and fauna, Cooper also depicted mermaids as representatives of 'what one might call the magic & the poetry of the sea', calling attention not only to the physical appearance of this underwater world but also to its symbolic and supernatural associations.[163] As previously discussed in the section on mother-of-pearl, Cooper equated the peaceful, dreamy quality of the sea's depth with femininity. Accordingly, Cooper again chose marine imagery to decorate objects intended for feminine use. Chased representational mouldings are extremely rare on Cooper's shagreen; they only appear on a few pieces executed between 1924 and 1933, mainly female toilet articles. The Waechter button hook is perhaps the most cleverly conceived item in the entire service (Plate 31). Designing the button hook to represent a fish from whose mouth extends a hook, rather than it being lodged inside, is a typical Cooper conceit. Such intellectual play, added to the pleasing design and workmanship of the piece, transforms the button hook into a little masterpiece.

METALWORK AND JEWELLERY

As recorded in his stockbooks, metalwork and jewellery were the last decorative media Cooper developed.[164] Though Cooper himself noted 1896 as the beginning of his metalwork career, only three of his recorded metal pieces were completed prior to 1901, all three dating between 1899 and 1900: two metalwork pieces; a silver frame and a seal; and one jewellery piece, a belt buckle.[165] In 1901, one metalwork item (a silvered copper frame) and two jewellery pieces (a belt buckle and bracelet) were executed. Only in 1903, when Cooper produced thirty-three pieces of jewellery and seven pieces of metalwork, did a steady output of metalware begin.

The earliest item, a silver frame, was exhibited at the Arts and Crafts Society exhibition of 1899.[166] An extant design for this piece indicates an oval-shaped frame, approximately four inches in height, with a rim composed of rope moulding and a teardrop repoussé design (Figure 31). In 1901, Cooper made a variant of this frame decorated with repoussé violet leaves (Figure 92).[167] Both of these frames also disclose the handiwork of Lorenzo Colarossi. Cooper, who created their designs, only executed the repoussé decoration; the rest of the work was completed by Colarossi.[168]

The execution of the 1899 frame set the pattern for the execution of all other metalware. Cooper provided the designs and his workmen, with the occasional help of craftsmen outside the studio (e.g. casters, enamellers, engravers, etc.), did most of the execution. Usually, Cooper only worked on the repoussé and chasing demanded by a design. In contrast to the gesso and mother-of-pearl work, May Cooper's role in the execution of metalware was minimal, even though she did make jewellery herself as indicated by several entries in Cooper's stockbooks; Cooper would, however, consult her as to the arrangement of stones on certain pieces.[169] A letter May wrote to Cooper on 8 June 1925 while he was travelling in Italy, testifies to her keen sensibility for the colour and appearance of stones: 'Laurie [Colarossi] is at work today, we have just decided he must use the pale foil at the back of the stones. It makes them look a tiny bit more orange which is not an advantage, but at the same time those looked alive & without foil they looked deader.'

Among these three pre-1901 metal pieces, completed in March 1900, was a belt buckle mounted with mother-of-pearl (Figures 32, 33).[170] The execution of this buckle is not listed in Cooper's costing books, so it is not known who worked on it. The piece was sold through Montague Fordham in 1901. In fact, approximately one quarter of all the metalware, primarily jewellery, that Cooper made between 1902 and 1906 was sold through Fordham and the later Artificers' Guild. In contrast, only one-tenth of the metalwork and jewellery executed between 1907 and 1915 was subsequently sold through the Artificers' Guild, even though Cooper's shagreen was selling extremely well in the same shop during this period. Only once, in 1903, did Fordham directly commission Cooper to execute metalware for him. The commission was for six brooches identical to one Fordham had previously sold. Likewise, only on two occasions did the Artificers' Guild commission Cooper to execute specific metal pieces: a necklace in

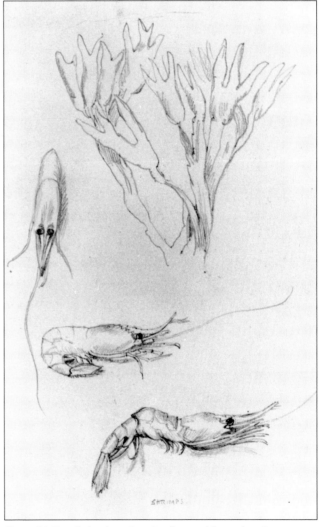

Figure 91 Pencil sketches of marine flora and fauna done in Sheringham, Norfolk, 1927. Cooper Family Archives.

1907 and a brooch in 1908. For both pieces, the Guild supplied the stones. In contrast to the metalware, the Guild ordered at least ten specific shagreen boxes from Cooper between 1907 and 1915. There is no indication that Fordham ever ordered any specific shagreen pieces from Cooper.

Cooper's extensive involvement with Fordham and, subsequently, the Guild poses interesting questions concerning the noticeable similarity between Cooper's and Edward Spencer's work. Spencer became the Guild's chief designer when Fordham purchased it in 1903. In about 1907, when Fordham severed his ties with the firm and the Guild took over his Maddox Street shop, Spencer became the Guild's director. Considering that Fordham's association with Cooper predated his business association with Spencer, Fordham's keen appreciation of Cooper's work, and the fact that Cooper's work sold extremely well through Fordham and the later Guild, it seems logical to assume that Cooper must have had some influence on the Guild's output. Moreover, Cooper and Spencer had similar artistic outlooks and at least two of Cooper's workmen – Colarossi and Charles Baker – also worked for the Guild.

Aesthetically, Spencer's metalwork tends to lack the balanced harmony of Cooper's more subtle decoration and surface treatment. Spencer's objects are often so over refined and attenuated that they negate the inherent solidity and mass of their silver material. His jewellery also often lacks the subtle motif and stone variations found in Cooper's work. No evidence exists in Cooper's archives that there was any frequent contact between the two artists. However, Francis Cooper did remember his father meeting Spencer on one occasion and expressing his displeasure at the Guild copying his designs.

As Cooper's earliest recorded piece of jewellery, the design for the mother-of-pearl belt buckle of 1900 conspicuously recalls enamelled buckles made by Edith (m. 1893) and Nelson Dawson (1859–1942).[171] However, instead of enamel, Cooper chose to decorate his buckle with mother-of-pearl, whose graining suggested a similar floral composition. The avoidance of enamel became typical of Cooper's subsequent work. Only on very rare occasions did Cooper employ enamelling to decorate his metalwork and jewellery. However, it does appear on a small group of Cooper's metalware executed between 1914 and 1915, the enamel decoration of which was carried out by workmen outside his studio.

The Dawson comparison is particularly pertinent in showing that Cooper's early jewellery and metalwork were not wholesale imitations and derivations of Henry Wilson's work. The close friendship between Cooper and Wilson, their mutual exchange of ideas, and their joint architectural projects during the 1890s while embarking on craft careers, account for some of the similarity between their work. Likewise, Cooper's use of Wilson's workmen (e.g. Colarossi and Romer) to execute his metalware designs and his brief silversmithing lessons in Wilson's studio during the summer of 1901 contributed to some resemblance between their work. In considering this issue, Francis Cooper wrote: 'By how much was Wilson my father's senior? My father definitely looked up to Wilson and no doubt being nearly the same age, they talked over many things together, which accounts for much of their early work being rather similar.'[172]

Figure 92. Frame in silver-plated copper, H 10.3, 1901. The photograph in the frame is of Cooper's sister Violet whose name is purposely alluded to in the chased violet leaves on the frame. Private Collection.

Throughout Cooper's career, Wilson had great admiration for him, an attitude hardly possible if Cooper had merely been capable of imitation. In 1901, Wilson wrote: 'Mr Paul Cooper . . . I consider, one of the most remarkable and gifted of my acquaintances.'[173] Wilson's mature work, in contrast to Cooper's, tended to be much more sculptural (i.e. plastic, almost baroque in feeling), often decorated with enamel to produce vibrant colour effects. The complexity of Wilson's richly opulent, stone-encrusted pieces is in direct opposition to the more subtle colouring and less dazzling technique seen in Cooper's work. Cooper's virtuosity lay primarily in the decorative chasing of monochromatic surfaces and in the delicate arrangement of subtly coloured stones.

Between 1896 and his first recorded pieces in 1899 and 1900, little information exists concerning Cooper's work in metal. One of Cooper's earliest metalwork projects (executed in 1896) was to chase an inscription on to a copper plate. This was followed by several other similar commissions from various architects. Among these were the inscriptions for Wilson's Welbeck Abbey lectern and baptistry gates in 1896 and for a tombstone panel designed by Arthur Grove in 1897.[174] Such work familiarized Cooper with metal as a medium and prepared him for executing the repoussé design on the silver frame of 1899. With confidence, Cooper was able to state in 1901 that, in executing chasing, he could now hold his own. Cooper's more specific interest in jewellery seems to have stemmed directly from Wilson's activities at his Vicarage Gate studio during the late 1890s.

The motivation for the aroused interest in silversmithing and jewellery by a number of artists in the late 1890s was explained by a plea that appeared in *The Studio* in November 1896:

> Of all the shop windows to-day the jeweller and silversmith (if he confines his wares to modern products) is least likely to arrest a lover of fine design. . . . We can hope that every one whose means permit will do his best to support a movement towards beauty in these needlessly degraded industries. It is a reproach to our wealthy country that its most costly products are beyond question the most hideous, that its devices in precious metals and jewels are, as a rule, not the least bit better than those produced in cheap imitations.[175]

A clipping of this review is among Cooper's personal papers. This same piece went on to praise C.R. Ashbee (1863–1942) as one of the first to produce artistically designed jewellery and silver tableware. By 1901 *The Studio* was crediting French jewellers, René Lalique (1860–1945) in particular, with instigating a revival of artistic jewellery: 'The pre-eminence of the French artists is evident in jewellery . . . they were the first to gain their freedom and to work as "moderns".'[176] In 1902 *The Studio* printed a special issue entirely devoted to jewellery and fans as further evidence of the revolution taking place in this art.[177]

Cooper's appointment to the metalwork post at the Birmingham Municipal School of Art in the autumn of 1901 propelled him to concentrate almost exclusively on metal during the following year. His artistic output for 1902 was marked by a substantial increase in metalware – thirty-four pieces of jewellery and seven pieces of metalwork.

Plate 1. Watercolour of Evington Hall, North Evington, Leicestershire, where Cooper's family lived during the 1880s and 1890s, 1901. Cooper Family Archives.

Plate 2. Watercolour design for harebell plasterwork at Maybury Cottage, Woking, seen in Figure 25, dated November 1894. Cooper Family Archives.

Plate 3. Watercolour of chapel with the tomb of Sir William Sharington in the Church of St Cyriac, Lacock, Wiltshire, submitted by Cooper for the 1893 Pugin Studentship. Cooper Family Archives.

Plate 4. Romanticized watercolour of the Infants' School Cooper designed in Whitwick, Leicestershire, c. 1898. Cooper Family Archives.

Plate 5. Entrance to the Infants' School, Whitwick, as it appears today.

Plate 6. Watercolour of Betsom's Hill, Westerham, Kent, dated 1912. Cooper Family Archives.

Plate 7. Perseus and Andromeda candlesticks in silver with moonstones, citrines, garnets and amethysts, H 26.3, 1913. Private Collection.

Plate 8. Casket with Ellen Terry's ashes in silver, H 22.5, 1913. St Paul's Church, Covent Garden, London.

Plate 9. Watercolour designs for ceiling and walls of Nursery Room at 1916 Arts and Crafts Society exhibition, 1916. Cooper Family Archives.

Plate 10. Altar cross, H 60.3, and candlesticks, H 33.8, in silver, 1918. St Paul's Church, Four Elms, Kent.

Plate 11. Altar cross in silver with various stones, H 98.4, 1925. The cross was designed for a chapel built as a memorial to the school's 'Old Boys' who had died in the First World War. Oakham School, Rutland.

Plate 12. The King's Royal Rifle Corps War Memorial in oak and patinated steel, H 34.9 × L 117.9 × W 80, 1921. The casket contains a leather-bound book, also designed by Cooper, which lists the names of men from the Royal Green Jacket Regiment who died during the First World War and the Second World War. Headquartered in Winchester, this regiment was founded in 1755 to fight the French and Spanish in North America. The Dean and Chapter of Winchester.

Plate 13. Reliquary commissioned by George Bernard Shaw in silver, H 26, 1931. Photograph by Robert Cotton used with permission of Stanbrook Abbey.

Plate 14. Watercolour of Coutances, France, 1925. Cooper Family Archives.

Plate 15.   Pastel of Bodiam Castle, East Sussex, 1912. Cooper Family Archives.

Plate 16. 'Seasons' workbox in Denoline with gilding, H 22.9 × L 20 × W 14.3, 1898–9. Private Collection.

Plate 17. *Pastel of jewel box in Denoline, c. 1899. Cooper Family Archives.*

Plate 18. *'Flowers' box in gesso with gilding, H 20.9 × L 18.1 × W 14.3, 1901. Photograph by Robert Cotton by courtesy of* The Magazine Antiques.

Plate 19. *'Porta Vitae' box in gesso with gilding, H 10.8 × D 16.5, 1903. Cooper Family Archives.*

Plate 20. *'Venus Mirror' frame in gesso with gilding, H 35.5 × W 18.4, 1904. Private Collection.*

Plate 21. Cardbox in ebony with mother-of-pearl, H 7.3 × L 24.8 × W 12.4, 1901. Private Collection.

Plate 22. Mirror with mother-of-pearl, H 79 × W 42.9, 1902. Trustees of the Cecil Higgins Art Gallery, Bedford.

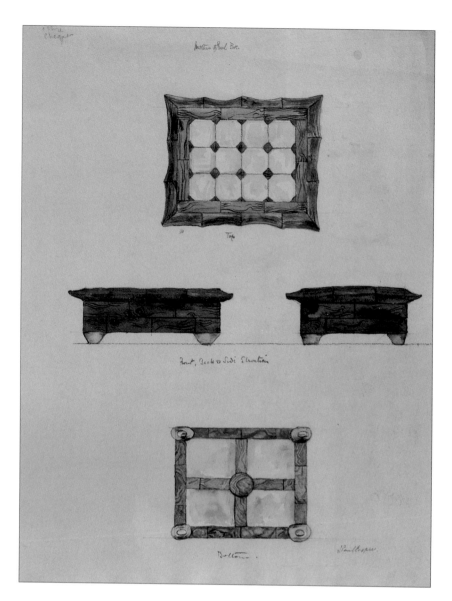

Plate 23. Watercolour design for stampbox in mother-of-pearl, 1904. Cooper Family Archives.

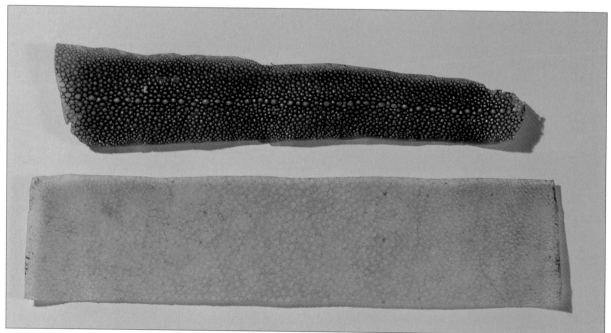

Plate 24. Natural-colour shagreen skins with the nodules intact, at the top, and with filed nodules, on the bottom. Private Collection.

Plate 25. Octagonal box in shagreen with silver, H 12.1 × D 13.6, 1906. Photograph by A.C. Cooper Ltd, by courtesy of The Magazine Antiques.

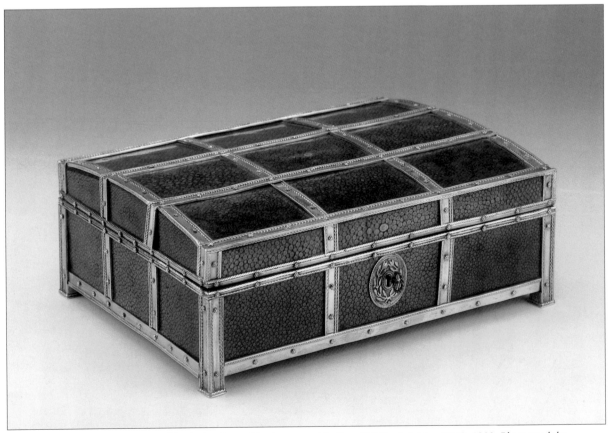

Plate 26. Writing box commissioned by Arthur Samuel in shagreen with silver, H 9.2 × L 25.4 × W 19, 1903. Photograph by A.C. Cooper Ltd, by courtesy of The Magazine Antiques.

Plate 27. Puzzle box in shagreen with silver and mother-of-pearl, H 2.4 × L 5.4 × W 5.4, 1913. Private Collection.

Plate 28. Oblong box in shagreen with silver, H 8.4 × L 22.1 × W 10.2, 1932. Fitzwilliam Museum, Cambridge.

Plate 29. Circular cigarette box in shagreen with silver, H 11.1 ×
D 8.9, 1932. Private Collection.

Plate 30. Lady Armatrude Waechter de Grimston toilet service in
shagreen with silver, 1925-1929. V&A Picture Library, London.

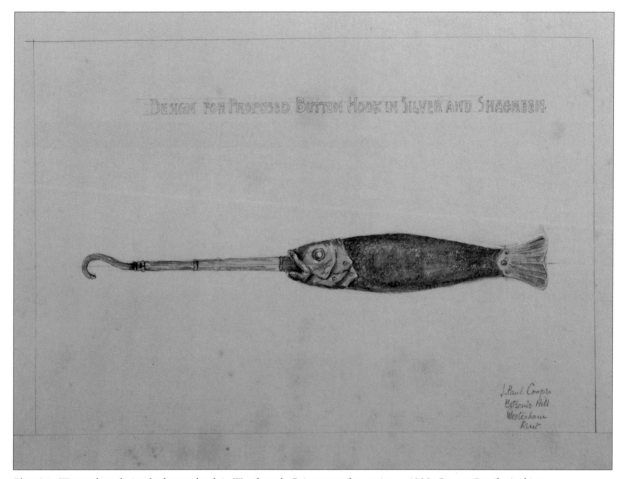

Plate 31. Watercolour design for button hook in Waechter de Grimston toilet service, c. 1928. Cooper Family Archives.

Plate 32. 'St Hubert' pendant in silver with sapphires and amethysts, L 5.7, 1905. Private Collection.

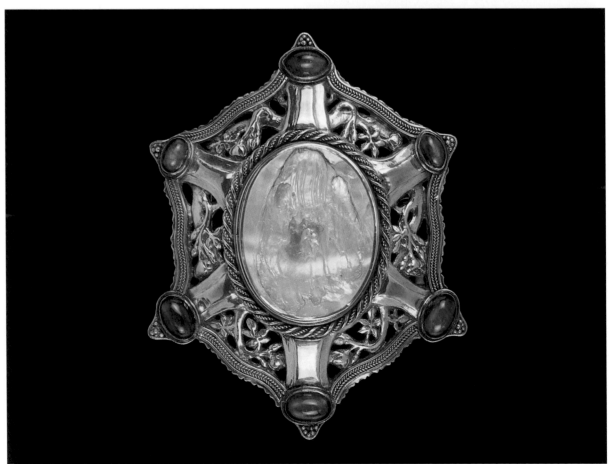

Plate 33. Belt buckle in silver with mother-of-pearl and labradorite, L 10.5, 1902. Fitzwilliam Museum, Cambridge.

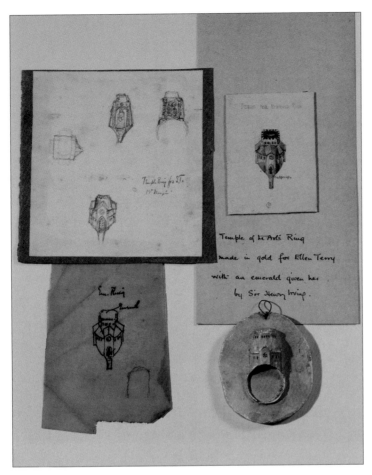

Plate 34. *Design and production stages for the execution of the Ellen Terry ring in Figure 99. Cooper Family Archives.*

Plate 35. *Belt buckle in silver with chrysoprases, L 8.2, 1905. Private Collection.*

Plate 36. Necklace in 18-carat gold with 384 seed pearls, L 36.8, 1905. Private Collection.

Plate 37. Altar cross in brass with sapphires, amethysts and crystals, H 119.4, 1905. With permission of Provost and Chapter of Birmingham Cathedra

Plate 38. Left: Matchbox in mokumé, H 4.8, 1906. Private Collection. Right: 'Hanging Moth' brooch in mokumé, D 4.1, 1906. Private Collection.

Plate 39. Bonbonnière in silver with coral, ivory and lapis lazuli, H 20.3, 1903–6. Private Collection.

Plate 40. Brooch in silver and gold with moonstones, pearls and tourmalines, L 3.5, 1908. Private Collection.

Plate 41. Pendant in silver and gold with rubies, opals, chrysoprases, sapphires and aquamarines, L 13.6, 1906. V&A Picture Library, London.

Plate 42. Double brooch in 15-carat gold with moonstones, rubies, chrysoprases and shell, L 14.3, 1908. Collection John Jesse.

Plate 43. Necklace in 15-carat gold with chrysoprases, sapphires, Ceylon zircons, opal and ruby, L 38.1, 1909. Tadema Gallery, London.

Plate 44. Necklace in 15-carat gold with garnets, chrysoprases and pearls, L 39.4, 1907. Private Collection.

Plate 45 Chalice in silver with garnets, chrysoprases and carbuncles, H 27.6, 1907. Leicester City Museums Service.

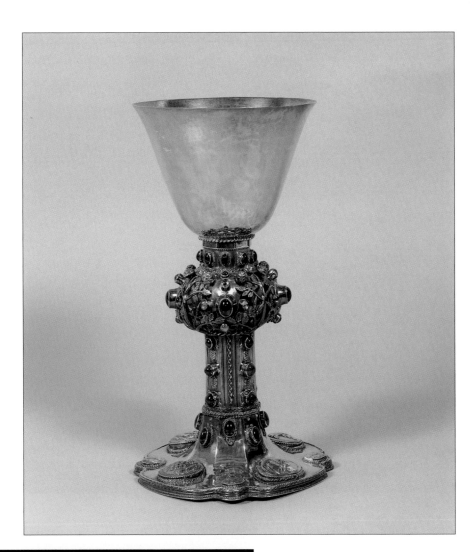

Plate 46. *Chalice in silver and parcel-gilt with garnets, Ceylon zircons and carbuncles, H 23.2, 1908. Trustees of the Cecil Higgins Art Gallery, Bedford.*

Plate 47. *Fruit stand in gilt-copper with shell and mother-of-pearl, H 19, 1908 (gilding added later). Private Collection.*

Plate 48. Covered jar in patinated copper, H 14.6, 1910. Private Collection.

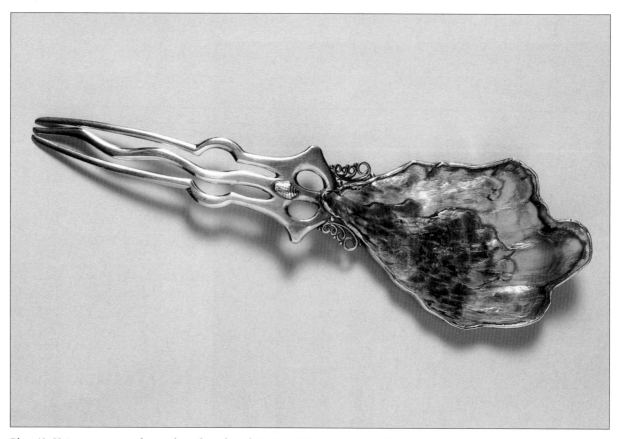

Plate 49. Hair ornament in silver with mother-of-pearl, L 16.8, 1909. Birmingham City Museum and Art Gallery.

Plate 50. 'Pomegranate'
necklace in 18-carat gold with
enamel, L 49.5, 1915. Private
Collection.

Plate 51. Right: Box in silver with moss agate and enamel, H 2.5 × L 5.1, 1915. Private Collection. Left: Box in silver with white
agate and enamel, H 2.5 × L 4.1, 1915, Private Collection.

Plate 52. 'Xmas' pendant in 18-carat gold with spinels and coral, L 5.7, 1913, Private Collection.

Plate 53. Right: fibula brooch in 18-carat gold with emeralds and pearls, L 4.4, 1911. Private Collection. Left: fibula brooch in 18-carat gold with emeralds and sapphires, L 4.4, 1911. Private Collection.

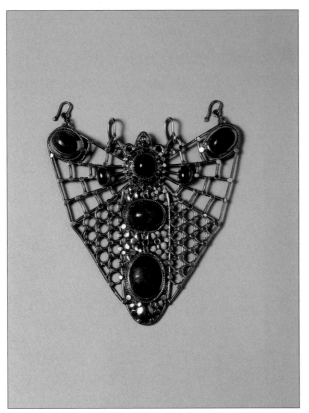

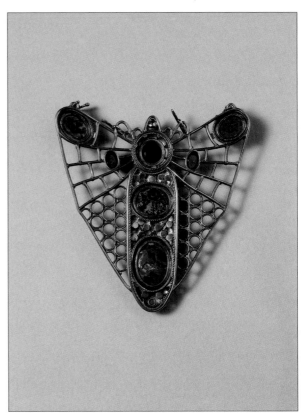

Plate 54. 'Moth' pendant in silver with azurite, lapis lazuli, amethyst, stained agate and garnets, L 8.9, 1912. Birmingham City Museum and Art Gallery.

Plate 55. Back view of pendant in Plate 54.

Plate 56. Watercolour of moth, dated 27 March 1912. Cooper Family Archives.

Plate 57. Necklace in 18-carat gold with emeralds, sapphires, tourmalines and pearls, L 36.8, 1912. Trustees of the Cecil Higgins Art Gallery, Bedford.

Plate 58. Coconut bowl mounted in silver with mother-of-pearl, H 16.2, 1915. V& A Picture Library, London.

Plate 59. Altar cross in brass and silver with various stones, H 111.8, 1915. Royal Holloway, University of London.

Plate 60. 'Justice' pendant in 18-carat gold with emeralds, sapphires, Ceylon zircons, garnets, moonstones and black pearl, L 11.4, 1921. Birmingham City Museum and Art Gallery.

Plate 61. Right: 'Cupid Triumphant' pendant in silver with chrysoprase and azurite, L 8.9, 1921. Private Collection. Left: Pendant in silver with chrysoprase and garnets, L 6.7, 1921. Private Collection.

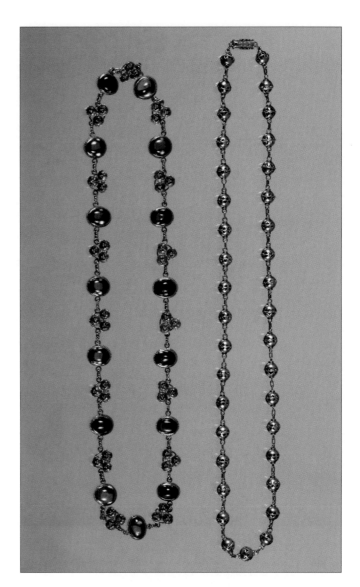

Plate 62. Left: Necklace in 18-carat gold with zircons, L 39.4, 1921. Private Collection. Right: Neckchain in 18-carat gold, L 41.9, 1922. Private Collection.

Plate 63. Pair of string boxes in brass and copper, D 7.6, 1922. Private Collection.

Plate 64. Pendant in 18-carat gold with moonstones, L 13.3, 1929. Tadema Gallery, London.

Figure 93. Pair of candlesticks and sugar bowl in silver, copper and mother-of-pearl illustrated in Der Moderne Stil *in 1903. Photograph in Cooper Family Archives.*

As a result, Cooper exhibited hollow ware (three-dimensional objects) and jewellery for the first time at the 1903 Arts and Crafts Society exhibition.[178] Two of the exhibited pieces – a candlestick and sugar bowl made of silver, copper and applied mother-of-pearl – were singled out for illustration by the German periodical *Der Moderne Stil* (Figure 93).[179] However, Cooper's metalware did not receive widespread British critical attention until the Arts and Crafts Society exhibition of 1906.

Between 1899 and 1906, excluding handles made for Gimson, Cooper's jewellery pieces outnumbered his metalwork three to one. Gradually, this ratio changed in favour of metalwork. Cooper's stockbooks record a total of more than 1,400 executed pieces of metalwork and jewellery. In reaching this total, metalwork was produced approximately one and a half times more frequently than jewellery (i.e. approximately 550 pieces of jewellery and 850 pieces of metalwork were made). The fact that jewellery was made more frequently than hollow ware during the early years of Cooper's career points to both his and his workmen's lack of proficiency in executing three-dimensional objects. Jewellery pieces, essentially two-dimensional in form when compared to hollow ware, were conceptually and technically easier to execute.

In the years between the Arts and Crafts Society exhibitions of 1903 and 1906, Cooper's theoretical views concerning the nature of metalwork and jewellery began visibly to influence his work, affecting both his designs and technical treatment. The majority of Cooper's lectures on silverwork and jewellery – delivered between 1903 and 1929, mainly to fellow craftsmen – stressed the romantic and magical origins of these arts.[180] According to Cooper, from prehistoric times to the Middle Ages metals, such as silver and gold, and precious stones were considered

Figure 94. 'Aladdin' pendant in
silver with moonstone, sapphire
and chrysoprases, L 6, 1903.
Illustrated in The Studio in 1906.
Clipping in Cooper Family
Archives.

sacred, 'as symbols or types of the Divinity, and as gifts to
man from the Gods themselves'.[181] As such, they were
employed to represent the power, wealth, and majesty of the
divinities. Expanding his theories further, Cooper stated that
'from looking upon metals as symbols of divinity it is but a
step to regard them as the dwelling place or body of some god
or spirit'.[182] Gold and precious stones came to be 'regarded as
possessing in themselves inherent magical qualities. Gold was
not only considered intimately connected with the sun &
silver with the moon. The precious stones themselves had
influence over men's destinies, some being preventatives of
vice, some guardians of virtue, whilst others were held to utter
warnings to their possessors of coming danger.'[183] Jewellery
functioned 'as charms, talismans or amulets to placate evil
spirits or to attract the attention of good spirits or as
memorials of some saint or hero whose virtue the owner
wished to attain or of whose personality he wished to be
continually reminded'.[184] Continuing to expound his ideas,
Cooper declared: 'It was but a step from regarding the metals
as sacred to investing those who worked in them with priestly
attributes . . . his [the goldsmith's] work was regarded rather
as a sacred mystery than as a secular trade'.[185] High esteem
was bestowed on goldsmiths and jewellers who, during pagan
times, were regarded as magicians and, during the Middle
Ages, became pious clerics attached to monasteries. In both
cases, their spiritual aim was to express and represent metaphysical truths
in their work. According to Cooper, with the coming of the Renaissance,
precious metals and stones gradually became more indicative of social
status rather than of spiritual and religious beliefs. As they became mere
signs of material wealth, their designs lost expressive power, which
resulted in a loss of aesthetic value. Commercialism was the final blow to
inspired goldsmiths' work.[186]

The loss of spiritual expression, which Cooper saw in much post-
medieval metalwork, had culminated in the tasteless and aesthetically
barren late nineteenth-century English trade jewellery and silverwork:

It isn't design that is needed today, as we are told, as much as finding out
what we want to say and saying it. Today there is a call in metalwork, as
in other arts, for plainness and simplicity; & a corresponding fear of
decoration. That is all very well if it is the result of wishing for plainness
and simplicity in our lives, but if it is because the metal work trade by
their overloading their work with meretricious ornament, has led to a
change of fashion in the opposite direction, then it is like calling for
plain Jane because one is sick of her overdressed sister.[187]

It was Cooper's firm belief that strong spiritual expression guaranteed a
good aesthetic design: 'In former days nobody troubled their heads as to
what [good] design was. When a person had something to say or express
he worked at it till it took the best form suitable for conveying the
impression he intended, and that final form we call the [good] design.'[188]

Related to the concept of precious metals and stones as sacred materials was the early belief that these materials were alive and possessed a soul. A by-product of early animism, which endowed inanimate matter with animate characteristics, the belief evolved 'that the life lying dormant in metals was evoked by the artist in his act of creation'.[189] A discussion of this belief had appeared in James George Frazer's *The Golden Bough*, which Cooper cited several times. This book was a source of inspiration for many Arts and Crafts artists, including W.R. Lethaby. Originally written in 1890, it was a multi-volume study of primitive superstitions, magic and religions. The book stressed the interrelationship of all these practices and ideas, and how each successive religious sect tended to modify and adapt previously held beliefs and customs. Cooper owned a copy of the second edition of this work published in 1900.

To support the validity of a modern belief that inanimate matter had animate characteristics, Cooper cited contemporary scientific experiments by the Indian physicist Professor Jagadis Chunder Bose (1858–1937) who proved that metal responded to outside stimuli in a similar way to living tissue.[190] Cooper mused about the influence such thinking could have on modern artists: 'What a different view we should take of the metal we worked in if we really felt that while working it we were dealing with life itself. We should endeavour to bring out its innate qualities & treat it feelingly & sympathetically. The artist does so unconsciously, but the effect is greater when done consciously, or rather it is more continuous.'[191] Cooper became a master at exploiting and asserting the innate qualities of his materials. The surfaces of his silver pieces deftly express both the inherent rigidity of their material as well as its possible fluidity when annealed. The subtle balance between these two contrasting features imbues Cooper's silver with a pulsating vibrance. Likewise, the discreet colouring and idiosyncratic shapes of his stones animate their settings.

It is in relation to theories concerning the magical and spiritual origins and connotations of metals and stones that Cooper's metalware must be considered. Repeatedly, Cooper voiced his admiration and preference for the pattern and ornament employed by early artists: 'Decoration in early art whether by means of figures, animals, foliage, or interlacing & other patterns were not used as mere ornament, ornament as we understand it can hardly be said to have then existed, it approached nearer to hieroglyphics. It was a language people could read.'[192] Applied to jewellery, such decoration precluded its function as mere adornment. Instead, jewellery was:

largely looked upon as symbols, as hieroglyphics, ideas expressed by symbols, portmanteau words, as it were, that carried as much meaning as the reader was capable of understanding. . . . The bee was a symbol of the soul. . . . The hawk was a symbol of Horus, on

Figure 95. Pendant in silver and copper with stones,1903, illustrated in The Studio *in 1906. Clipping in Cooper Family Archives.*

account of its soaring & upward flight. And among plants the rose with its thorns symbolized love & the lily and lotus the productive power of nature.[193]

The jeweller . . . not only emphasized [such] symbols in his chasing, carving, enamelling and inlay, but the stones he used were carefully used for the symbology of their colour, or as charms or for the magical qualities they possessed, or were supposed to possess. But, they were not only symbolic on account of their colour, but were thought to be in intimate connection with the stars, and as stars had influence on man's destinies, the stones affected by certain stars could increase or lessen the influence according to circumstances.[194]

The subject matter and stones of Cooper's metalwork and jewellery were similarly intended as 'sign language'. Visually pleasing, they invariably carried symbolic associations that were meant to increase their aesthetic value. Cooper owned a copy of George Frederick Kunz's *The Curious Lore of Precious Stones* (1913), which detailed the symbolic, superstitious, and magical associations of various stones. In March 1928, he published his own article on jewellery and superstition.[195]

Strong symbolic expression in early metalwork and jewellery was achieved not only by the depicted imagery but also by the artistic rendering of such motifs. As Cooper pointed out, 'the symbolic animals, plants, etc. were not treated naturally to represent animals in nature, they were treated what one might call rhythmically'.[196] According to Cooper, 'rhythmic' treatment meant the stylization and simplification of motifs in opposition to visual verisimilitudes and technical virtuosity. Such rhythmic rendering, enhanced by the aesthetic appropriateness of a motif to the surface it decorated and its material (i.e., truth to materials, functions and form), helped evoke metaphysical associations, turning ordinary motifs into hieroglyphics (i.e. sign language).

As a result of such thinking, Cooper employed only the most basic decorative motifs and silversmithing techniques. His son Francis explained: 'While searching to recapture something of early times, which he felt had been lost, he built up his designs using simple units – silver beads and domes, twisted wires and simple shapes which could be raised by hammer. He did not use spinning or die stamped parts.'[197] Hand raising, repoussé and chasing were the primary techniques used to execute most of Cooper's work. Even casting was seldom utilized. When it was employed, the rough, molten quality of the melted metal was carefully preserved in the final cast, a quality that also appealed to Wilson.[198] Machine-like finish was strenuously avoided: 'My father [John Paul Cooper] was suspicious of all machine work, as making for deadness. Polishing in our workshop had to be done on an old treadle lathe, the only machine we had. Exhaustion took over long before it was possible to polish away too much metal surface and so risk removing marks left by the hand.'[199]

Cooper's back-to-basics technical approach in metalwork also extended to his jewellery. Almost exclusively, he used polished cabochon (i.e., convex-cut and unfaceted) stones set in plain bezels, just as ancient and

Figure 96. Hair ornament in silver and gold with chrysoprases, rubies and opals, 1905, illustrated in The Studio *in 1906. Clipping in Cooper Family Archives.*

medieval jewellers had. Faceted stones were used only when provided by a client for a specific commission. In Cooper's opinion:

> glitter is valuable, but it should not supersede the expression of ideas, & it should not hide the workmanship. By rights every jewel has an expression of its own which it should be the lapidary's business to bring to light, the present aim of the lapidary seems to be to forget all qualities except that of brilliance, & to reduce the stone as nearly as possible to the appearance of paste, so that only an expert can tell the difference & that not always by sight alone.[200]

A cabochon cut best expressed the individual characteristics of a stone. In addition to the importance of its individual appearance, a stone, according to Cooper, should 'grow out of the metal . . . & have not the appearance of being plastered on'.[201] Stones should not dominate their settings, but instead should 'take their place in the general scheme & be servants not rulers'.[202] In constructing a piece of jewellery, Cooper suggested that: 'the first thing is to get your stones, not make settings & when the work is finished buy the stones to fit, & arrange them so as to get a pleasing effect of colour, making them play on one another as two notes of music, and then make a setting for joining them together with metal.'[203]

As stated earlier, Cooper's metalwork and jewellery began receiving extensive British critical acclaim at the 1906 Arts and Crafts Society exhibition. In reviewing this exhibition, a critic deplored 'the absence of

Figure 97. 'St George and Dragon'
belt buckle in silver, D 7.6, 1903.
Birmingham City Museum and Art
Gallery.

strong exhibits in the department of craft relative to domestic architecture
and domestic equipment', and condemned the Society's failure 'to contend
for improvements in the practical necessities of domestic comfort'.[204]
Instead the Society's artists had turned their attention to the dilettante fields
of bookbinding, needlework and jewellery. The exhibition was particularly
dominated by jewellery. In design after design, *The Studio* critic found:

> one motif worked to death viz. the pearl attached to the design by a
> chain. . . . In hardly any pendant has the designer been able to resist the
> temptation of this hanging pearl . . . [such] devices are repeated again
> and again without restraint until they are staled. . . . There is too great a
> tendency in modern jewellery to make large things. . . . Much of the
> jewellery made now by good designers it neglected by the ordinary
> purchaser on the score of its being so large and called to itself so much
> attention.[205]

In opposition to these criticisms, the same critic cited three jewellery pieces
by Cooper:

> . . . certain designs by Mr. Paul Cooper, indicate a skilfully finished and
> sculptural treatment of the metal on a miniature scale which is
> altogether pleasant. Mr. Cooper's lantern pendant [Figure 94] gives to

Figure 98. 'Squirrel' belt in silver, buckle D 6, 1903. Private Collection.

his work a happy invention and variety escaping the formulas controlling so many designers around him. He has conceived some of his designs [Figure 95] in a spirit of quaintness which we cannot help finding attractive. . . . In referring to Mr. Cooper's designs, mention should . . . [be] made of the hair ornament [Figure 96]. . . . It is apparent that it is restrained and simple, but, like the foregoing piece of jewellery, the accents of colour arrived at in arranging the stones give to it a valuable and rare effect. As a hair ornament it has the merit of not being too heavy; so many of the modern hair ornaments are so weighty that it would be difficult to wear them.[206]

Like the balance of objects in this 1906 exhibition, Cooper's own output between 1902 and 1906 was dominated by jewellery. The majority of these Birmingham period pieces, particularly the brooches and belt buckles (Cooper made more buckles during these years than at any other time) were decorated with representational imagery, repoussé and chased by Cooper himself. The St George buckle in Figure 97, executed in 1903, the squirrel belt in Figure 98, and the pendants in Figures 94 and 95, and Plate 32 are all dominated by chased figural imagery.

The buckle in Figure 97 is decorated in high relief with an image of St George and the Dragon, a popular subject with Arts and Crafts artists and one that Cooper himself defined as 'an endless fight' with 'a symbol of evil'.[207] This same decorative motif appears on a round gesso box Cooper executed in December 1902.[208] Such a free exchange of subjects and decorative motifs between various media is typical of Cooper's work. The depiction of St George was meant to recall the patron saint of England and the deeds of the Red Cross Knight in Edmund Spenser's *The Faerie Queene* (1590–6), a popular source for Arts and Crafts imagery. In addition, the composition's rendering cleverly reinforces the circular shape of the buckle, which in turn symbolizes the eternity of the struggle. Similarly in Figure 98, the plumpness of the squirrel and the positioning

Figure 99. Ring commissioned by Ellen Terry in 18-carat gold with green stone, L 4.4, 1905. The National Trust, Smallhythe Place.

Figure 100. Pencil sketch of buildings in Luynes, France, dated 1904. Cooper Family Archives.

of its tail emphasize the roundness of the buckle on the belt.[209] Simultaneously, the angle of the squirrel's pose gives a sense of spatial recession.

Between 1902 and 1906, when Cooper added stones to the figurative compositions of his jewellery, gems were of subsidiary importance. They merely functioned to enhance the significance of the centrally chased scene, as seen in Figure 94 and Plate 32. According to a sketch notation, the composition of the pendant in Figure 94 depicts Aladdin with his magic lamp.[210] Typically, Cooper gave even such quaintly charming imagery a symbolic connotation, related here to the Arabian Nights character whose magic lamp became a source of wealth and good fortune. Similarly, the stag in Plate 32 represents St Hubert (d. 727), the patron saint of hunters.[211] According to legend, as a young man, Hubert was hunting on Good Friday when he was suddenly confronted by a white stag bearing a crucifix between its antlers. This vision converted him to

Figure 101 Pencil sketch of Le Puy, France, dated 3 August 1902. Cooper Family Archives.

Christianity and he later became Bishop of Maastricht and Liège. The cult of the stag, the pre-eminent sacred beast among Central Asian tribes, reached Hittite Anatolia probably *c.* 1800 BC[212] It was adopted by Greeks in about the 6th century BC, and they depicted it with an eagle of Zeus between its antlers. In Christian imagery, the eagle was replaced by a crucifix.

In the same vein, it is interesting to speculate what the bird on the pendant in Figure 95 was supposed to represent. Perhaps it was a symbol of the Egyptian god Horus, familiar to Cooper as the sparrow-hawk in Egyptian art. According to Gerald Massey, one of Cooper's favourite late nineteenth-century mystical interpreters of the Bible, the attributes and exploits of Horus became associated with Jesus in Christian theology, effectively making the two gods interchangeable.[213] Massey, like Frazer and Cooper, believed that each successive civilization adapted and modified previously established beliefs and ideas. As a result, the attributes of a Christian deity could easily be traced to an earlier pagan god as had also been the case with St Hubert's stag.

On the rare occasions when figurative imagery was rejected for the decoration of jewellery pieces made between 1902 and 1906, their aesthetic impact remained substantially the same. The composition of the Fitzwilliam buckle in Plate 33 is as sculpturally bold and expressive as that of contemporary pieces with chased representational imagery.[214] Such early pieces, which relied on their stones and non-figurative settings for decorative effect, were tightly, often symmetrically composed, and outlined by a solid, unbroken contour. Characteristic of Cooper's preference for suggestive, idiosyncratic stones is the central mother-of-pearl piece whose graining alludes to a mountain shape.

One of Cooper's earliest jewellery commissions came in 1905 from the actress Ellen Terry.[215] She asked Cooper to mount an emerald given to her by Henry Irving (Figure 99). The ring's setting is in the form of a centrally planned, turreted structure. The crenellations of its central tower act as claws to hold the stone in place. According to archival notes, the ring's setting was meant to represent a 'Temple of the Arts', Cooper's homage to the talents and careers of both Terry and Irving. In an inventory compiled by Ellen Terry's daughter, it is referred to as the 'Globe Ring', after Shakespeare's famous theatre.[216] Slightly prior to Terry's ring, Cooper had designed a smaller version of its 'temple' setting in silver mounted with an amethyst for his wife, May, whose artistic abilities he likewise admired.[217] Such architectural settings, which also recall seventeenth-century Jewish marriage rings, appear on rings designed by Charles Ricketts (1866–1931) in about 1903.[218]

Cooper was particularly attracted to medieval fortress architecture and his sketchbooks are full of drawings of such buildings which inspired various designs (Figure 100).[219] Terry's ring's setting is also similar to the twelfth-century Chiesola Reliquary in the treasury of St Mark's, Venice, which Cooper must have seen on one of his numerous visits to that cathedral. Originally designed as an incense burner in the shape of a domed building, probably a garden pavilion, it eventually came to house a phial of Christ's blood.[220] As a centrally planned structure, it is circumscribed by alternating circular and angular turrets similar to Terry's ring.

A surviving series of designs for the Ellen Terry ring illustrate the procedure followed in Cooper's studio to realize a commissioned piece of jewellery (Plate 34). First, Cooper would make several quick sketches of his initial design ideas (Plate 34, upper left). He would then make a finished watercolour design to show his client (Plate 34, upper right). From this finished design, Cooper would make a tracing for his workmen to use (Plate 34, lower left). If high relief was involved, a plasticine model would be made and May consulted as to the placement of the stones. Finally, a plaster cast would then be created in order to give an exact idea of the necessary height for the relief work (Plate 34, lower right).

Cooper's adaptation of other non-Italian imagery he encountered during his various trips to Europe is clearly seen on the buckle in Plate 35.[221] The chased scene here represents the French church of St Michel in Le Puy en Velay, near Lyons, which Cooper visited in 1902. A drawing of this site exists in one of Cooper's sketchbooks (Figure 101).[222] There are striking similarities between these two images, right down to the stairs that wind around the mountain. However, the depiction of water surrounding the mountain base on the buckle isolates the image and suggests a deeper, hidden significance. No longer is the composition a mere recording of a geographical site. Is this church-clad-mountain piercing the 'oversea' Lethaby described as existing above the earth's sky in his *Architecture, Mysticism and Myth*, and thereby providing a glimpse of a heavenly world? Are faith and spirituality, symbolized by the church, depicted as man's 'rock of stability' amid 'troubled waters'? Typical of other Birmingham-period jewellery pieces, the buckle's shape and decoration are bold and expressive, the stones being subsidiary to the chased representational imagery.

In addition to Cooper's jewellery, *The Studio* reviewer of the 1906 Arts and Crafts Society exhibition also singled out a piece of his hollow ware, a teapot, for praise (Figure 104).[223] One of the more ambitious pieces of domestic plate Cooper produced between 1902 and 1906, the teapot is characteristic of the domestic plate that dominated his output at this time: a finely balanced, simple shape with equally simple and restrained chased decoration. The scale pattern on its handle and the applied rope moulding around its neck became standard decorative motifs on Cooper's metalwork. The spout, which has been given the most extravagant decoration on the teapot, represents a dragon, purposely evoking the exotic Chinese origins of tea and a dragon's hot, steamy breath.

The culmination of the visual boldness and three-dimensional expressiveness seen in Cooper's Birmingham-period pieces was reached in two mixed-media objects more aptly labelled sculpture than hollow ware: a coral and ivory bonbonnière and an ivory and shell fruit stand (Plate 39, Figures 105 and 106).[224] The colourful, multi-material, sculptural quality of these two pieces comes closer to Wilson's metalwork than any other object Cooper ever executed. These two pieces also recall trophy designs by Alexander Fisher (1864–1936), who had formed a brief partnership with Wilson during the late 1890s.

The happy variety of materials used to construct these pieces and their mounted stones relate directly to a request by *The Studio* magazine that colour be added to contemporary silverwork:

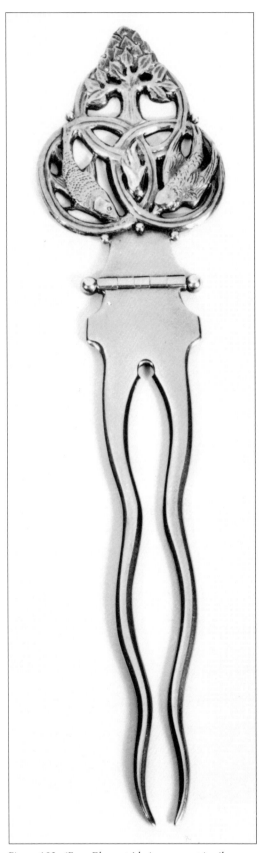

Figure 102. 'Four Elements' hair ornament in silver, L 13.6, 1904. Private Collection.

. . . craftsmen must think of it [silver] always in connection with other things that run strongly counter to the industrial methods and finish. Thus silver, for example, must be thought of in relation to colour. There are many felicitous ways in which it may be employed with other substances, all beautiful and many-hued . . . in art old things become new in new combinations . . . and it then makes us wish that modern metalworkers would employ these gay ornaments [precious and semiprecious stones] more often then they do at the present moment.[225]

Cooper's dramatic use of silver, coral, walrus tusk, and lapis lazuli to form the bonbonnière in Plate 39 give it a bold, sculptural feeling, considerably more daring than anything seen in his previously discussed pieces. As a result of this unusual combination of materials, the silver portions are given a new appearance and significance. Particularly striking are the lapis lazuli stones set in high bezels on the base. Their applied vertical mouldings give them the appearance of jelly fish, carefully redolent of the marine origins of both the coral and walrus tusk. Such high bezels are typical of Cooper's early, emotionally charged work.

The blackberry fruit stand in Figures 105 and 106 is likewise composed of texturally and structurally contrasting materials. The base is mounted with three amethysts and two chrysoprases again set in high bezels. The stem, composed of ivory with trailing silver blackberry vines, is surmounted by a shell. Originally, the bowl had been constructed of silver but, in 1907, it was replaced by a shell for greater aesthetic impact. Edward Spencer used similar ivory stems for his trophies and presentation cups that were designed subsequent to Cooper's blackberry fruit stand which was sold through the Artificers' Guild in 1913.[226] An unidentified source praised the blackberry fruit stand's subtle colour coordination:

The bonbonnière, like Mr Cooper's work in shagreen, is a colour invention; the rough ivory, the silver of bramble branches, of the cup, and of the beaded settings of the jewels at the base, as well as the jewels, realising an idea of harmonious colour prepared to receive addition from colour of fruit in the bowl . . . an art that has vitality, inspiration, bringing always a new material from the actual and intellectual spheres of the artist's domain.[227]

In both the bonbonnière and blackberry fruit stand, Cooper's sensitivity to the physical properties of each of their incongruous materials enabled him to achieve aesthetic unity. This talent for understanding and exploiting the innate characteristics of his various media brought Cooper his greatest critical accolades.

In 1905, Cooper received his first public commission: an altar cross for Birmingham Cathedral (Plate 37).[228] Such a commission gave Cooper an ideal opportunity to express his consuming interest in symbolic imagery, numerology, and colour. Cooper considered the cross 'a figure of perfect balance . . . perhaps the oldest symbol known . . . [whose] use is universal'.[229] It had always, regardless of its shape variations or cultural

adaptations, signified resurrection. In Christianity, 'the Cross has symbolized on the one hand the suffering of Our Lord, on the other hand the glories of the resurrection'.[230] About four feet in height, the Birmingham cross is constructed of brass, its base being hammered from a single piece and mounted with amethysts, sapphires and crystals. The centre of the cross has an applied chased roundel depicting the Virgin and Child with signs of the Passion chased on each of its arms.

Figure 103. Matchbox in silver with agate, H 2.5 × L 5.1 × W 3.5, 1904. The box's mouldings recall those found on Cooper's contemporary shagreen boxes. Private Collection.

Among Cooper's surviving sketches, there exist watercolours of a model posed identically to the Virgin in the chased roundel. Such watercolours must have served as preparatory studies for the relief. No factual information exists about what inspired Cooper to pose his model in this manner. Perhaps, he was thinking of similar reliefs by Donatello (*c.* 1385/6–1466). Cooper had mentioned seeing casts of sculptures by Donatello at the Royal Architectural Museum. This Florentine sculptor was noted for his masterful *schiacciato* reliefs, which incorporated spatial and emotional realism. In fact, Cooper's roundel does recall Donatello's *Madonna of the Clouds* (now in the Museum of Fine Arts, Boston) where the placement of the Madonna and the prominent rendering of her lap in which the Christ Child sits are identical to Cooper's composition.

The knob on the Birmingham cross's shaft is formed by an entwined serpent, the cause of man's eternal damnation, overcome by the surmounted cross, the symbol of Christ's redemption. Directly above the subjugated

Figure 104. Teapot in silver,
H 13.6, 1906. Private Collection.

serpent is a rose briar, the symbol of triumphant love, which nourishes the base of the Tree of Life, an allegory of man's salvation through the love of Christ.

The thirteen amethysts mounted on the arms of the cross, near the signs of the Passion, represent a number indicative of unfaithfulness and betrayal, Judas being the thirteenth disciple at the Last Supper. The violet of the amethysts symbolizes the passion and suffering of Christ. The seven sapphires in the chased roundel represent a number associated with completion and perfection; their colour is intended to suggest the heavenly abode of both Christ and the Virgin. The five mounted crystals on the base recall the five wounds Jesus suffered· on the cross, their colour representing the holiness and purity of Christ.

In addition to this rudimentary explanation of the cross's decoration, taken from Cooper's personal copy of F. Edward Hulme's *Symbolism in Christian Art* (1899) (which gave detailed interpretations of the images, colours and numbers used in Christian art), each motif, its number and colour, would have been imbued with additional superimposed layers of progressively more obscure symbolism, an intellectual game Cooper believed would eventually expose the ultimate universal unity of all thought and matter.

Stylistically, the cross's robust, exaggerated proportions and minimal chased decoration give it a bold, forceful quality, typical of Cooper's Birmingham metalware. This vigour and forceful expressionism are also evident in a copper and silver cross Cooper executed in 1907 and in a pair of copper candlesticks from 1906 (Figures 107, 108).[231]

Between 1902 and 1906, Cooper's most numerous commissions, particularly in 1903 and 1904, came from Ernest Gimson and were for silver and brass handles to be mounted on furniture designed by him.[232] The majority were ring handles with decorated round backplates (Figure 109). In addition to these, Cooper also executed three distinct types of drop handles for Gimson. The first type, made of silver, was mounted with coral or lapis lazuli. The second type was composed of three radiating scrolls, and the third type depicted two hieratic bird heads. For the ring handles, Gimson sent Cooper specific designs. The drop handles, on the other hand, were largely designed by Cooper himself.

In completing the discussion of Cooper's metalwork between 1902 and 1906, which formed the first phase of his stylistic development, mention must be made of a unique group of pieces executed in the mokumé technique. This Eastern process employed thin layers of different coloured metal bonded together to form a sandwich. Either the underside of this metal sandwich was punctured with a blunt tool and the resulting surface nodules were then filed down to expose concentric rings of different coloured metal or the top was gouged leaving a cavity that exposed the different-coloured layers.

Cooper's interest in mokumé stemmed both from his high regard for Japanese metalware and from a series of lectures organized by Wilson in 1905–6 at the Royal College of Art; the lectures on oriental metalwork were given by the artist Unno Yoshimori, known as Bisei for short, a professor at the Tokyo Fine Art School.[233] Living in Birmingham at the time, Cooper was not able to attend the Bisei lectures. Instead, he recopied notes taken by Henry Wilson and George Sedding. Cooper's copy of Wilson's *Silverwork and Jewellery* contains numerous handwritten notations concerning Japanese metal casting, patination and mokumé techniques. In addition to mokumé, Cooper's experiments with copper patination between about 1908 and 1915 also seem to have been inspired by these lectures.

Primarily executed in 1906, Cooper designed approximately twelve pieces in the mokumé technique, including brooches, napkin rings, and match cases (Plate 38).[234] In these objects the exposed metal layers are mainly composed of silver and different copper alloys which Cooper purchased already laminated; the notations in Cooper's costing books indicate that the material was purchased by weight.

The output of Cooper's Hunton studio between 1907 and 1910 marked a transitional phase in the style of his metalware. It was characterized by a gradual shift away from stiff, forceful expressionism towards a lighter, more refined, lyrical style. In jewellery, this gradual transition was

Figure 105. Fruit stand in silver with ivory, amethysts and chrysoprases, 1902. Clipping in Cooper Family Archives.

designated by less emphasis on chased representational imagery and a greater emphasis on mounted stones, which then became more essential to the overall aesthetic effect. A comparison between a Le Puy brooch executed in 1908 and the previously discussed Le Puy buckle made in 1905 (see p. 107) effectively illustrates the changes which took place in Cooper's jewellery (Plates 35, 40).[235] The general effect of the 1908 brooch is one of greater opulence and richness of colour due to the variety and prominence of the stones. The open work between the mounted stones gives a new feeling of lightness, resulting in a sense of even greater elegance.

The Mother and Child pendant in Plate 41 likewise exemplifies the more strenuous integration of stones with chased decoration during this period in Cooper's work.[236] The stones here have become pigments with which the monotone silver surface is coloured, giving the pendant a new sense of colour diversity. The open work of the starry ring adds characteristic lightness to the entire composition. The inspiration for this pendant seems to have been a ceramic medallion based on the same subject by Luca della Robbia in the Church of Orsanmichele, Florence. Cooper's sketchbooks contain an early watercolour of this image (Figure 110).[237] Cooper had spent time exploring Florence during his 1893 Italian trip, when he specifically mentioned seeing a particularly fine Luca della Robbia *Coronation of the Virgin*, and in 1899 with Wilson and Whall. The watercolour must have been executed during one of these visits.

Cooper also owned a book on Luca della Robbia, published in 1900, which contained an illustration of this same Madonna and Child. According to this book, it was typical of Luca to place the Child to the right of the Virgin for a greater sense of realism.[238] An interesting aspect of Cooper's composition is the extreme naturalism of the way the Virgin holds the Christ Child, as an ordinary mother would hold her baby. This feature, despite the otherwise summary rendering of the two figures, gives a distinct humanity to the composition, typical of Cooper's religious depictions and expressive of the essential union between all earthly and heavenly mothers.

Figure 106. Same fruit stand as in Figure 105 but with the silver bowl now replaced by a shell, 1907. Photograph in Cooper Family Archives.

During the Hunton period (1907–10), a new style of design emerged in a small group of Cooper's brooches and pendants. Related to the contemporary creations of Georgie and Arthur Gaskin, this 'romantic hedgerow' style was composed of scrolling metal tendrils and leaves, among which were mounted stones. Cooper's new manner can be seen in the double brooch in Plate 42 and in the brooch fragment in Figure 111.[239] This new stylistic treatment produced compositions that were looser and more improvisational than those dating between 1903 and 1906. Such 'hedgerow' designs, which primarily functioned as backgrounds for the mounted stones and required little representational chasing, were generally the work of Cooper's studio workmen.[240]

A comparison between Cooper's 'hedgerow' designs and those of the Gaskins', however, discloses some striking differences. The Gaskin designs are much more consciously symmetrical, having a central focus surrounded by a radiating, symmetrical arrangement of stones. Cooper's compositions are distinctly asymmetrical. Unlike the Gaskins', they are never set with faceted stones or enamel work. Cooper's journals mention several social visits to the Gaskins while both families were living in Birmingham. As headmaster of the Vittoria Street School between 1903 and 1924, Arthur Gaskin's jewellery style had a profound influence on the school's students. In fact, the 'romantic hedgerow' style also became known as the Birmingham style because it was so commonly seen on jewellery produced there.

The new trend, where the metal portions of a jewellery piece began functioning primarily as settings for the stones rather than the stones being sparse accents to the metalwork, found its greatest expression in contemporary necklaces. When compared to the necklace in Plate 36 from Cooper's Birmingham period, the Hunton necklace in Plate 43 clearly shows how much the metal portions have now become subsidiary to the stones and how much more interest there is in and variety of stone combinations.[241] The metalwork of the Hunton necklace, typically light and airy, provides a lacy foil to the solidity of the stones and contributes to the general sense of refined opulence. Also typical of Cooper is the placing of the rose ruby opposite the sapphire to create a purposeful tension amid an otherwise symmetrical composition. The contrasting colours of these two stones recall Cooper's statement that stones should play off each other like musical notes (see p. 101).

Also during the Hunton period, the typical composition format for Cooper's necklaces became thoroughly established: a long central pendant with a centralized cluster of stones, and two smaller pendant clusters on either side, all attached to a chain of metal beads often alternating with stones. The beginnings of this pendant-cluster format, which created distinct focal points along the length of the necklace, can be seen on an earlier Hunton period necklace in Plate 44.[242]

From 1908 Cooper gradually began to produce more hollow ware than jewellery. As he had with shagreen, Cooper now also developed the commercial possibilities of his metalwork. He began producing numerous spoons and napkin rings, the quick production and relative cheapness of which made them easily saleable studio staples. Between 1907 and 1933, Cooper produced over 300 of these items. Cooper's Hunton metalwork,

Figure 107. Pair of candlesticks in patinated copper, H 22.2, 1906. Private Collection.

still dominated by domestic plate, was now more frequently punctuated by elaborate, eye-catching pieces whose designs and execution displayed a greater confidence and sophistication than is seen in his Birmingham period work. The chasing that had been so prominent on his early jewellery was now transferred to his metalwork.

A hot water jug Cooper originally completed in January 1906 (Figure 112) and then reworked in October 1906 (Figure 113) provides a singular example of the gradual change which took place in Cooper's hollow ware style between Birmingham and Hunton.[243] The reworked version has been given a more slender, elegant shape, its more prominent decoration cleverly disguising the jug's longer neck. The two chalices in Plates 45 and 46, executed only one year apart, also exemplify the shift towards a greater delicacy and elegance of shape and decoration during the Hunton period.[244] Likewise, a 1908 fruit stand (Plate 47), which recalls the bonbonnière (Plate 39) and blackberry fruit stand (Figure 106) from Cooper's Birmingham period, possesses a more relaxed, slender profile.[245] Its simplified use of non-metal materials further illustrates the transition which took place among such mixed-media pieces during the Hunton period: from sculptural exuberance towards a more calm aesthetic restraint.

The gradual transition towards greater lightness and refinement of shape and decoration that took place between 1907 and 1910 is further illustrated by a comparison between the blackberry fruit stand before its silver bowl was replaced by a shell and a pair of fruit dishes made in 1907 (Figures 105, 114).[246] The earlier expressive exuberance and dynamism seen in the twisting stem and scalloped bowl has been pacified in the 1907 pair. In the fruit dish pair, the careful proportioning of the base, stem and bowl has produced a new sense of grace and elegance. No longer is the exoticism of the non-metal materials thrust at the viewer. Instead, the crystal columns and the mounted stones quietly take their place among the silver portions of the stem. Likewise, the representative chasing on the fruit dishes contributes more prominently to the overall decorative effect than on the earlier piece. In fact, the applied reliefs on their bases recall brooches Cooper had designed between 1902 and 1906. As with the necklace in Plate 43, Cooper has slightly varied the chased decoration and stone colour between the pair to produce a pleasing asymmetrical tension.

An inkstand Cooper designed for his sister Violet in 1908–9 provides another good example of the prominence chasing was now given on Cooper's hollow ware (Figure 115).[247] The body of the inkpot is composed of eight chased medallions, the representative imagery of which recalls Cooper's Birmingham period jewellery. Indicative of Cooper's interest in symbolism and metaphysical expression, this inkpot's decoration was carefully coordinated to reflect its recipient. According to Cooper's design notations, the incised hieroglyphics around the neck of the inkpot spell out Violet's name. The images around its body symbolize qualities of character Cooper associated with his sister; for example, the olive branch represents peace, the owl wisdom and the cock courage. The elephant, which forms the structural supports and, by implication, sustains the above symbols, signifies strength and endurance.[248]

Figure 108. Altar Cross in patinated copper with silver and mother-of-pearl, H 59, 1907. National Museums and Galleries on Merseyside.

As stated earlier, Professor Bisei's lectures on oriental metalwork not only inspired Cooper to try mokumé but also encouraged his interest in copper patination. In the early 1910s, Cooper produced numerous copper pieces, the patinations of which were carefully noted in his stockbook entries.[249] Such entries cite the recipe number of the stain used to patinate their surface. Cooper had already sporadically experimented with copper patination between 1906 and 1910; during the 1920s, he continued periodically to produce patinated copper pieces. Not one copper piece designed by Cooper has a bright, highly polished finish; all, without exception, were patinated. In his copy of Wilson's *Silverwork and Jewellery*, Cooper wrote extensive notes and recipes for colouring copper.

The 1910 jar in Plate 48 is a typical and particularly successful example of his patinated copper work.[250] In homage to the cultural origins of its patination process, the shape and decoration of the jar recall oriental models. Its arrowhead plant decoration is based on drawings Cooper made directly from nature (Figure 116)[251] and the sensitivity of the sketch points to his life-long interest in vegetation. The plant's more schematic and stylized rendering on the jar demonstrates Cooper's belief that artistic expression is not attained by mere realism but by the careful correlation of a motif to the shape and material of the surface it is intended to decorate. The jar's colour gives it a mellowed worldliness suggestive of the metaphysical spirituality Cooper associated with oriental metalwork and Eastern philosophy: 'This oneness of life . . . has been long acknowledged by Eastern nations. The Chinese, the Japanese, the Indian "understood the continuity of the universe; he recognized the kinship between his own life and the life of animals and birds and trees and plants. And so he approached all life with reverence, giving each its due value".'[252]

During the 1910s, especially prior to the First World War, the stylistic trends already discussed in relation to Cooper's Hunton output became intensified. In jewellery, this meant an ever greater sense of luxury, opulence and decorative refinement, particularly encouraged by the addition of translucent enamel. Stones were now often mounted in open settings, increasing their light refraction and making the back of the jewellery as colourful and attractive as the front.

Only a small group of Cooper's metalware, primarily executed between 1914 and 1915, has enamel decoration (Plates 50, 51).[253] Applied to Cooper-designed pieces for the first time, this translucent enamel work was executed by Sidney G. Wiseman, a workman in Henry Wilson's St Mary Platt studio. Cooper's general philosophy concerning enamelling mirrored that of Alexander Fisher, one of the leading Arts and Crafts exponents of the medium: he preferred translucent enamels to opaque ones for small pieces and favoured their application as jewels to give sparkling accents of colour. Speaking to his students in Birmingham, Cooper stated: 'I wish it to be understood that . . . Enamel is to be treated as a jewel, not as a picture painted on glass – an end in itself. . . . Enamel is no more to be considered solely as painting than a cameo is to be considered as sculpture.'[254]

In Cooper's 1910s jewellery, the stones attained ultimate unity with the representational portions of their metal settings. In Plate 52 the pendant's

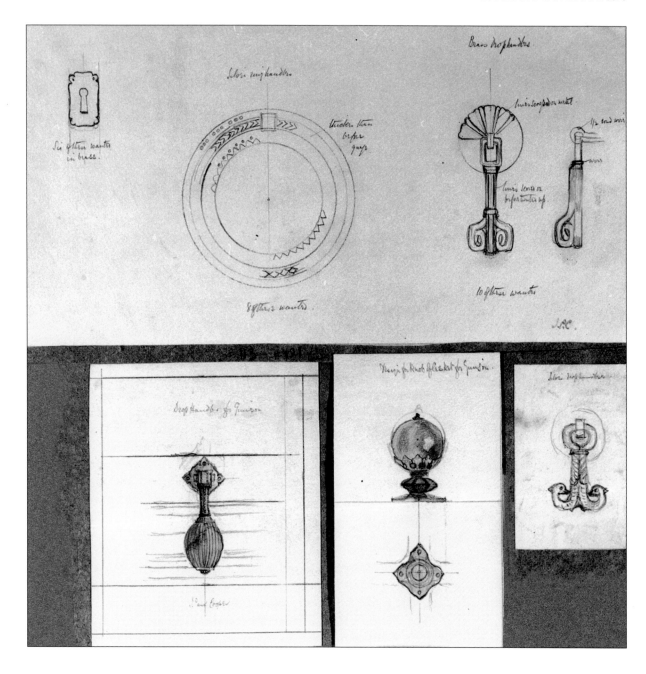

spinels are not used merely to indicate colour but have in fact become the actual holly berries, making the stone and representational image one and the same.[255] The extreme lightness and delicacy of the pendant are also characteristic of Cooper's jewellery of the 1910s. The moth pendant in Plates 54 and 55 also demonstrates the ethereal elegance and delicacy which prevailed in Cooper's jewellery of the period.[256] As with the holly pendant, all separation between image and stone is removed, the stones becoming the actual markings on the moth's wings. The moth's wirework provides the ultimate means of making the front and back of the pendant virtually identical. During the 1910s, Cooper made numerous watercolour sketches of moths. The earliest of these, dated 27 March 1912, seems to

Figure 109. Handle designs for Ernest Gimson, 1902–1906. Cooper Family Archives.

have been the catalyst for the use of this motif on subsequent jewellery and metalwork (Plate 56).[257]

Another distinctive feature of Cooper's jewellery from 1910 to 1915 is a group of four fibula brooches (Plate 53).[258] This was the first and one of the rare instances where Cooper directly copied a distinctly historic jewellery prototype.[259] The reliance in the form of these 1911 brooches on a purely geometrical shape demonstrates the extent to which Cooper's jewellery designs were now conceived in terms of abstract shapes and colourful stone arrangements, not as primary vehicles for representational imagery. A geometric, rather than representational, arrangement of stones also characterized Cooper's necklaces from the 1910s, a trend started in his Hunton studio. The majority of these necklaces followed a compositional format introduced between 1907 and 1910 (see p. 114): The design and flawless execution of the necklace in Plate 57 make it a consummate example of the stylistic refinement and elegance that emerged between 1907 and 1910.[260]

As with the jewellery, the stylistic trends initiated in Cooper's Hunton period metalwork culminated in objects produced between 1910 and 1915. Chased decoration became even more profuse and elaborate, dominating the surfaces it ornamented. Its placement, execution and integration with other decorative elements, such as stones and castings, reached a new level of intricacy and sophistication. The Perseus and Andromeda candlesticks in Plate 7 demonstrate this stylistic intensification.[261] Here, Cooper's chasing effectively conveys the essential elements of the mythological tale: the bound Andromeda; the all-encompassing monster; and the battle-ready Perseus. Simultaneously, the placement of the chased decoration emphasizes the shape of the candlesticks: the entwined monster accentuates the roundness of the base; the upright figures of Andromeda and Perseus stress the verticality of the shafts; while their focused attention pulls the viewer's eye around the circumference of the shaft; the horizontal bands of mounted stones harmoniously restrain and balance this verticality. As a result, the narrative, ornament and shape of the candlesticks are fused into a tasteful aesthetic whole, typical of Cooper's pre-war metalwork.

The chased decoration on the candlesticks also demonstrates that certain Cooper imagery was derived directly from photographs. The 'monsters' on the bases of the candlesticks bear a striking resemblance to the photographed alligators and caimans in Figure 118. Similarly, the jagged cliffs illustrated in Figure 119 resemble the rocky formations behind Andromeda and Perseus. The frieze on the bowl of the Ascot Cup, likewise, draws its inspiration directly from photographs of actual horse races held at Lingfield and Kempton Park (Figures 42, 120, 121). Cooper kept numerous files with such photographs and illustrations.

A cormorant fruit bowl executed in 1915 demonstrates the prominence chased ornament was given on metalwork of the 1910s (Figure 122).[262] In comparison to the 1907 fruit bowls in Figure 114 the surface is now dominated by chased decoration. The chasing also has a greater spatial fullness and sculptural roundness. Being more directly and purposefully related to the shape of the bowl and the applied three-dimensional ornament, the chasing has become a major component of the object's

Figure 110. Watercolour of Luca della Robbia's roundel in Orsanmichele, Florence. Cooper Family Archives.

marine theme. In contrast, the chasing on the 1907 bowls remains limited and tentative, lacking any dominant aesthetic force or prominent thematic purpose. The cast cormorants are based on sketches Cooper made of such birds during a family seaside holiday in 1913 (Figure 123).[263] These cormorants only appear on Cooper's metalwork dating from 1914–15 and in 1926 mounted on a coconut bowl.

Probably the best known metalwork piece Cooper executed during the 1910s was a silver casket that now contains the ashes of Ellen Terry (Plate 8).[264] An octagonal box, it is surmounted by a cast figure of Ceres, the protectress of agriculture, holding sheaves of grain. The body of the box is dominated by eight chased panels representing different land and water fowl, dependent on the grain provided by Ceres. The subjects of the panels include pheasants, peacocks, ducks, grouse, doves, swans and chickens. As with the Perseus and Andromeda candlesticks, the figural and ornamental decoration is evocative and tightly linked to the shape, proportions and narrative theme of the box. The careful and purposeful manipulation of the chased decoration produces a sense of harmonious opulence. Such an intimate and lyrical

Figure 111. Bottom portion of double brooch in 18-carat gold with emeralds, moonstone and ruby, L 1.9 × W 2.5, 1909. Tadema Gallery, London.

expression of elegance and refinement was rarely achieved in metalwork that postdates the First World War.

In Cooper's stockbook, this casket is labelled as being a biscuit box. This is not an error; it originally had been intended for such use. However, its expensive price, offered at £100 in 1920, kept it from being easily sold. Ellen Terry's sudden death in 1928 forced the immediate need for an ash receptacle. This biscuit box was one of the very few Cooper pieces instantly available to serve such a function. Its iconography particularly appealed to Terry's son and daughter who thought it characterized their mother's love of nature and nurturing character: especially the panel depicting a hen with her young which they found 'symbolic of . . . [their] mother, who was always surrounded by young people whom she always treated like her chicks'.[265] There also exists an octagonal gesso box by

Cooper with decorative panels which duplicate some of the ones on the Terry casket; no factual or artistic evidence exists as to which of these boxes was executed first.

In 1912, Cooper completed one of his most important secular commissions, the Leicester Freedom Casket (Figure 124).[266] The elaborately decorated box was presented to William Wilkins Vincent (1843–1916), Mayor of Leicester 1902–3 and 1910–11. Its rich, intricate decoration, so typical of Cooper's pre-war 1910s metalwork, is closely tied to its function. On the hexagonal body of the box are represented: the Leicester coat-of-arms; King Lear, the mythical founder of Leicester; Simon de Montfort, representing the Earldom of Leicester and the military history of the town; Cardinal Wolsey on his way to Leicester Abbey bent down with sickness, representing the ecclesiastical history of the town; Lady Jane Grey and Roger Ascham, representing the acquisition of knowledge; William of Wigston, representing the giving forth of knowledge; and four trees, representing the forests that surround the city. On the lid are Virtues associated with a great town: Prudence, Cheerfulness, Chastity, Justice, Charity, Mercy, Temperance, Liberality, Faith and Hope.

Between 1911 and 1915, there also appeared in Cooper's work, for the first time, a group of silver mounted coconut bowls.[267] The designs for these pieces typically consisted of the following elements: a circular foot; a stem whose height and style were dictated by the coconut's natural shape and the desire to achieve a particular proportional effect; and the actual coconut which had been previously cleaned and polished. Fourteen mounted coconut pieces were made during this period. The two earliest were purchased by the Scottish architect Sir Robert Lorimer, whose surviving correspondence with Cooper indicates that he was as interested in Cooper's mounted coconuts as in his shagreen work. In 1913, Lorimer even supplied Cooper with some of his own unused polished coconuts and advised him where he could acquire more. In a letter, Lorimer counselled Cooper on how they should be mounted: 'I do hope you will try mounting some as to get a very dumpy proportion.'[268] Cooper's mounted coconuts, however, tended to have rather high stems, minimizing any sense of heaviness. Only during the 1920s, when another twenty-one mounted coconuts were executed, did Cooper put a significant number on short stems to give them the dumpy proportions suggested by Lorimer.

The Victoria and Albert coconut bowl in Plate 58, with its tasteful, luxurious use of mother-of-pearl, and the Bedford coconut bowl in Figure 125, with its prominent chasing, again typify Cooper's metalwork from the 1910s.[269] The starkly simple, rhythmic design chased on the stem and foot of the Bedford piece also illustrates Cooper's interest in the expressive possibilities of rudimentary, almost primitive ornament.

In 1914, Cooper received his second major liturgical commission: an altar cross for the chapel of the Royal Holloway College in Surrey (Plate 59).[270] The resulting brass and silver cross presents a striking contrast to the Birmingham cross made a decade earlier even though both are roughly the same size (Plate 37). Rather than being hollow like the Birmingham cross, the Holloway one's arms are constructed of brass

Figure 112. Hot water jug in silver, January 1906. Clipping in Cooper Family Archives.

sheets pinned to a wooden core, a technique Cooper was to employ for all his subsequent crosses. The more evident display of chased ornament, the decorative colour play between the silver and brass, the profusion of mounted stones and the lighter proportions make the Holloway cross an elegant and opulent work, firmly rooted in Cooper's stylistic manner of the 1910s.

Figure 113. Hot water jug in silver, H 18.7, October 1906. Reworked version of jug in Figure 112. Private Collection.

The Holloway cross was followed by a commission for liturgical plate for St Paul's Church, Four Elms, Kent. The Four Elms cross, the surface of which is now entirely of silver, also has arms constructed of silver sheets pinned to a wooden core (Plate 10).[271] Like Cooper's 1910s domestic plate, the cross relies strongly on the prominence, placement and execution of its repoussé and chased decoration for symbolic and aesthetic

Figure 114. Right: Fruit dish in silver with crystals and amethysts, H 18.3, 1906. Photograph © The Detroit Institute of Arts. Opposite: Fruit dish in silver with crystals and Ceylon zircons, H 18.3, 1906. Birmingham City Museum and Art Gallery. Both these objects appear as no. 373 in the stockbook page illustrated in Figure 2 and in the costing book page illustrated in Figure 4.

impact. However, unlike most of Cooper's other metalwork, this cross was almost entirely executed by Cooper himself due to the shortage of skilled labour during the First World War. Only the cross's base was not executed by him; it was made by William Hazlewood, an ex-Cooper workman, who was now living in Birmingham and working in a munitions factory. By post, Cooper sent him instructions and the necessary silver to execute the base. Cooper himself spent 289½ hours working on the cross, and the high quality of its workmanship testifies to the state of his silversmithing skills at the time:[272] despite the fact that Cooper generally executed only repoussé and chasing, he was cognizant enough of basic silversmithing techniques to be able to employ them when necessary.

Subsequently, Cooper received a series of liturgical commissions during the 1920s and early 1930s. For at least eleven different chapels and churches, Cooper executed liturgical plate, such as altar and processional crosses, candlesticks, altar vases, chalices and patens, verges, a warden's wand and a tabernacle. These eleven ecclesiastical locations were: St James's, Muswell Hill, London (1920); St Mary's Cathedral, Edinburgh (1920–2); Rochester Cathedral, Kent (1921); Pembroke College, Cambridge (1924); Oakham School, Rutland (1925); Eton College, Windsor (1925/1927); St Mary's, Tatsfield, Surrey (1926); Korea Cathedral, Seoul (1926); Canterbury Cathedral, Kent (1928); St Andrew's, Limpsfield Chart, Surrey (1930); and St James's and St Basil's, Fenham, Newcastle-upon-Tyne (1931).

Cooper's stylistic preferences, sparked by his interest in the expressive content of pre-Renaissance art, as well as his use of symbolic and evocative imagery, made him an ideal designer of such ecclesiastical plate.

*Figure 115. Inkstand in silver,
H 13.6 × L 24.4 × W 16.5,
1908–9. The Fine Art Society,
London.*

Such tendencies in the Arts and Crafts Movement as a whole made its adherents the most likely group of artists to which patrons needing religious accoutrements would turn. Rarely did the liturgical work of Arts and Crafts artists receive the critical derision reserved for some of their domestic designs. When Cooper submitted a silver candlestick design for Arthur Samuel's approval, his client wrote back: 'The candlestick . . . I do not like at all! It is too tall for a writing table – my purpose in view . . . and the shaft appears a wee bit heavy in diameter. But my main objection is that it possesses the flavour . . . of a church altar.'[273]

During the 1920s and early 1930s, a new coolness and detachment gradually began to permeate Cooper's jewellery and metalwork. The intensified outburst of chasing and stone mounting seen during the 1910s slowly became more calm and more quiet. Simplification, compartmentalization, and repetitive ornament, often characterized by a shallow, geometric crispness, came to dominate Cooper's metal surfaces. Contemporary with this stylistic shift, new descriptive observations began appearing in Cooper's journals. His commentary on the architecture and art that he admired was now punctuated with such adjectives as 'simple', 'quiet', and 'dignified'.[274] The reasons for this new perceptual bias were numerous, not the least of which was Cooper's own maturing age; he was now well into his fifties. The war, whose developments Cooper followed avidly, collecting various press cuttings on its incidents, also had a sobering effect. Likewise, his work in Benson's factory, the emergence of abstract art and the gradually worsening national economy must have contributed to his visual rethinking. The elegance and opulence of the 1910s was now replaced by a streamlined stoicism that put a curb on all decorative lavishness.

In jewellery made between 1920 and 1925 this new orientation was marked by a dominance of figural imagery in pendants which recalled

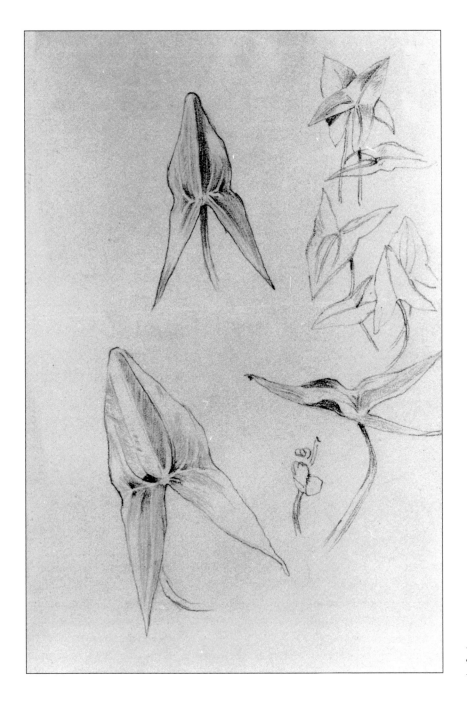

Figure 116. Pencil sketch of arrowhead plant, 1909. Cooper Family Archives.

Figure 117. Pot pourri jar in copper and silver, H 12.7, 1908. Trustees of the Cecil Higgins Art Gallery, Bedford.

Cooper's 1906 Mother and Child pendant (Plates 60, 61, 41).[275] However, in contrast to this Victoria and Albert Museum piece, the focus of their compositions was more determinedly on the figure. Subsidiary ornamental motifs (e.g. architecture, vegetation and stones) were now minimized and simplified, being compositionally situated below the figures' eye-level. In contrast to the expressive exuberance of Cooper's Birmingham period jewellery, the compositions now displayed a quiet, detached passivity.

Likewise, during the 1920s, the lavishness seen in the necklaces of the 1910s was suppressed. The earlier luxurious and dazzling display of stones disappeared. The majority of necklaces made after 1920 were, by true definition, mere neckchains, composed of repetitive ornamental metal links (Plate 62).[276] Even when stones appeared on a necklace, they were usually of one repetitive type, no longer the purveyors of opulent colour combinations.

Between 1925 and 1933, Cooper's jewellery output dramatically dropped to a total of approximately thirty pieces.[277] He now only designed and executed jewellery for specific commissions. Among these were three from the Ashbee family. In 1930, C.R. Ashbee, known as 'Crashbee' in the Cooper family, ordered a silver and turquoise hat brooch-pendant, and in 1931 and 1933 his wife ordered two stone-set pectoral crosses.[278] Mrs Ashbee had already bought a stone-set pectoral cross from Cooper in 1924.[279] One cross was given to each of Ashbee's three eldest daughters.

Obviously, Cooper's jewellery talents were not unnoticed by his fellow craftsmen. In fact, in June 1906, having decided to resign from the Birmingham School of Art, Cooper had been approached to become manager of the jewellery department, Ashbee's special province, at the Guild of Handicraft in Chipping Campden.[280] Cooper refused the offer.

One of the more important pieces among this last chronological grouping of jewellery was a gold moonstone pendant made for Mrs Thomas Bowhay (Plate 64).[281] Mrs Bowhay's husband, who died in 1925, was a self-proclaimed spiritual guru who, during the early 1920s, gave lectures in a house rented for the summer near Betsom's Hill.[282] Cooper's archives contain numerous transcripts of Bowhay's lectures, known as 'August Talks'. Bowhay's mixture of Christianity, Eastern mysticism and clairvoyance was close to Cooper's own thinking about spirituality and reincarnation. Predictably, the imagery and stones of the pendant correlated with the beliefs of its recipient, who shared her husband's philosophy. The circular snake symbolized eternity, man's constant spiritual and physical renewal through reincarnation. The moonstones were considered sacred in India and believed to bring good fortune.[283] In fact, the entire composition of the snake encircling the oval-shaped moonstones recalls a passage from a book on symbolism owned by Cooper: 'As organic substance was represented by the symbol of the egg, so the principle of life, by which it was called into action, was represented by that of the serpent; which having the property of casting its skin, and apparently renewing its youth, was naturally adopted for that purpose. We sometimes find it coiled round the egg to express the incubation of the vital spirit.'[284] Visually, the pendant's wirework has been reduced to a series of interconnected geometric shapes and its stones to one type and colour. Such abstracted simplification, the ultimate expression of both physical and mental transcendentalism, typifies the conclusion of Cooper's jewellery style.

In metalwork, a comparison between the cormorant fruit bowl of 1915 in Figure 122 and the mermaid bowl of 1931 in Figure 126 immediately reveals the new stylistic tendencies that emerged during the 1920s.[285] The shape of the mermaid bowl has become more solid and

Figure 118. Group of alligators and caimans with Director Accarezzando Fatma at the Indo-African Aquarium in Florence. Photograph in Cooper Family Archives.

compact. The lighter, more elegant profile of the bowl on top of the cormorant dish has been replaced by a heavier, plainer bowl with a repetitive, non-representational, linear design which serves to emphasize the metallic nature of the material. The stem of the mermaid bowl has likewise been simplified and given a more even profile. Though this stem is chased with a representational scene, the uniformity of its shape and the pattern-like repetition of the shells and stalactites negate any sense of spatial proportion. The undulating stem and the cast birds on the cormorant dish produce a greater feeling of roundness and three-dimensional interplay.

The deliberate, repetitive rendering of the fish on the foot of the mermaid bowl reaches its climax in two bowls executed in 1930.[286] Here, the stylized multiple depictions of the datura plant in Figure 127 and the repetitive rendering of the dragon tree bark in Figure 128 have transformed naturalistic forms into an abstracted ornamental pattern. The decorations for both of these bowls were inspired by sketches Cooper made during a holiday in the Canary Islands in 1930. The direct, crisp rendering of these natural forms evokes the cold, metallic nature of the silver to a degree not seen before in Cooper's work.

A similar effect is achieved on the foot and stem of the mounted coconut in Figure 129.[287]

Similarly, the boldness of design in the two copper and brass string boxes of 1922 in Plate 63 would have been unthinkable in Cooper's pre-First World War work.[288] The pure geometry of their shapes and the deliberate simplicity and restraint of their decoration give them a startlingly modern appearance. Another group of three silver vases, completed in 1932 and characterized by simple geometric forms and the abandonment of all decoration, rank as Cooper's most progressive metalwork (Figure 130).[289] Their unusually modern designs again indicate a stylistic influence outside Cooper's normal sphere of inspiration: it is tempting to speculate that Cooper's war work at Benson's factory might have inspired their creation.

Not only Cooper's domestic plate but also his contemporary liturgical silver displayed his new stylistic preferences. The Oakham cross of 1925 presents a striking contrast to the Royal Holloway and Four Elms crosses of nearly a decade earlier (Plates 11, 59, 10).[290] All sense of plastic, sculptural chasing has now disappeared. The grapes on the Oakham cross have been

Figure 119. Coastline with cliffs. Clipping in Cooper Family Archives.

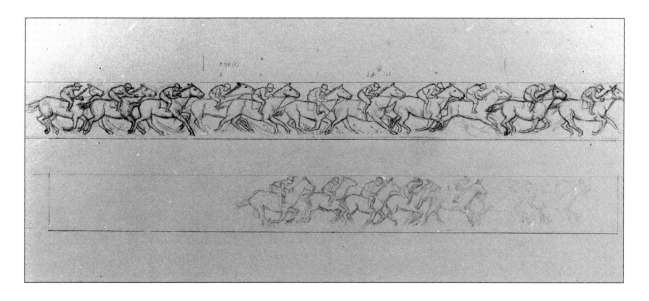

Figure 120. Pencil design for frieze of Ascot Gold Cup in Figure 42, c. 1926. Cooper Family Archives.

simplified and stylized to the point of becoming abstracted patterns. The profile on the cross is likewise completely angular. The silver moulding that outlines the face of the cross serves further to organize, compartmentalize and flatten the surface. An interesting aspect of this cross's decoration is the fact that the mounted stones came from jewellery collected from grieving mothers, widows and sweethearts of Oakham 'old boys' who had died in the First World War. In many instances, Cooper mounted the stones in their original settings on to the cross. Despite the immense diversity of these settings, Cooper masterfully integrated them into the general design of the cross.

Perhaps the most interesting commission Cooper received during this last stylistic phase of his metalwork came from George Bernard Shaw (1856–1950) for a reliquary to be presented to Dame Laurentia (1866–1953), Abbess of Stanbrook Abbey and close friend of both Shaw and Sydney Cockerell (Plate 13).[291]

On a trip to Israel in 1931, Shaw had picked up two pieces of limestone rock outside the Church of the Nativity in Bethlehem. Thinking that they might have been stepped on by the baby Jesus, Shaw decided to throw one rock, while blindfolded, into the garden of Stanbrook Abbey. The other rock was to be mounted in the reliquary and given as a gift to Dame Laurentia. In May 1931 Shaw wrote to Cooper:

I have brought back from Bethlehem a small stone: a common scrap of limestone rock which I want to present to an Abbess as a relic, she having asked me to bring her something of the sort. A relic should have a reliquary. Could you – or rather would you – do something with it for me? Our friend Sydney Cockerell has suggested that you might.[292]

In his journals, Cooper described his subsequent meeting with Shaw:

He [Shaw] came into the room with two small pieces of limestone chippings just under 1½ in. One rough & the other smooth, the latter I at once fixed on as the one most suitable, & I found it was the one he preferred. 'The one you don't choose I'll throw in the garden' he said. . . . He [then] said . . . that it *was* possibly a piece of stone that Christ's feet had touched. . . . He did not want it mounted to wear, & did not want a cross on it. A baby with a halo possibly in a cradle. The Stone underneath? It was to be open no glass possibly a canopy over, as I mentioned dust. . . . I asked if he had any slight idea of what he thought of spending [for the commission] & he said about £50.[293]

When Shaw received the finished reliquary, he wrote to Cooper: 'Lovely! The drawing looked a bit Victorian; but the realization is perfect twelfth century, though not the less Cooperesque.'[294]

In comparison to objects from the 1910s such as the Ellen Terry casket, the 'Cooperesque' manner had become more boldly geometric, angular and detached. The reliquary's body is composed of clearly distinguishable

geometric shapes: a cone, cylinder, and circle. Such an obvious division between component parts is missing in the Terry casket (Plate 8). No longer used to render compositional scenes, the chased decoration on the Shaw reliquary has been transformed into repetitive ornamental patterns. The cast figure of Christ is simplified and faces directly forward, thereby lacking the spatial complexity and plasticity of the more fully modelled, seated Ceres figure. The elegance and lyricism of the Terry casket, with its intimate depictions of the natural world, are replaced by a timeless and impersonal rendering that echoes the implications of the Bowhay pendant: as Cooper approached the end of his career, he transcended the need for temporary and idiosyncratic artistic expression.

Figure 121. Views of various horse races published in The Illustrated Sporting and Dramatic News, *1925–6. Clippings in Cooper Family Archives.*

CHAPTER THREE

ASSESSMENT

*Paul Cooper is not only a craftsman – and an excellent one – but he
is also an artist. This much abused word still retains its real meaning
. . . for those who know, . . . that 'expression' reaches out beyond the
most perfect craftsmanship.*

F. Ernest Jackson[1]

Cooper's career in the decorative arts was largely the result of
fortuitous circumstance. His initial ambition to become a writer
had been opposed by his father. Forced to choose an alternative
vocation, he decided to study architecture in London. There, he
was apprenticed to J.D. Sedding, a prominent advocate for the revival of
architectural craft and handiwork.[2] Sedding's office, located above
Longden & Company – a wrought iron manufacturer that often
participated in the early Arts and Crafts Society exhibitions – and next
door to the showroom of Morris & Company, was managed by Henry
Wilson, another active supporter of the contemporary Arts and Crafts
Movement. In response to such influences, Cooper's own artistic
sensibilities were guided by the aesthetic outlook and theoretical doctrines
of this movement. His son Francis described his father's evolving
convictions:

> . . . these young architect-trained students saw the red light for the way
> the crafts were developing in an industrial world. Don't forget my
> father, at all events, had seen that industrial world at first hand through
> his father's eyes and had rejected it as a way of life for himself. It was
> abhorrent to him in all its aspects. For comparison he saw the
> traditional crafts still lingering on, in small town and country
> workshops throughout the country, with craftsmen using traditional
> designs and tools as they had been doing uninterrupted for past
> centuries.[3]

Surprisingly, Cooper spent very little time discussing William Morris,
the spiritual leader of the Arts and Crafts Movement, in his writings. The
only lengthy mention of him occurs in connection with Sydney Cockerell,
who was the secretary of Morris's Kelmscott Press during the 1890s:

> He was working at the time with William Morris, for whom he had
> great admiration, & would bring sheets of new printed books to show.

These floral pages I could not get up any enthusiasm for. One day Cockerell said Morris had broken out into a new line, he had introduced a bird among the foliage. Wilson used to say that Morris had stuck just where he was when [in 1856] he left Street's office [the architect Edmund Street to whom Sedding had also been apprenticed]. We used to see him sometimes come to his shop . . . in a blue shirt & a bag slung over his shoulder, & the Socialists' procession when they had their meetings in Hyde Park if they passed his shop used to cheer.[4]

Only on two other occasions did Cooper briefly mention Morris in his writings. Rather than Morris or even Ruskin having any explicit influence on Cooper, it was Sedding and W.R. Lethaby that had the most direct impact on the formulation of Cooper's thinking and on his adoption of the Arts and Crafts creed. Cooper's writings are full of admiration and

Figure 122. 'Cormorant' fruit bowl in silver, H 17.8, 1915. Private Collection.

Figure 123. Pencil sketch of cormorant, 1913. Cooper Family Archives.

reverence for these two artists. After Sedding's death, Cooper relied more heavily on the artistic advice of Lethaby who was directly responsible for Cooper's receiving several commissions, including the Four Elms and Muswell Hill liturgical plate orders.[5]

With Sedding's sudden death in 1891 and the transfer of his practice to the more 'decorative-minded' Wilson, Cooper experienced another career modification. Wilson's increasing focus was on the decorative arts and he encouraged Cooper to follow his lead. The immediate outcome of Cooper's emulation was gesso-decorated boxes executed during the 1890s.

With his chance appointment to the metalworking post at the Birmingham Municipal School of Art, Cooper's fate as a decorative artist, primarily as a silversmith and jeweller, was sealed. Cooper's lack of metalworking experience makes it astonishing that he served the position. However, it demonstrates the strong theoretical inroads made by the Arts and Crafts Movement into British art schools at the turn of the century when teaching posts at numerous institutions throughout Great Britain were infiltrated by Arts and Crafts artists who insisted that their students not only learn conceptual design (emphasizing drawing from nature) but also acquire the necessary technical skills (i.e. the understanding of the materials they were working with) to execute such designs.[6]

This new insistence on practical workshop training revolutionized British art education. Its irreversible effects are still felt today. It seems paradoxical that Cooper, who had so little practical metalworking experience at the time, should have been hired to teach this subject in a school that stressed manual training. In fact, Cooper epitomized what Walter Crane acceptably referred to as a 'mental craftsman' and what Robert Catterson-Smith (1853–1938), principal of the Birmingham Municipal School of Art between 1903 and 1920, described as an 'appreciative workman' with an all-round knowledge, not actual practical experience, of technique. According to such Arts and Crafts artists,

Figure 124. Leicester Freedom Casket presented to Sir William Wilkins Vincent in silver, 1912. Photograph in Cooper Family Archives.

technical knowledge, not manual dexterity, characterized an artist as a craftsman. Most Arts and Crafts artists, like Wilson and Cooper, had an understanding of their materials and tools, but left the main execution of their pieces to hired, manually experienced workmen. Today, such practices would classify artists like Wilson and Cooper as designers rather than craftsmen, even though their designs were individually executed by hand and not mass produced. Correspondingly, in turn-of-the-century writings, the phrase 'industrial arts' refers to hand, not machine, executed work.

Though it steered Cooper's career towards the decorative arts, chance, however, was not responsible for his success; his conspicuous artistic ability quickly secured that distinction for him. Significantly, the very first object Cooper exhibited – a gesso-decorated box at the 1893 Arts and Crafts Society exhibition – received a favourable published notice. By the turn of the century, again almost immediately after he took up the medium, Cooper's shagreen work was receiving flattering acknowledgements. Less than six years after he had executed his first metal piece, Cooper's silver and jewellery were also attracting sporadic but favourable reviews.[7] This early critical attention confirms the astonishingly quick development of Cooper's artistic talents. No doubt his mother's artistic inclinations and tutelage in matters of taste and culture had provided an early stimulus for the evolution of Cooper's own aesthetic faculties. His design capabilities were already fully evident in his early pieces, even though their workmanship sometimes lacked dexterity and finesse (Plates 41, 47).

Between 1906 and 1912, Cooper's exhibited work began to receive steady, widespread published recognition (Figure 131). It was regularly mentioned in such magazines as *The Studio* and *The Art Journal*. It even received an appreciative review in the April 1911 issue of the *Deutsche Goldschmiede-Zeitung*.[8] These admiring reports were frequently punctuated by such adjectives as 'elegant', 'refined', and 'tasteful'.[9] Such words became the descriptive hallmarks of Cooper's work in subsequently published reviews, which he carefully collected throughout his life.

The growing respect for Cooper's work contrasted sharply with the critical disapproval for succeeding Arts and Crafts Society exhibitions. In 1912, the Tenth Exhibition signalled to many contemporary critics that the Society had lost energy and sense of purpose. It seemed to be in the midst of a directional crisis: its members, as noted by numerous contemporary publications, were still following and repeating the same themes and motifs established by the Society's founders in the early 1890s. A review in *The Studio* described the 1912 exhibition as giving 'a general impression of skilled craftsmanship following recognized and respected lines, with a corresponding output of good and frequently interesting work, but all unstirred by any fresh emotion . . . no great designer or craftsman rises above the ruck to lead the way to fresh fields of invention.'[10]

Since the early 1890s nothing new or innovative had been introduced to link the Society's output more directly to the needs and wants of the contemporary public. As architectural critic, John Betjeman (1906–84) noted: 'In the 1900s and earlier, these [Arts and Crafts Society] exhibitions at the New Galleries rivalled the Academy in importance. By 1912, it was a failure, even unfashionable. "Arty-craftiness" became an expensive joke.'[11] Despite the negative critical appraisal of the 1912 exhibition as a whole and its noticeable revenue deficit, Cooper's own work sold very well, totalling over £131 and making this his best ever Society exhibition.[12]

The Society's continuing refusal to recognize the necessity of industrial design and machine production and its inability to innovate within the craft tradition resulted in increasingly unfavourable published reviews and contributed to *The Architectural Review*'s perception that the Society was doomed for extinction; in fact, in 1911 the magazine mistakenly concluded that the Society had ceased to exist.[13] When the Society held its Fifteenth Exhibition in 1931 even *The Studio*, an earlier ally of the Society's aims and aesthetic doctrines, published no mention of the show.

Cooper's exhibited work, however, continued to receive favourable notice and recognition. Between 1912 and 1925, his pieces at the various

Figure 125. Coconut bowl mounted in silver, H 14.6, 1914. Trustees of the Cecil Higgins Art Gallery, Bedford.

Figure 126. 'Mermaid' bowl in silver, H 15.9, 1931. Leicester City Museums Service.

Arts and Crafts Society exhibitions were always singled out for special praise. In addition, a review of the British Arts and Crafts section at the Ghent International Exhibition of 1913 concluded that Cooper's 'work on the altar-screen, and his shagreen boxes and silverwork further down the gallery, are among the most perfect examples of taste and skill to be seen'.[14] At the 1914 Paris exhibition of British Arts and Crafts, Cooper's work was again singled out for specific praise in both British and French publications.[15] Likewise, during the Arts and Crafts Society exhibition of 1916, considered by many historians to be the swansong of the movement,[16] Cooper's work again received widespread acknowledgment.[17]

The British description of the 1916 exhibition as the swansong of the Arts and Crafts movement also reached American shores when *The Nation* noted that 'with the organization of this exhibition in war-time, the Society seems to have exhausted its enterprise'.[18] Uniquely, the Society's 1916 exhibition included a room with commercial wares sponsored by the Design and Industries Association (DIA), an English equivalent of the *Deutscher Werkbund*, founded in 1915 to foster good industrial design among machine-made consumer goods. These commercial wares were included:

> . . . as a direct concession to the new movement for the appropriation of German trade and German industry and German art. The war having given Englishmen a sharp reminder of how they have lagged behind, the desire is to profit by it and to be prepared for peace and the commerce it will bring . . . [but] the members of the Society have still far to go before they can hope to compete with the German commercial methods of 'before the war.' The complaint is that Germans appropriated the ideas and the initiative of English arts and craftsmen. But, then, Germany turned them to practical use, which is just what the Arts and Craftsmen themselves have not done.[19]

The British newspaper, the *Star*, summarized the situation similarly:

> There has been in the last twenty years a remarkable revival of English handicrafts, but the unpleasant fact is that Germany stole our ideas and exploited them. The German Government sent representatives to our art schools, and those representatives went back with our designs and our methods; their manufacturers saw the commercial possibilities of the triple alliance of art and science and industry, and they set about capturing the world market in decoration, and furniture, and books, pottery, and metal work. The war has interrupted their attempt, and given our own manufacturers the chance to awaken to the fact that art in industry pays.[20]

Though English manufacturers were to become increasingly aware of the need for artistic beauty in machine-made products, and such organizations as the DIA actively promoted a union between craftsmen and industry, the Arts and Crafts Exhibition Society increasingly turned its attention away from commercial production and emphasized the need for continued hand workmanship. Instead of fulfilling its original aim of improving the general artistic level of consumer goods, now easily achieved on a major scale by means of machine production, the Society retreated further into its handwork shell. At an executive committee meeting held in 1928, it was resolved that no objects predominantly made by machine would be allowed in future exhibitions.[21] In 1931 the committee resolved that no artist whose work was machine-made would be allowed to become a member.[22] Cooper never joined the DIA, which so actively supported the thorough integration of craft and industry. However, during the 1920s he did exhibit with the British Institute for Industrial Art, founded in 1919, which clearly differentiated between machine-made and handmade objects and promoted the equal need for both side by side.

In 1923 the Royal Academy devoted its entire Winter Exhibition to the decorative arts, giving the Arts and Crafts Society its own space for the display of members' work. Again, critics bemoaned the lack of any new

Figure 127. 'Datura' bowl in silver, 1930. Photograph in Cooper Family Archives.

design ideas in the majority of the Society's exhibits: '. . . the Arts and Crafts Society is forced to feed on memories of the past, and is sadly lacking in new blood. . . . And the survivors of this highly efficient and accomplished band of art-workers continue to work on familiar lines, producing variation upon variation of worn-out motives, and rarely introducing a fresh idea. It is as though their attention were centred on perfection of craftsmanship to the exclusion of all original invention.'[23] However, another similar review commended Cooper's exhibited work, in particular his jewellery: 'Mr Cooper's jewellery is of such delicate and exquisite workmanship, based on sound knowledge of the essentials of the craft and fine design, that it almost persuades one that the golden age of jewellery is not yet past.'[24]

Subsequently, the Arts and Crafts Society exhibitions of 1926, 1928, and 1931 received less and less published attention. The consensus of such published critiques as did appear was that the Society's members were no longer in touch with contemporary *Zeitgeist*. Being once at the forefront of decorative arts reform, the Society's exhibited work now appeared distinctly old-fashioned: '. . . the general atmosphere was one of sentimental loyalty to ideas and methods which provide no inspiration to the younger generation. . . . The galleries seemed peopled with ghosts of the past. . . . We [*The Studio* staff] do not want imitations of these old-master craftsmen. We want designers with initiative and an unfettered outlook.'[25] Craftsmanship also continued to outweigh the importance of design in the Society's pieces: 'Many finely made objects, and material beautiful in itself, are stultified either by over abundance of ornament or its diffused application, and by the inappropriate mixture of modern and ancient motives.'[26]

The popular press's reaction to the artistic quality of the Society's output was not the only negative one: following the 1928 Society exhibition at the Royal Academy, the president of the Academy, Sir William Llewellyn (1858–1941), warned the Society that unless the quality of its exhibitions improved the Royal Academy would refuse the use of its galleries for future exhibitions.[27] In fact, the Academy suggested postponing the next exhibition until the autumn of 1931 so that a strong show could be organized.[28] It was following this 1931 exhibition that Cooper and May Morris, along with numerous other artists, resigned from the Society in protest at the new vetting policies which seemed to favour younger artists. By 1932, there was a consensus on the Society's executive council that reorganization was necessary, particularly since it was increasingly difficult to show the work of younger and older craftsmen together in the same exhibition. A suggestion was even put forth that membership in the Society be terminated after a certain number of years.[29]

The most obvious feature that differentiated the work of the younger members from that of the older generation of craftsmen was the skill of execution. For the younger artists the quality of execution, rather than the design itself, was of paramount importance for the aesthetic success of an object. Echoing Cooper's own feelings, F. Ernest Jackson noted this changed outlook:

Figure 128. 'Dragon Tree' bowl in silver, H 6.3, 1930. Leicester City Museums Service.

Figure 129. Carved coconut mounted in silver, H 29.2, 1931. Private Collection.

The too great emphasis placed – in our day – upon technical accomplishment so frequently results in the achievement of a material finish which leaves the mind and senses tired and somewhat bored. . . . Modern methods of training in the artistic crafts tend to obscure the vision by over concentrating on a point of activity, with the result that technique becomes mechanical, and the craftsman, whilst loudly cursing the machine, makes a machine of himself.[30]

The younger generation of craft artists had been trained in art schools which, reformed by Arts and Crafts doctrines, now stressed technical accomplishment. Consequently, these emerging craftsmen were technically proficient and expected flawless execution in handmade objects. Cooper's

Figure 130. Vases in silver, 1932. Photograph in Cooper Family Archives.

generation of craftsman, on the other hand, had begun craft work without any formal training and viewed slight execution irregularities as indications of a maker's individuality rather than clumsy defects that detracted from the aesthetic significance of a piece. According to Cooper, it was the design of an object, not the machine-like precision of its execution, that determined its aesthetic value.

While the critics largely condemned the artistic relevance of the Arts and Crafts Society, Cooper's work was still continuing to receive favourable appraisals. In particular, during the late 1920s and early 1930s, his shagreen boxes were singled out for complimentary remarks. The interest in Cooper's shagreen pieces was no doubt due to the understated decorative sleekness and geometric design of their silver mounts, which appealed to sensibilities increasingly accustomed to machine-inspired designs.

During the 1920s, Cooper's work was most frequently discussed in lengthy reviews of his various one-man exhibitions at the Three Shields Gallery and Walker's Galleries.[31] Without exception, these reviews were highly complimentary, stressing Cooper's sensitivity to the inherent characteristics of his materials and the dominant sense of design, not mere craftsmanship, in his exhibited pieces. By the end of the 1920s, Cooper was receiving even greater accolades: 'In silver alone Mr Cooper is about the only English craftsman who consistently rivals the Danes – chiefly because, like them, he appears to think in silver.'[32] As the Arts and Crafts Exhibition Society faded into popular obscurity, Cooper became regarded as one of the most, if not *the* most, important contemporary British silversmith: 'With the keenest appreciation for the intrinsic qualities of his materials Mr Cooper has the most perfect taste in design. Nobody in England is handling silver with greater felicity.'[33]

The inverse relationship which developed between the critical response to the Arts and Crafts Exhibition Society, on the one hand, and to Cooper's exhibition work, on the other, is significant for assessing Cooper's importance. The insistence by numerous contemporary publications that the Society's artists were weak in design and merely content to emulate, with minor variations, the work of the Society's founding members such as William Morris and Walter Crane does not pertain to Cooper. Nor does it pertain to other Society artists, such as Edward Spencer, whose work during the 1920s showed a marked shift towards a new abstracted simplification. Likewise, in the late 1920s and 1930s the silver of Harry G. Murphy began displaying stylistic characteristics that now frequently cause it to be classified as Art Deco. Though Cooper remained faithful throughout his career to the basic Arts and Crafts doctrine of hand craftsmanship – utilizing ornament derived from nature rendered in a spontaneous, forthright manner – there were evident changes in his style which reflected both his gradual artistic maturity and his response to the changing artistic environment surrounding him.

As demonstrated in the jewellery and metalwork section of Chapter Two, Cooper's Birmingham period work was characterized by a bold, expressionistic style, analogous to the daring pioneer spirit of the early Arts and Crafts Exhibition Society. By the 1910s, his work became more refined, elegant and opulent, more closely conforming to contemporary Edwardian tastes. During the 1920s and early 1930s simplification, repetition and detachment began to permeate his pieces, reflecting the machine-inspired abstraction popularized by the Art Deco style.

As well as these stylistic variations, Cooper's pieces also display a strong sense of design. The subtle modulations in their proportions, in their placement of decoration and in the colour and texture of their materials were always carefully planned by Cooper in order to create aesthetically pleasing and interesting pieces. The mere craftsmanship of their execution was never allowed to overpower their design or become their sole *raison d'être*. Such skilful design modulations and the subtle adaptation of Cooper's style to changing artistic influences attracted reviewers to his work and were responsible for eliciting favourable critiques. Though Cooper may not have been at the forefront of the innovative machine-inspired design, preferring to remain faithful to his Arts and Crafts roots, his mature pieces still convey a sense of artistic importance and merit that contemporary art critics were quick to recognize.

In 1933, Cooper's work was shown posthumously at the Exhibition of British Industrial Art in Relation to the Home. Held at Dorland Hall in London, the exhibition featured both hand- and machine-made objects side by side. The show – an outcome of a report on industrial design compiled by a departmental committee set up by the Board of Trade under the chairmanship of Lord Gorell (1884–1963) – was meant to display well-designed accessories for the home, particularly those produced through a collaboration between artists and manufacturers.[34] *The Studio* gave the following appraisal of the exhibition:

The word 'industrial' is evidently key to the exhibition's purpose, though perhaps this might have been made somewhat clearer, as both machine and hand-made products were shown. The dictionary, it is true, does not make any hard and fast divisions between handicraft and machine production in defining 'industrial'. Yet evidently the modern problem and the problem which an exhibition of this sort should attempt to solve is largely that of designing for the machine. Perhaps greater emphasis might have been laid on this point and given a more pronounced idea of purpose.[35]

The obvious disappointment expressed in *The Studio* at the inclusion of handmade objects, primarily executed by Arts and Crafts Society artists, again points to the then growing belief that modern reform of public taste could only be achieved through mass-produced objects and that any attempt at reform by means of handmade objects was ineffectual and long outdated. In reviewing the Society's 1928 exhibition, *The Studio* had proclaimed: 'The Arts and Crafts Exhibition Society, now occupying Burlington House, will do little towards persuading an opponent of the movement as to its utility. There is little that the machine could not do as well, and a regrettable disregard of present-day housing conditions.'[36]

In fact, the 1933 Dorland Hall exhibition signalled to many intellectuals the dawn of a new era of partnership and cooperation between artists and manufacturers, a change of direction that the Crystal Palace exhibition had failed to achieve. Instead of ushering a new era of cooperation between art and industry, the 1851 exhibition had actually witnessed the end of this genial partnership:

On October 15, 1851, the Great Exhibition was brought to an end and with it an epoch too . . . the end of his [Prince Albert's] Exhibition was also the end of friendly relationships [between art and industry]. For it had been a purely a Georgian affair. It was conceived by Royalty, it was a risk and and a poetic dream. Manufacturing was still largely in the hands of the enlightened, or rather there was still an aristocracy of class which laid claim to an authority in taste. Commerce was still a splendid new pet which had not grown dangerous. There have been other Exhibitions in England since then; but they have been commercial undertakings. Commerce has displayed its taste and it has been found unpleasant. It has shown its claws and the Prince Alberts have been massacred. Commerce put its smelly paw on the objects of the Great Exhibition. It broke those objects in two: one half it smelled out as 'Art' and the other as 'Use.' The question then arose as to how much 'Art' was needed to make the 'Use' a paying or commercial proposition. . . . Let us see . . . whether the Dorland Hall Exhibition, . . . may be looked upon as the dawn of another era such as that which the Great Exhibition of 1851 brought to a close.[37]

Similarly, committee chair Lord Gorell, noted:

We are coming, in fact, to a turning point. In the old days of the master-craftsmen, art and industry walked harmoniously hand in hand: the greatest artists of their times were often quite simply and naturally designers also: the lesser folk took a pride in their handicraft. Then came the age of the machine and the separation between art and industry: the artist scorned the manufacturer, the manufacturer had little or no use for the artist. William Morris and others of his mind saw and deplored the separation, and endeavoured zealously to span the widening rift: but no man can set back the hands of the clock, and with mass production the old conditions were gone. So has arisen a new movement to meet new conditions, a gathering body of opinion to emphasize the great truth, that the need both artistically and industrially today is for full recognition of the fundamental importance of design – for the artist to understand the requirements of the manufacturer in this machine age and for the manufacturer to appreciate that without the brain of an artist, he is fatally handicapped in the race for commercial success.[38]

In view of the public campaign launched by the Dorland Hall exhibition in support of machine production, it seems prophetic that Cooper should have died shortly before its opening. This exhibition became, in essence, the officially sanctioned debut of British industrial design. The reformist torch was now publicly placed into the hands of the

Figure 131. Display case containing Cooper's metalwork at the 1910 Arts and Crafts Society exhibition. Case includes objects illustrated in Figures 55 and 115, and Plate 45. Photograph in Cooper Family Archives.

industrial designer. Subsequently, craft artists, such as Cooper's son Francis, retired to their individual studios and quietly continued to execute their work, no longer dominating public debates concerning social and artistic reform.

Though Cooper's career focused on handicraft, his views concerning the machine were not entirely antagonistic, particularly as stated in a lecture he gave to the Art-Workers' Guild in 1929. Here, Cooper explained his belief that handicrafts and machine production were two distinctly separate endeavours: 'There is a tendency I think in some quarters to do away with the distinction between the tool & the machine & to bridge the difference between the handicrafts & machine production, instead of regarding them as two streams running side by side each useful in its own way.'[39] To achieve their respective maximum potentials, of which Cooper believed both were capable, handicrafts and machine production were each to pursue a line of development most characteristic and faithful to their respective execution methods:

> The handicrafts set the machine going but now that it is properly set going, what seems to be required is to let those who manage it learn what they can do well, improve their methods & invent new ones & let the handicrafts advance in their own direction to arrive at a quite different destination. In fact, the time has come when it is wisest for them to decide each on its own course & to pursue it.[40]

> Machine production has created almost a new craft & should I think be left to run its course & to solve its own problems. It is not a graft on the tree of the handicrafts but rather a cutting from that tree which has struck roots of its own & is in no way dependent on the parent tree for its future existence, or for the quality of its fruit.[41]

Though both handicraft and the machine were capable of satisfying their respective aesthetic potentials, Cooper clearly thought that handicrafts were capable of higher artistic expression than the machine. According to him, art was an activity of the soul, expressive of its creator's intuition and spirituality. A craftsman's emotions and passions, clearly absent in an inanimate machine, endowed the handicrafts with higher aesthetic merit:[42] 'To design for the machine as done at present, is to place the executant of the work in the position of a lifeless tool, a sort of lever to move the machine. It is like placing a non-conductor between designer & the finished product – a non-conductor of expression. The result is something so nearly lifeless that it may be said to cease to have any artistic expression.'[43] The craftsman's hands imparted individuality to a piece and thereby gave it a greater artistic impact: 'We have been told, . . . that the machine is only a tool. The difficulty is that a tool is not merely a machine. "A machine is an existing something which can do what it can do always in the same way & is incapable of doing any more, it is limited and fixed in its usefulness." A tool in a workman's hand is on the contrary like another hand or finger. It can do what it can do in innumerable ways. It does what the individual craftsman makes it do.'[44]

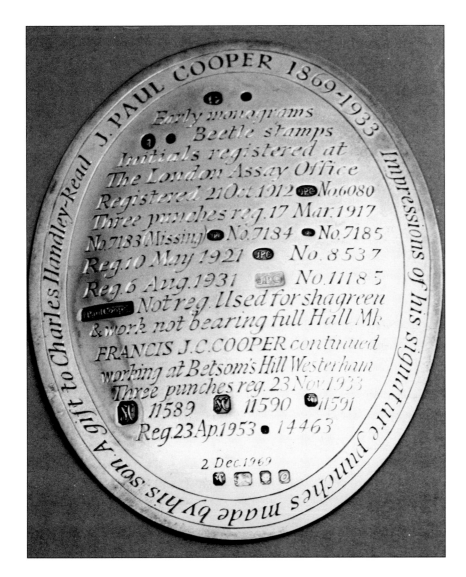

Figure 132. Silver plaque with signature punches of John Paul Cooper and his son Francis made by Francis Cooper, L 11.1, 1969. Trustees of the Cecil Higgins Art Gallery, Bedford.

According to Cooper, the reasons a craftsman chose traditional methods of workmanship, preferring his hand tools to the machine, were further based on the respect he had for the material being worked. Again, the machine was incapable of such sentiment:

He [the craftsman] abjures the use of the machine, because he can't get it to sufficiently do what he wants to bring out the quality of the metal. He prefers to respect his metal by hammering rather than spinning because spinning stretches the metal without consolidating it, & leaves it as if it had been rolled into shape instead of coaxed. . . . He does not refuse, as a rule, to use facetted stones because they are faceted, but because they are so mechanically cut that except when used as a conglomeration of brilliants arranged to sparkle they as a rule kill his work. With unfaceted stones the individuality which each stone really possesses is not lost to the same extent. It is the same with metal, he has a respect for its texture for the way it is capable of receiving impressions, & the way it responds when sympathetically, one might say affectionately, treated. It does not even in such cases resent file marks.[45]

Following Cooper's argument, it would seem that the hard-edged Art Deco style in metal evolved more from the appearance and production methods of the machine than from a conscious effort by the designer to express the inherent rigidity of the material.

The essential humanism of Cooper's view – that only the artist-craftsman, and not the industrial designer, was able to impart artistic expression to an object – stemmed from his and other Arts and Crafts artists' distrust of materialism and commercialism. Contemporary trade silversmiths and jewellers were quick to begin employing machines in order to reduce their costs and increase their production and thereby make their products more commercially attractive. As a result, commercialism and the machine became permanently linked together in Arts and Crafts minds. The degradation and loss of human values, which inevitably resulted from expanding commercialism, likewise became associated with the introduction of the machine. Having seen such conditions first hand in his father's business, Cooper's distrust of commercialism and materialism, which he characterized as the 'love of show & love of competition [;] the doctrine that human life is not actually but normally a struggle for existence, in which each person must strive to elevate himself at the expense of others,' also then became associated with the machine.[46] Commercialism and the machine became interchangeable terms, equally void of artistic possibilities.

Cooper's own personality and interests were likewise incompatible with commercialism and with repetitive, standardized machine production. A true child of *fin-de-siècle* thought, his interests in symbolism, mysticism and astrology all exemplified an independent, intuitive mind, interested in expressive, subjective thought. Artists as diverse as Henry Wilson and René Lalique also shared Cooper's predilection for thought and imagery evocative of the non-material. Cooper often reflected on the lack of spiritual motivation in his contemporary world: 'The advent of machinery is often blamed for the destruction of romance in workmanship, but it would be more reasonable to blame the philosophic & scientific teaching that has taken place on positive and materialistic grounds, which denied the existence of the hidden side of life, on which the artist depends for his inspiration.'[47]

The contradiction between Cooper's own dislike of machine-generated commercialism, and the comfortable lifestyle that the income from his father's business allowed him, never seems to have bothered Cooper. It might have been this very contradiction that pushed him into his private inquiries concerning mysticism and spirituality rather than into instigating social reforms in a similar way to William Morris and C.R. Ashbee. Cooper's natural shyness and modesty precluded his involvement in any large-scale, orchestrated campaigns for artistic or social reform.[48] He was satisfied to work privately in his own studio as an individual crusader for aesthetic reform in the decorative arts. It was this kind of individualism, in an increasingly commercially amalgamated world, that contributed to the Arts and Crafts Exhibition Society's downfall. Writing in 1915, C.R. Ashbee had warned that:

our traditions, training & methods for the last 20 years have all been against concerted action of any sort. . . . We have all of us been running our own little workshops & side shows in our own way, without believing in the good intentions, or the ideas, or the 'bona fides' of 'the other fellow'. . . . In so doing we have, I fear, destroyed, for the sake of a petty individualism, the life and the principles of our Society. . . . Our difficulty indeed is not one of aesthetics it is one of organization, – of livelyhood, – of adjusting the conditions under which the Arts & Crafts can be practised to the mechanical environment of our time. In that sense our difficulty is social, human, ethical.[49]

Despite his considerable artistic reputation and the critical acclaim for Cooper's metalwork and shagreen during the late 1920s and early 1930s, he increasingly turned his attention towards watercolours. In 1922, the artist John Wright (1857–1933) took a cottage near Betsom's Hill and gave Cooper several lessons in watercolour to improve his technique. By the end of the 1920s Cooper's holiday sketchbooks were filled with preparatory studies for his paintings. His written account of these holidays also became dominated by quick sketches of local people and scenery he encountered. In 1932, Cooper went to see Turner's sketchbooks at the British Museum.

By this time Cooper had recognized the expanding dominance of commercially generated ideas in the decorative arts and discerned that industrial design and mass production would increasingly dictate their stylistic direction. Impersonal machine production, solely meant to satisfy utility, did not meet Cooper's definition of artistic objects where personalized spiritual expression was paramount for aesthetic impact: 'art is intuition & intuition is individuality & individuality can never be repeated.'[50]

Paralleling Cooper's beliefs, the opening quotation to this chapter, taken from F.E. Jackson's writings, also stated that an artist should mainly concern himself with expression, communicating ideas and feelings to his viewers, rather than concentrating on execution technique. Published reviews criticizing the Arts and Crafts Society's output had reported that the technical execution of its members' exhibited pieces was good but that they lacked a sense of design. This lack of purposeful content, expressive of the contemporary social environment, was at the epicentre of the crisis experienced by British decorative arts: the Arts and Crafts ideals appeared outdated in an industrialized world, and the machine aesthetic was too cold and impersonal.

In watercolour, Cooper found a medium that could solely be employed for subjective expression and one that he could conceive and execute totally by himself. Utility, an ever present consideration in the decorative arts, was absent in watercolours. Consequently, Cooper's artistic sensibilities were no longer pragmatically restrained. Gordon Craig had pointed out that Cooper's watercolours were like letters written in paint: personalized descriptions of various geographical sites which stirred Cooper's imagination and emotions, better characterized as 'breathless exploration' rather than as architectural renderings.[51] Taste, after all, Cooper had concluded was 'the power of appreciation of the feeling which is put into a work of art by the executor'.[52]

The word 'taste' serves as a suitable epitaph for Cooper who, throughout his life, endeavoured to discern and emulate the best in nature, literature, architecture and handicraft. Though largely unacknowledged by succeeding generations, Cooper's success was fortunately recognized by his contemporaries. As an obituary to him concluded: 'He aimed in all his work to embody all that is best and highest in life, with a beauty of creation that stamped him a great artist.'[53]

APPENDIX A
SIGNATURE MARKS

A. UNREGISTERED MARKS

1. Monogram stamps:

2. Beetle stamps:

3. Full name stamp:

B. REGISTERED MARKS

1. Initials stamp, registered as No. 6080 at the London Assay Office on 21 October 1912.

2. Initials stamp, registered as No. 7184 at the London Assay Office on 17 March 1917.

3. Initials stamp, registered as No. 7185 at the London Assay Office on 17 March 1917.

4. Initials stamp, registered as No. 8537 at the London Assay Office on 10 May 1921.

5. Initials stamp, registered as No. 11185 at the London Assay Office on 6 August 1931.

CRAFTSMEN EMPLOYED BY JOHN PAUL COOPER

A. STUDIO WORKMEN

1. *Lorenzo Colarossi (1879–1965)*
Employed 1899–1911, 1913–15 and 1919–33; prior to 1899, employed in Wilson's Vicarage Gate studio; executed jewellery, metal, and shagreen work; taught 1901–7 at the Birmingham Municipal School of Art; employed 1911–13 at the Artificers' Guild; after 1933 continued working for Cooper's son Francis.

2. *George Romer*
Employed 1900–7; prior to 1900, employed in Wilson's Vicarage Gate studio; mainly executed jewellery and technically difficult metalwork; taught 1901–14 at the Birmingham Municipal School of Art.

3. *William Hazlewood (b. 1886)*
Employed 1904–17; executed jewellery, metal and shagreen work; former student of the Birmingham Municipal School of Art.

4. *George Bertram Middleton (b. 1880)*
Employed 1906–9; executed jewellery, metal and shagreen work; former student of the Birmingham Municipal School of Art.

5. *Bernard Instone (1891–1987)*
Employed 1911–12; executed jewellery, metal and shagreen work; former student of the Birmingham Municipal School of Art.

6. *Charles J.C. Baker*
Employed 1913–15; executed jewellery, metal and shagreen work; also employed at the Artificers' Guild.

7. *Gwendoline Ethel Rendle (a.k.a. Sah Oved) (1900–83)*
Employed 1922–1923; executed jewellery and metalwork.

8. *Francis Cooper (1906–80)*
Employed 1924–1933; executed metal and shagreen work.

B. OUTSIDE WORKMEN

1. *Augustus H. Mason*
Workshop located at 112 Chiswick Lane, Chiswick, London.
Employed 1899–1916 to execute wood, inlay, and shagreen work.

2. *G. Fiorini*
Workshop located at The Foundry, Winders Road, Battersea, London.
Employed 1907–1933 to execute metal castings.

3. *Arthur S. Willis*
Workshop located at 151 Highbury Hill, Highbury, London.
Employed 1914–27 to execute metal engraving.

4. *Sidney G. Wiseman*
Workman in Wilson's Vicarage Gate and St Mary Platt studios.
Employed 1913–15 to execute enamel work; employed 1926–1933 to execute metalwork.

5. *Laurence A. Turner (1864–1952)*
Workshop located at 42 Lamb's Conduit Street, London.
Employed 1917–33 to execute wood and shagreen work.

6. *E. Newton*
Workshop located at Silverstead Cottage, Westerham Hill, Kent.
Employed 1926–33 to execute wood work.

7. *G.T. Friend (1881–1969)*
Workshop located at 321 High Holborn, London.
Employed 1928–33 to execute metal engraving and signature punches.

ARCHITECTURAL COMMISSIONS

1. Manor House, Thurnby, Leicestershire
   Date of specifications: November 1891
   Client unknown
   Alterations and additions to existing structure

2. Tower Cottage, Winchelsea, East Sussex
   Date of specifications: February 1896
   For Ellen Terry
   Alterations and additions to existing structure, including a new porch,
      cellar window, and gate

3. St Margaret's Works, Leicester
   Date of specifications: February 1898
   For Messrs Cooper, Corah and Sons
   Enlargement of west factory shed and toilets

4. St Margaret's Cottages, Leicester
   Date of specifications: May 1898
   For Messrs Cooper, Corah and Sons
   Erection of toilet building

5. Cottages, North Evington, Leicester
   Date of specifications: September 1898
   For John Harris Cooper
   Erection of six residential cottages

6. St Margaret's Works, Leicester
   Date of specifications: October 1898
   For Messrs Cooper, Corah and Sons
   Alterations to administrative office

7. St Margaret's Works, Leicester
   Date of specifications: November 1898
   For Messrs Cooper, Corah and Sons
   Enlargement of west factory shed

8. St Margaret's Works, Leicester
    Date of specifications: January 1902
    For Messrs Cooper, Corah and Sons
    Erection of three-storey building at southeast corner of complex

9. Infants' School, Whitwick, Leicestershire
    Date of specifications: March 1902
    For James Mackenzie and Mr Boothe
    Erection of school building

10. 39 Holland Street, London
    Date of specifications: August 1909
    For Fanny Loder Cooper
    Alterations to existing structure, including new chimneypiece

11. Smallhythe Place, Tenterden, Kent
    Date of specifications: May 1910
    For Ellen Terry
    Addition of toilet to second floor

12. Betsom's Hill, Westerham, Kent
    Date of specifications: October 1910
    For John Paul Cooper
    Erection of two-storey residence and studio

13. Smallhythe Place, Tenterden, Kent
    Date of specifications: November 1911
    For Ellen Terry
    Erection of new roof and three interior oak posts

PUBLISHED WRITINGS BY JOHN PAUL COOPER

1. '"The Toy Town"', *The Architectural Review*, 2, June–November 1897, 284.
2. 'King John's Dinner Hour', *The Architectural Review*, 3, December–May 1897–8, 273–4.
3. 'The Relation of Journalism to the Arts', *The Architectural Review*, 3, December–May 1897–8, 109.
4. 'The Work of John Sedding, Architect', *The Architectural Review*, 3, December–May 1897–8, 35–41, 69–77, 125–33, 188–94, 235–42; 4, June–November 1898, 33–6.
5. '"The Architect's Eden: Much Ado About Nothing" at the St James's Theatre', *The Architectural Review*, 4, June–November 1898, 37–43, 87–92.
6. 'The Castles of "The Three Musketeers": No. 1: Porthos, His Château of Pierrefonds', *The Architectural Review*, 5, December–May 1899, 2–14, 67–76.
7. 'The Town and Castle of Annecy', *The Architectural Review*, 7, January–June 1900, 168–77, 283–92.
8. 'Notes on Masons' Marks', *The Architectural Review*, 8, July–December 1900, 187–90.
9. 'Opera Glasses', *Mask*, 1, May–June 1908, 54.
10. 'Inigo Jones', *Mask*, 1, July 1908, 99–102.
11. 'Masques', *British Architect*, 70, August 1908, 105–6.
12. 'Various Objects in Shagreen', *Catalogue of a Loan Collection of Antique Furniture, Medieval Tapestries, and Allied Domestic Arts*, New Gallery, Edinburgh, 1917, 27–8.
13. 'Local Societies of the Arts and Crafts', *Handicrafts and Reconstruction. Notes by Members of the Arts and Crafts Exhibition Society*, London, 1919, 113–18.
14. 'A Chance for South Kensington', *The Arts and Crafts Quarterly*, l, May 1920, 13.
15. 'The Madonna of Orvieto, or the Making of a Museum', *The Arts and Crafts Quarterly*, 1, May 1920, 9–13.
16. 'The Present Position of Symbolism and Allegory', *The Architects' Journal*, 57, May 1923, 915–17.
17. 'Jewellery and Superstition', *Oxted and Limpsfield Signpost*, 1, March 1928, 85–7.

JOHN PAUL COOPER'S WORK

IN BRITISH AND AMERICAN COLLECTIONS

GREAT BRITAIN

Bedford:	Cecil Higgins Art Gallery
	gesso, mother-of-pearl, jewellery, metalwork
Birmingham:	Birmingham City Museum and Art Gallery
	shagreen, jewellery, metalwork
	Cathedral Church of St Philip
	metalwork
Cambridge:	Fitzwilliam Museum
	shagreen, jewellery
	Pembroke College
	metalwork
	Trinity College
	lighting fixture
Canterbury:	Cathedral Church of Christ, St Martin of Tours Chapel
	metalwork
Cheltenham:	Cheltenham Art Gallery and Museum
	shagreen, jewellery
	Cheltenham Ladies' College
	metalwork
Edinburgh:	Cathedral Church of St Mary
	metalwork
	Huntly House Museum
	Sir Douglas Haig Sword
	Royal Museum of Scotland
	shagreen
Egham, Surrey:	Royal Holloway College, University of London
	metalwork
Four Elms, Kent:	Church of St Paul
	metalwork
Leicester:	Leicester Museum and Art Gallery
	gesso, shagreen, metalwork
Limpsfield Chart, Surrey:	Church of St Andrew
	metalwork
Liverpool:	Liverpool Museum

	metalwork
London:	Church of St James, Muswell Hill
	metalwork
	Church of St Paul, Covent Garden
	metalwork
	Royal Aeronautical Society
	Airship R38 Memorial
	Victoria & Albert Museum
	shagreen, jewellery, metalwork
	The Worshipful Company of Goldsmiths
	shagreen, metalwork
Newcastle -upon-Tyne:	Church of St James and St Basil, Fenham
	metalwork
Norwich:	Castle Museum
	metalwork
Oakham, Rutland:	Oakham School
	metalwork
Richmond, Surrey:	Church of St John Divine
	metalwork
Rochester:	Cathedral Church of Christ and the Blessed Virgin
	metalwork
Tatsfield, Surrey:	Church of St Mary
	metalwork, war memorial
Tenterden, Kent:	Ellen Terry Memorial Museum
	jewellery
Winchester:	Cathedral Church of the Holy Trinity and of St Peter and St Paul and of St Swithun
	King's Royal Rifle Corps War Memorial
Windsor:	Eton College
	metalwork
Worcester:	Stanbrook Abbey
	metalwork

UNITED STATES

Detroit:	The Detroit Institute of Arts
	metalwork
Miami Beach:	The Wolfsonian-Florida International University
	metalwork
New York:	Cooper-Hewitt National Design Museum
	shagreen

NOTES

FOREWORD

1 All the quotations, unless otherwise indicated, are taken from Natasha Kuzmanović's text.
2 W.R. Lethaby *Philip Webb and His Work*, (Oxford, Oxford University Press, 1935); quoted from Gillian Naylor *The Arts and Crafts Movement* (London, 1971), p. 164.

INTRODUCTION

1 John Paul Cooper (JPC), 'Metal Work and Jewellery' (unpublished manuscript, n.d.), p. 1.
2 Gillian Naylor, *The Arts and Crafts Movement* (London, 1990), pp. 5–7 and Peter Stansky, *Redesigning the World* (Princeton, 1985), pp. 14–21, 266–9. Both authors tackle the paradox of this complex issue, and how social and political structure affected and impeded the outcome of this self-analysis. The historical survey presented in the following introduction is intended as a generalized summary of the major artistic events that contributed to the development of the Arts and Crafts Movement. It is a broad synopsis which condenses extensive information and simplifies the complex issues prevalent during the second half of the nineteenth century.
3 *The Art-Journal Illustrated Catalogue of the International Exhibition* (London, 1862), pp. 6–7.
4 'Art Metal-Work at the Chicago Exhibition', *The Art Journal Supplement* (1893), xxi.
5 *Ill. Cat. of Int. Exh.* (1862), p. 11.
6 Quoted in Gilbert R. Redgrave, 'Art Education during the Past Fifty Years', *The Art Journal* (June 1887), 221.
7 Quoted in *Ill. Cat. of Int. Exh.* (1862), pp. 7–8.
8 *Ill. Cat. of Int. Exh.* (1862), p. 13.
9 *The Art-Journal Catalogue of the Paris Universal Exhibition* (London, 1867), pp. 37–8.
10 *The Illustrated Catalogue of the Paris International Exhibition* (London, 1878), p. 39.
11 Quoted in *Ill. Cat. of Paris Int. Exh.* (1878), p. 37.
12 A. Harris, 'The Technical Commission and Industrial Art', *The Art Journal* (October 1884), 304.
13 Lewis F. Day, 'Victorian Progress in Applied Design', *The Art Journal* (June 1887), 188.
14 Harris, 'The Technical Commission and Industrial Art', pp. 309, 312. This article goes on to recommend that 'this great central school of Industrial Art would have to be based on a wider foundation. It would include not only the teaching of the principle of Art as applied to industry, but the application of those principles to work. The school-room and the workshop would be placed along side each other, and as knowledge was gained in the former, it would be applied in the latter.'
15 Oscar Lovell Triggs, *Chapters in the History of the Arts and Crafts Movement* (Chicago, 1902), pp. 11–17.

16 William Morris (ed.), *The Nature of Gothic. A Chapter of the Stones of Venice by John Ruskin* (Hammersmith, 1892), p. i.

17 Triggs, *Arts and Crafts*, p. 62. Noted art historian Alan Crawford very aptly commented on this quote in a recent letter: 'Morris would not have been outraged if he had read that he "originated almost nothing in point of theory, the socialism with which he was identified himself being Ruskin's" because he was a generous man and loved Ruskin. But Morris became a revolutionary Marxist, and though the starting point from which he came was a very Ruskinian one, Ruskin did not travel that road. There is a great deal that is distinctly new about Morris in the wake of Ruskin. Oscar Lovell Triggs, who is quoted here, had his own American individualist agenda in writing about Morris, and it shaped his view. Any modern historian would say it mis-shaped his view.'

18 Gillian Naylor (ed.), *William Morris By Himself* (Boston, 1988), pp. 37–8. The efforts of architect A.W.N. Pugin were largely responsible for the renewed serious interest in decorative design.

19 Philip Henderson (ed.), *The Letters of William Morris to His Family and Friends*, (London, 1950), pp. 65–6.

20 Quoted in Stansky, *Redesigning the World*, p. 151.

21 H.J.L. J. Massé, *The Art-Workers' Guild 1884–1934* (Oxford, 1935), pp. 7, 17, 22.

22 Gillian Naylor, 'Formative Years of the Arts and Crafts Exhibition Society 1888–1916', *Craft History* 1 (1988), 1–3 and Stansky, *Redesigning the World*, pp. 67–8, 206–7.

23 Lewis F. Day, 'Arts and Crafts', *The Art Journal* (November 1893), 330.

24 Arts and Crafts Exhibition Society, *Catalogue of the First Exhibition* (London, 1888), pp. 7–8.

25 The Fine Art Society Ltd, *Jewellery and Jewellery Design 1850–1930 and John Paul Cooper 1869–1933* (London, 1975), cat. nos. 192–300. This slender catalogue accompanied a selling exhibition of Cooper's work in London and contains an outline of his career. As such, it was the only study of Cooper and his work published before this monograph.

CHAPTER ONE: BIOGRAPHY

1 Francis Cooper, 'John Paul Cooper and the Arts and Crafts Movement', letter to Tricia Laurie, February 1979, Cooper Family Archives, p. 10.

2 Keith Jopp, *Corah of Leicester 1815–1965* (Leicester, 1965), pp. 11–20, 42–3.

3 JPC, Journal IV, pp. 258–9.

4 Kanty Cooper, 'Father, Family and Friends', unfinished manuscript, Cooper Family Archives, pp. 2–3.

5 JPC, Journal IV, p. 256.

6 JPC, Journal IV, pp. 259–60.

7 JPC, Journal IV, p. 260.

8 Edward Gordon Craig, 'Writing in Water-Colour', *Walker's Monthly*, 39 (March 1931), 1. In the quotation, Craig is describing the Coopers' London house at 42 Inverness Terrace, Hyde Park, during the early 1890s.

9 JPC, Journal IV, p. 249.

10 'The Late Mr. W. Jackson', *Leicester Daily Post*, 16 July 1894, n. pag.

11 JPC, Journal IV, p. 249.

12 K. Cooper, 'Father, Family and Friends', p. 3.

13 JPC, Journal II, p. 322.

14 JPC, Journal IV, p. 237A. Cooper's birth in London rather than in Leicester was probably due to his illegitimacy.

15 JPC, Journal IV, p. 237A.

16 JPC, Journal IV, p. 237A.

17 JPC, Journal IV, pp. 250–1.

18 JPC, Journal I, p. 59.

19 JPC, Journal I, p. 74.

20 JPC, Journal I, p. 67.

21 JPC, Journal III, p. 94.

22   W. Houghton, *Country Walks of a Naturalist With His Children* (London, 1870).

23   JPC, Journal I, p. 74.

24   JPC, Journal I, p. 74.

25   JPC, Journal I, p. 74.

26   JPC, Journal I, pp. 26, 55.

27   Enrolment records at Bradfield College, Berkshire.

28   JPC, Journal III, p. 109.

29   JPC, Journal III, pp. 96, 103.

30   JPC, Journal I, pp. 64–5.

31   JPC, Journal III, p. 102.

32   Edward Gordon Craig, *Index to the Story of My Days* (London, 1957), p. 78.

33   Craig, 'Writing in Water-Colour', p. 1.

34   JPC, Journal III, p. 102 and Journal IV, p. 151.

35   Craig, *Index to the Story of My Days*, p. 103.

36   JPC, Journal IV, pp. 149, 157–8.

37   JPC, Journal III, p. 114. During the 1890s until he acquired his Aubrey Walk studio, Cooper often used his family's London house at 42 Inverness Terrace, Hyde Park, as his professional address. He seems also to have lived there on and off during this period.

38   Geoffry Lucas, 'Obituary. Walter John Nash Millard', *Journal of the Royal Society of British Architects* 44 (1936–7), 152, 247.

39   JPC, Journal IV, p. 179.

40   W.H. Hewish, 'Notes on Classes', *The Architectural Association Notes* 2 (November 1887), 150.

41   JPC, Journal IV, p. 181.

42   JPC, Journal IV, p. 181.

43   JPC, Journal IV, p. 181.

44   Quoted in W.R. Lethaby, 'A Note on the Artistic Life and Work of John D. Sedding', *The Builder*, 10 October 1891, 271.

45   For further discussion of Mackintosh's career see: Alan Crawford, *Charles Rennie Mackintosh* (London, 1995); Wendy Kaplan (ed.), *Charles Rennie Mackintosh* (Glasgow and New York, 1996); and Bille Wickre, 'Collaboration in the Work of Margaret and Frances Macdonald, Charles Rennie Mackintosh, and J. Herbert McNair' (unpublished PhD dissertation, University of Michigan, 1993).

46   JPC, Journal IV, p. 183.

47   JPC, Journal IV, p. 183.

48   JPC, Journal IV, p. 202 and Mary Comino, *Gimson and the Barnsleys*, London, 1980, p. 34. Ernest Barnsley (1863–1926), another well-known pupil of Sedding's, had left the office in the middle of 1887 and moved to Birmingham.

49   JPC, Journal IV, p. 182.

50   JPC, Journal IV, p. 189.

51   JPC, Journal IV, p. 183.

52   Cooper visited France in 1890 (French Riviera, Calais, St Omer), 1891 (Abbeville, Rue, St Riquier), 1894 (Caen), 1896 (Amiens, Beauvais), 1897 (Avignon, Nîmes, Arles, Annecy), 1900 (Amiens, Paris, Ypres), 1902 (Le Puy), 1904 (Chartres, Le Mans, Loire valley), 1912 (Avignon, Toulouse), 1914 (Laon, Rheims, Paris), 1920 (Caen, Havre), 1921 (Loire valley), 1923 (Rouen, Lisieux), 1924 (St Malo, Dinan), 1925 (Coutances, Bayeux), and in 1933 (Menton). Cooper visited Italy in 1893 (Milan, Venice, Florence, Padua, Ravenna, Siena, Rome), 1898 (Milan, Perugia, Assisi), 1899 (Florence), 1908 (Pisa, Genoa, Florence), 1922 (Milan, Naples, Sicily), 1923 (Venice, Padua), 1925 (Dolomites), 1926 (Piacenza, Parma, Ravenna, Venice), 1931 (Dolomites), and in 1932 (Genoa, Rome, Pompeii, Amalfi).

53   JPC, Journal IV, p. 185.

54   John Summerson, *The Architectural Association 1847–1947* (London, 1947), pp. 35–7. Summerson was curator of Sir John Soane's Museum from 1945–84.

55   JPC, Journal IV, p. 195.

56   JPC, Journal IV, p. 196.

57   'Heatherleys', *The Studio* 94 (September 1927), 227.

58 JPC, Journal IV, p. 197. Crompton was principal between 1888 and 1908.
59 JPC, Journal IV, p. 195.
60 JPC, Journal IV, p. 198.
61 Arts and Crafts Exhibition Society, *Catalogue of the Fourth Exhibition* (London, 1893), no. 244.
62 Cynthia Manton, 'Henry Wilson (1864–1934): His Work and Influence' (unpublished PhD dissertation, Brighton Polytechnic, 1985).
63 JPC, Journal IV, pp. 197–8.
64 JPC, Journal IV, p. 198.
65 JPC, Journal IV, p. 197.
66 Royal Institute of British Architects, *The Kalender of the Royal Institute of British Architects*, 58th sess. 1893–4, (London, 1893), 237–8.
67 'The Prize Drawings at the Institute. The Pugin Studentship', *The Architectural Association Notes* 7 (February 1893), 102.
68 JPC, Journal IV, p. 208.
69 JPC, Journal III, pp. 14–84.
70 Alfred Powell, 'Owen Jones Studentship. Memoir, December 1893', The British Architectural Library, London, Msfo 1893–(079J)72.03(45).
71 JPC, Stockbook II, pp. 17, no. 769: 'Silver Inkstand', May 1914.
72 JPC, Stockbook II, pp. 16, no. 750.
73 Letter to JPC from Alexander Graham, 14 March 1894, and Royal Institute of British Architects, Ordinary General Meetings Minutes, vol. 1 (1885–94), British Architectural Library, London, p. 397.
74 Letters to JPC from Henry Wilson, 11 January 1894 and 16 January 1894.
75 JPC, Journal III, p. 13.
76 JPC, Journal I, p. 166.
77 JPC, Journal IV, p. 219.
78 JPC, Journal I, p. 176.
79 JPC, Journal I, pp. 87, 154.
80 JPC, Costing Book I, (1896–1906) and Stockbook I (1896–1914).
81 JPC, Journal I, p. 153 and Journal IV, p. 216.
82 JPC, Journal I, p. 152.
83 JPC, Journal I, p. 153 and Journal IV, p. 216.
84 JPC, Journal I, p. 87; letter to JPC from Henry Wilson, 1 June 1896; and JPC, Stockbook I, p. 1.
85 See Appendix C.
86 JPC, Journal I, p. 155.
87 JPC, Journal I, p. 87.
88 J. Paul Cooper, 'The Work of John Sedding, Architect,' *The Architectural Review* 3 (December–May 1897–8), 35–41, 69–77, 125–33, 188–94, 235–42; 4 (June–November 1898), 33–6.
89 JPC, Journal IV, p. 199.
90 See Appendix D.
91 JPC, Journal IV, p. 200. In his later years, the poet Massey studied ancient Egyptian civilization in which he thought to trace psychic and spiritual problems to their source and thereby find their true solution.
92 George Hart, *A Dictionary of Egyptian Gods and Goddesses* (London, 1986), pp. 108–10
93 See Appendix A.
94 JPC, Journal I, p. 91.
95 JPC, Journal I, p. 101. Also see Appendix C.
96 JPC, Costing Book I, p. 4 and Journal I, p. 101. In 1898, for the first time, Cooper gives a summary of his yearly accounts. That year he received £489 16s 9d, £300 of which was his allowance, and spent £411 13s 3d.
97 JPC, Journal I, p. 100.
98 Letter to JPC from Andrew Tuer, 28 December 1899. Tuer died in February 1900. Shortly afterwards, Cooper made a shagreen box for his wife, mounted with a skin which Tuer had dyed himself (JPC, Stockbook I, p. 23, no. 46).
99 JPC, Journal I, p. 125.
100 JPC, Journal I, p. 127. Interestingly, the catalogue to the 1899 International Society exhibition makes no mention of Cooper exhibiting shagreen, only gesso and mother-of-pearl work: The International Society of Sculptors,

Painters and Gravers, *Catalogue of the Exhibition* (London, 1899), cat. nos. S24, S32.

101 Arts and Crafts Exhibition Society, *Catalogue of the Sixth Exhibition* 1899, pp. 92–3.

102 Henry Wilson, 'The Arts and Crafts Society: With Especial Reference to Certain Exhibits,' *The Architectural Review* 6 (June–December 1899), 213–14.

103 JPC, Journal I, p. 27: 'Feb. 1 [1899]. To work at Wilson's.'

104 JPC, Costing Book I, (1896–1906).

105 JPC, Journal I, p. 27 and '"Corri" Legion Steward Was Famous Craftsman', *Sevenoaks Chronicle*, 13 February 1948, p. 4. According to Colarossi, he began working for Cooper in 1897. Also known as 'Laurie', he followed Cooper to Birmingham where he both taught at the Municipal School of Art and worked in Cooper's private studio. He continued to work for Cooper in Kent until June 1911 when he briefly worked for Emil Lettré in Berlin and then at the Artificers' Guild until the outbreak of the First World War. Following the war, Colarossi returned to work at Betsom's Hill. After Cooper's death, he continued working for Francis, Cooper's son, whom he had taught silversmithing.

106 Arts and Crafts Exhibition Society, *Catalogue*, (1899), p. 92.

107 Letter to JPC from Eleanor Rowe, 26 July 1900, and letter to H.J.L.J. Massé from Paul Cooper, 20 July 1900, National Archive of Art and Design, London, AAD1/508–E15/17. Cooper had been proposed for membership by woodcarver Eleanor Rowe and seconded by Walter Crane.

108 JPC, Journal I, p. 126 and Stockbook I, p. 3, no. 5 where the date for the buckle is given as 1899–1900.

109 JPC, Journal I, p. 27.

110 K. Cooper, 'Father, Family and Friends', p. 23.

111 F. Cooper, 'John Paul Cooper', p. 9.

112 JPC, Costing Book, p. 13 and Journal I, p. 129. Also Appendix B.

113 JPC, Journal I, p. 126.

114 Charlotte Gere, 'Edward Spencer and the Artificers' Guild' lecture given at The Decorative Arts Society Symposium, Art Workers' Guild, 21 November 1992, and current research being conducted on the Artificers' Guild by Muriel Wilson and Anne Shannon at the Goldsmiths' Company, London.

115 JPC, Artificers' Guild Book. This ledger records Cooper's transactions with the Guild between 1903 and 1915.

116 Vittoria Street School for Jewellers and Silversmiths Minutes, vol. 1 (1901–7), Birmingham School of Art Archives, pp. 28–9.

117 Birmingham Municipal School of Art Management Sub-Committee Minutes, vol. 6 (1900–1901), The Birmingham School of Art Archives, p. 223 and JPC, Journal IV, p. 221.

118 JPC, Journal IV, p. 220.

119 Birmingham Art School Management Minutes, vol. 6 (1900–1), p. 244. This post had been rendered vacant by the death of Louis Movio, a previous foreman in Henry Wilson's Vicarage Gate studio.

120 JPC, Journal IV, p. 220. The workman referred to was John Innocent.

121 JPC, Journal I, p. 129.

122 JPC, Journal IV, p. 222.

123 Birmingham Art School Management Minutes, vol. 6 (1900–1), pp. 274–5.

124 Birmingham Art School Management Minutes, vol. 8 (1903–4), p. 168.

125 Birmingham Art School Management Minutes, vol. 6 (1900–1), pp. 251–2.

126 JPC, Costing Book I, p. 45 and Costing Book III, no. 849. Also see Appendix B.

127 Shelagh Wilson, 'Art Into Industry, The Birmingham Experiment: The Attempt to Unify Art with Manufacturing in the Birmingham Trade 1860–1914' (unpublished MA thesis, Royal College of Art, 1991).

128 JPC, Journal IV, p. 221.

129 JPC, Journal IV, pp. 222–4. It is curious that in his journals Cooper emphasizes so strongly the fact that the metalwork department at the Municipal School previous to his employment had been so unprogressive in adopting Arts and Crafts ideals. Alan Crawford, who is very familiar with the development of the

Arts and Crafts Movement in Birmingham, has unequivocally stated that at this time 'Birmingham was ahead of other British arts schools in focusing teaching on actual making, with training in designs for particular materials being introduced in the late 1880s, and workshops for the execution of designs specially built and opened in 1893. When plans were afoot for the establishment of the Central School of Arts and Crafts in London, Lethaby and others went to Birmingham to see how this practical aspect of teaching was handled.'

130   Birmingham Art School Management Minutes, vol. 6 (1900–1), pp. 274–5.

131   Birmingham Art School Management Minutes, vol. 8 (1903–4), p. 55.

132   Birmingham Art School Management Minutes, vol. 9 (1904–6), pp. 279–80.

133   Birmingham Art School Management Minutes, vol. 7 (1901–3), pp. 169–70 and vol. 8 (1903–4), p. 97.

134   Birmingham Art School Management Minutes, vol. 9 (1904–6), p. 279.

135   JPC, Stockbook I, pp. 3, 33–6, 39–43.

136   See Appendix B.

137   JPC, Journal I, pp. 17–18. G. Middleton, along with Colarossi and Hazlewood, moved to Kent with Cooper in 1907. Middleton was employed by Cooper until 1909. Also see Appendix B.

138   In November 1911, Cooper was appointed a member of the London County Council's Consultive Committee on Goldsmiths', Silversmiths', Jewellers' and Allied Trades. The members of this committee, which met every two weeks, visited schools and classes teaching silversmithing and jewellery, and wrote reports of findings and recommendations. Cooper resigned from the committee in 1930. Between 1913 and 1923, Cooper also annually awarded the Messinger Prize for outstanding student metalwork at the Birmingham Municipal School of Art.

139   John Farleigh, *The Creative Craftsman* (London, 1950), pp. 152–3. Cooper's son Francis (d. 1980) followed in his father's footsteps and became a silversmith. He worked with Cooper and, following his father's death, took over the studio and unfinished commissions. Katharine 'Kanty' Cooper (d. 1993) also initially pursued an artistic career, studying sculpture with Henry Moore. Cooper's youngest child Ursula (1913–93) became an accomplished silk weaver.

140   Letter to JPC from Henry Wilson, 29 December 1906. Between 1901 and 1912, Wilson taught goldsmithing at the Royal College of Art under W.R. Lethaby. In 1903, Wilson published *Silverwork and Jewellery*, a practical craftsman's manual still in use today.

141   Farleigh, *The Creative Craftsman*, p. 150.

142   Letter to JPC from Henry Wilson, 16 February 1906.

143   Letter to JPC from Henry Wilson, 5 September 1906.

144   Letter to JPC from Henry Wilson, 9 October 1906.

145   JPC, Stockbook I, pp. 91–117.

146   JPC, Exhibition/Approval Book I, pp. 27, 31.

147   JPC, Exhibition/Approval Book I, pp. 41–2, 51 and *Deutsche Kunst und Dekoration* 24 (April–September 1909), 295.

148   JPC, Journal IV, p. 189.

149   JPC, Journal I, p. 198.

150   JPC, Journal I, pp. 37–8.

151   JPC, Account Book III (Household Accounts), January 1910–May 1916. This book includes a detailed summary of accounts concerning the erection of Betsom's Hill. Price of the site and various legal fees was £566 6s 9d. The price of converting the existing bungalow into a workshop and living quarters for the servants was £55 9s 9d. Cost of erecting the house was £1,600. Cost of soil removal from building site was £14 10s. Installation of heating cost £136 and of the electricity £110 5s 11d. Adding to the above amounts another £23 8d for various house extras brought the total cost to £2,502 13s 1d. Arthur Grove helped design the house.

152   JPC, Journal I, p. 43.

153   JPC, Time Book I, n. pag. Instone stayed in Cooper's workshop from October 1911 to November 1912. Colarossi left Cooper's employment and joined the Artificers' Guild on 24 August 1911; he remained with the Guild until 14 January 1913.

154   F. Cooper, 'John Paul Cooper', pp. 8–9.

155   Letter to JPC from Otto Pullich, 19 April 1910 and Graham Hughes, *Modern Silver* (London 1967), pp. 138, 237. An artist-craftsman, Lettré worked in Vienna, Budapest and Paris before moving to Berlin. In 1933, he became the Director of the Staatliche Akademie in Hanau.

156   JPC, Exhibition/Approval Book I, pp. 75, 87, 94.

157   JPC, Exhibition/Approval Book I, p. 108.

158   'British Arts and Crafts at Ghent. French Official Interest', *The Times*, 20 August 1913, n. pag.

159   Letter to JPC from Henry Wilson, 13 April 1913.

160   Letter to JPC from Henry Wilson, 19 January 1914. Between 1912 and 1914 Wilson lived mainly in Venice, executing the sculptural commissions that now came to dominate his artistic output.

161   Arts and Crafts Exhibition Society, *Catalogue of the Eleventh Exhibition* (London, 1916), pp. 89–92 and letter to JPC from Henry Wilson, 27 April 1916.

162   John Paul Cooper, 'A Proposal for the Reorganization of the Arts and Crafts Exhibition Society', 27 January 1913, National Archives of Art and Design, London, AAD1/21–1980.

163   J.P. Cooper, 'A Proposal for Reorganization', pp. 2–3.

164   'British Arts and Crafts,' *Morning Post*, 23 April 1914, n. pag.

165   JPC, Journal I, p. 209. Jean Jacques Reubell (d. 1933) was a distinguished Parisian amateur who, in 1926, gave his collection of court swords and daggers to the Metropolitan Museum of Art in New York.

166   M.P. Verneuil, 'L'Exposition des Arts et Métiers (Arts and Crafts) de la Grande-Bretagne au Pavillon de Marsan', *Art et décoration* 35 (May 1914), 129, 145.

167   Letter to Sir Isidore Spielmann from Paul Alfassa, 29 November 1920, Cooper Family Archives. Translation: 'The cup you sent me will be cherished by the memories it will remind me of; also by its beauty. I have liked the works of M. Paul Cooper for a long time, 2 or 3 of which I already possess . . . tell him [Cooper] how much I love having this piece of metalwork of such a noble design and of such perfect execution.'

168   JPC, Journal II, pp. 56–8.

169   *The Times*, 15 November 1932, n. pag.

170   JPC, Stockbook II, pp. 26–64.

171   Letter to JPC from the British Department of Overseas Trade, 2 February 1926.

172   Alphonse Brégor, 'L'Art décoratif à la Walter [*sic*] Art Gallery de Liverpool', *Revue du vrai et du beau* 4 (December 1925), 26. Translation: 'The metal objects . . . by Paul Cooper . . . [are] of an extremely high style and of the finest execution. All objects personally handmade are of a rare elegance. That is why they hold a leading position in the realm of applied art.'

173   Letter to JPC from George Hughes, 2 June 1926.

174   Letter to JPC from the Goldsmiths' Company, 1 February 1927: 'Mr. A.M. Samuel, who of course knows your work well, is very anxious to show your cup to the King personally at the opening of the exhibition.'

175   Letter to JPC from the Goldsmiths' Company, 18 January 1929.

176   JPC, Exhibition/Approval Book III, pp. 32–51, 100–25. The most successful of the Hutton exhibitions was the one held in 1927 where Cooper sold over £700 worth of work. During the 1929 exhibition, he sold over £500 worth of work.

177   JPC, Stockbook III, nos. 784, 911, 930, 973–5.

178   Walker's Galleries, *An Exhibition of Water-Colour Drawings, Shagreen and Silverwork by J. Paul Cooper* (London, 1931).

179   'Art Exhibitions,' *Morning Post*, 19 March 1931, n. pag.

180   Craig, 'Writing in Water-Colour', p. 1. There is a sense of tongue-in-cheek in Craig's wording.

181   Letter to JPC from Walker's Galleries, 24 March 1931.

182   Arts and Crafts Exhibition Society, General Committee Minutes, 20 November 1917, National Archive of Art and Design, London, AAD1/53–1980, n. pag. and Arts and Crafts Exhibition Society, General Committee Minutes, 9 May 1929, AAD1/62–1980, p. 9.

183 Arts and Crafts Exhibition Society, General Committee Minutes, 26 January 1932, AAD1/62–1980, 100. Aside from Cooper, his wife, May, and sister, Violet Cooper, who exhibited embroidery, also resigned on the grounds that they no longer supported the policies of the Society.

184 JPC, Stockbook II, p. 49, no. 1241: 'Pair of Silver Candlesticks for F.A. Koenig of Tyringham Hall for Music Chapel', 27 July 1929 and Arts Council of Great Britain, *Lutyens. The Work of the English Architect Sir Edwin Lutyens (1869–1944)* (London, 1981), p. 143. The Tyringham estate was largely designed by John Soane between 1794 and 1800. However, between 1924 and 1928, Lutyens designed a pool and two pavilions for its owner F.A. Koenig (1867–1940), a wealthy Silesian banker. Cooper's candlesticks stood on a side altar inside the Temple of Music, one of the Pavilions. Lutyens considered this interior faultless and enjoyed sitting there alone.

185 JPC, Journal IV, pp. 84–5. Having established his own studio in 1913, Murphy rose to prominence during the 1920s and 1930s as one of the leading British exponents of the Art Deco style in silver.

186 Arts and Crafts Exhibition Society, General Committee Minutes, 30 October 1931, AAD1/62–1980, p. 90; letter to JPC from May Morris, 7 February 1932; letter to JPC from Emery Walker, 21 December 1931; and letter to Violet Cooper from May Morris, 29 January 1932, Cooper Family Archives.

187 Cooper's entry in personal diary for 3 May 1933.

188 'Death of Mr. J. Paul Cooper', *Westerham Herald*, 6 May 1933, p. 5.

189 JPC, Exhibition/Approval Book III, p. 276.

190 Robert Dunthorne & Son, Ltd, *Memorial Exhibition of Silverwork, Shagreen and Water-Colour Drawings by the Late J. Paul Cooper* (London, 1933).

CHAPTER TWO: STYLISTIC DEVELOPMENT

1 F. Ernest Jackson, foreword to Robert Dunthorne & Son Ltd, *Memorial Exhibition of Silverwork, Shagreen and Water-Colour Drawings by the Late J. Paul Cooper* (London, 1933), n. pag. Ernest Jackson (1872–1945), a well-known lithographer, taught life drawing to Francis Cooper.

2 JPC, Stockbook I, pp. 5–6.

3 F. Cooper, 'John Paul Cooper and the Arts and Crafts Movement', p. 4.

4 JPC, Costing Book I, pp. 6, 11, 53.

5 Walter Crane, 'Notes on Gesso Work', *The Studio*, 1 (May 1893), 45. Plaster work, according to Crane, was a 'close cousin' of gesso.

6 Aymer Vallance, 'The Revival of Tempera Painting', *The Studio* 23 (August 1901), 156–7.

7 Arts and Crafts Exhibition Society, *Catalogue of the Second Exhibition* (London, 1899), pp. 39–40.

8 Crane, 'Notes on Gesso', pp. 45–9.

9 Letter to JPC from Eleanor Rowe, 20 February 1900.

10 Matthew Webb, 'On Gesso', *The Studio* 13 (August 1894), 153–9.

11 'The Arts and Crafts Exhibition Society at the New Gallery, 1893', *The Studio* 2 (October 1893), 20.

12 Letter to JPC from Augustus Mason, 13 October 1916. Mason was a skilled cabinet maker who resided at 112 Chiswick Lane, Chiswick. In 1916, he gave up woodworking, which included various inlay work and covering objects in shagreen, to begin selling second-hand furniture at 226–228 King Street, Hammersmith. From this date on, confirmed by existing receipts, the majority of Cooper's important wooden articles were made by Laurence A. Turner of 42 Lamb's Conduit Street, London WC1. During the 1920s Turner supplied Cooper with a steady stream of wooden boxes for his shagreen work. According to Francis Cooper, a local Westerham craftsman named E. Newton also occasionally supplied wooden boxes.

13 JPC, Sketchbook 10 (1892), n. pag.

14 Letter to JPC from Henry Wilson, 4 October 1893.

15 Letter to JPC from Sydney Cockerell, 10 October 1893.
16 Arts and Crafts Exhibition Society, *Catalogue of the Fifth Exhibition* (London, 1896), cat. no. 42.
17 JPC, Costing Book I, p. 2: 'Sep. Workbox in Denoline', and Stockbook I, p. 5, no. 6: 'Workbox, Peacock top', 1896.
18 Crane, 'Notes on Gesso', p. 46.
19 JPC, Journal I, p. 155.
20 JPC, Journal I, p. 155.
21 JPC, Journal I, p. 187.
22 JPC, Journal I, pp. 92–94 and E.R. and J. Pennell, *The Life of James McNeill Whistler*, vol. 2 (London, 1908), p. 206.
23 JPC, Journal I, pp. 154, 156.
24 JPC, Sketchbook 10, n. pag.
25 Crane, 'Notes on Gesso Work', p. 46.
26 Crane, 'Notes on Gesso Work', p. 48.
27 Crane, 'Notes on Gesso Work', p. 48.
28 Letter to JPC from Eleanor Rowe, 3 February [1890s].
29 Webb, 'On Gesso', p. 155.
30 Webb, 'On Gesso', p. 158.
31 Webb, 'On Gesso', p. 158.
32 JPC, Costing Book I, p. 4 and Journal I, p. 86.
33 JPC, 'Shagreen, Mother-of-Pearl and Tortoiseshell', paper read to the Art Workers' Guild, 19 February 1915, p. 10.
34 Letter to JPC from Alice Radcliffe, 8 September 1899.
35 JPC, Journal I, p. 27.
36 *Builder's Journal and Architectural Record*, 14 (October 1901), 204.
37 JPC, Stockbook I, p. 5, no. l: 'Workbox in Denoline. Seasons', 1898–9. It is not known whether this was one of the two gesso boxes Cooper exhibited at the 1899 Arts and Crafts Society exhibition. Stylistically at least, it must have been similar to the ones exhibited.
38 JPC, Stockbook I, p. 5, no. 2: 'Jewel box. Denoline' and Stockbook I, p. 118. This gesso box was sold in 1900 at a Leeds Arts and Crafts exhibition.
39 JPC, Stockbook I, p. 36, no. 44.
40 These chased silver panels are now all at The Wolfsonian-Florida International University, Miami Beach, Florida (acc. nos. TD1990.227.1–14).
41 Natasha Kuzmanović, 'John Paul Cooper (1869–1933): Arts and Crafts Artist', *Wolfsonian Bulletin* 2 (Spring–Summer 1994), 2–3.
42 Pliny, *The History of the World*, trans. Philemon Holland, 2 vols (London, 1634).
43 Pliny, *The History of the World*, vol. 2, p. 614H.
44 Pliny, *The History of the World*, vol. 2, p. 609F.
45 Pliny, *The History of the World*, vol. 2, p. 619D.
46 Pliny, *The History of the World*, vol. 2, p. 605E.
47 John Paul Cooper, 'The Present Position of Symbolism and Allegory', *The Architect's Journal* 57 (May 1923), 915–17.
48 J.P. Cooper, 'The Present Position of Symbolism and Allegory', p. 915.
49 J.P. Cooper, 'The Present Position of Symbolism and Allegory', p. 917.
50 JPC, Stockbook I, p. 5, no. 4: 'Gesso box for Miss Cochran like no. 8', 1899–1900.
51 E. Cobham Brewer, *Dictionary of Phrase and Fable* (London, 1894), p. 368.
52 JPC, Stockbook I, p. 5, no.10: 'Octagonal flowers round', September 1901.
53 JPC, Costing Book I, p. 53.
54 Crane, 'Notes on Gesso Work', p. 48.
55 J.P. Cooper, 'The Present Position of Symbolism and Allegory', p. 915.
56 Aymer Vallance, 'British Decorative Art in 1899 and the Arts and Crafts Exhibition. Part III', *The Studio* 18 (December 1899), 192.
57 The Fine Art Society Ltd, *The Earthly Paradise* (London, 1969) and JPC, Journal II, p. 167.
58 JPC, Stockbook I, p. 6, no. 18: 'Porta Vitae Octag. Box', 1903.
59 JPC, Costing Book I, p. 53.
60 JPC, Stockbook I, p. 6, no. 19: 'Venus Mirror (Love in Mist & Venus looking glass)', January 1904.

61   Webb, 'On Gesso', p. 158.
62   JPC, Exhibition/Approval Book II, p. 70.
63   JPC, Journal II, p. 261.
64   The Fine Art Society Ltd, *Jewellery and Jewellery Design 1850–1930* and *John Paul Cooper 1869–1933* (London, 1975), cat. nos. 199, 200.
65   JPC, Journal I, p. 192.
66   JPC, Sketchbook 3A, n. pag.
67   JPC, Journal I, pp. 24–26.
68   The following section deals only with pieces grouped under the heading of 'Mother-of-Pearl' in Cooper's stockbooks. Here, Cooper included only wooden objects decorated with mother-of-pearl, excluding all metalwork with such decoration. Metalwork decorated with mother-of-pearl is discussed in the metalwork and jewellery section of this chapter.
69   JPC, Stockbook I, p. 6, no. 16 and p. 13, nos. 1, 2.
70   JPC, Costing Book I, pp. 16, 46–7, 57–8.
71   JPC, Stockbook I, pp. 13, 15.
72   Arts and Crafts Exhibition Society, *Catalogue of the Seventh Exhibition* (London, 1903), pp. 56, 80, 98. With these mother-of-pearl pieces, Cooper simultaneously exhibited metalwork decorated with mother-of-pearl.
73   JPC, Stockbook I, p. 13, no. 3: 'M of P Jewel Box (minus key)', 1899–1900.
74   JPC, 'Shagreen, Mother-of-Pearl and Tortoiseshell', paper read to the Art-Workers' Guild, 19 February 1915, p. 9.
75   JPC, 'Shagreen, Mother-of-Pearl and Tortoiseshell', p. 11.
76   JPC, 'Shagreen, Mother-of-Pearl and Tortoiseshell', p. 11.
77   JPC, Stockbook I, p. 13, no. 4: 'M of Pearl & beetle wing stampbox', May 1903. A design related to this box is dated 26 December 1900.
78   JPC, Costing Book I, p. 14.
79   Arts and Crafts Exhibition Society, *Catalogue* (1903), cat. no. 294 and JPC, Stockbook I, p. 15, no. 12: 'M of P & gold frame', 22 December 1902. The asking price for this frame at the exhibition was over £47.
80   Philippe Garner, 'Unpublished Notes on Gesso by Frederick Marriott', *Bulletin of the Decorative Arts Society 1890–1940* 1 (1975), 28–34.
81   Garner, 'Unpublished Notes on Gesso by Frederick Marriott', p. 33.
82   JPC, 'Shagreen, Mother-of-Pearl and Tortoiseshell', p. 12.
83   JPC, 'Shagreen, Mother-of-Pearl and Tortoiseshell', p. 3.
84   Letter to JPC from Montague Fordham, 4 November 1901.
85   JPC, Stockbook I, p. 13, nos 6–8. These pieces were completed on 22 December 1901.
86   W.R. Lethaby, *Architecture, Mysticism and Myth* (London, 1892), pp. 9–31.
87   JPC, Stockbook I, 15, no. 11: 'Stampbox white & green', September 1901.
88   JPC, 'Shagreen, Mother-of-Pearl and Tortoiseshell', p. 12.
89   This box apparently was never executed.
90   JPC, Sketchbook 29, n. pag. Cooper made sketches of various pavements throughout his life as seen in his Sketchbook 28, dated September 1899, and Sketchbook 80, dated October 1923.
91   Lethaby, *Architecture, Mysticism and Myth*, p. 215.
92   JPC, Stockbook I, 15, no. 14: 'M of P stampbox with feet', March 1904.
93   Lethaby, *Architecture, Mysticism and Myth*, pp. 15, 201–13.
94   Lethaby, *Architecture, Mysticism and Myth*, p. 217.
95   'Mr. Paul Cooper', *The Times*, 19 March 1931, n. pag.
96   John Paul Cooper, 'Various Objects in Shagreen', *Catalogue of a Loan Collection of Antique Furniture, Medieval Tapestries and Allied Domestic Arts* (New Gallery, Edinburgh, 1917), p. 28 and JPC, Technique Notebook 6, n. pag.
97   J.P. Cooper, 'Various Objects in Shagreen', p. 28.
98   J.P. Cooper, 'Various Objects in Shagreen', pp. 27–8.
99   J.P. Cooper, 'Shagreen, Mother-of-Pearl and Tortoiseshell', pp. 2–3, 48.
100 JPC, 'Shagreen, Mother-of-Pearl and Tortoiseshell', p. 6.
101 JPC, 'Shagreen, Mother-of-Pearl and Tortoiseshell', pp. 6–8.
102 J.P. Cooper, 'Various Objects in Shagreen', p. 28.
103 JPC, Stockbook I, pp. 7–8.
104 JPC, Technique Notebook 6, n. pag.

105 JPC, Technique Notebook 6, n. pag.

106 JPC, Technique Notebook 6, n. pag.

107 Arts and Crafts Exhibition Society, *Catalogue of the Sixth Exhibition* (London, 1899), p. 15.

108 JPC, Stockbook III, p. 25. Even though the number of the last shagreen entry is 1048, Cooper actually executed one hundred fewer boxes. In chronologically numbering his shagreen objects, Cooper accidentally skipped one hundred numbers during 1910, box 236 being followed by box 337. Cooper's shagreen output was only about 454 pieces fewer than his metalwork and jewellery.

109 JPC, Costing Book I, pp. 19, 27 and Stockbook I, p. 23, nos. 41–42.

110 JPC, Costing Book I, p. 12.

111 JPC, Stockbook I, p. 8, no. 1: 'Green with beetle on top sent to A & C Ex.,' 1899.

112 JPC, Stockbook I, pp. 7–8.

113 JPC, Stockbook I, pp. 119–20.

114 'Studio-Talk', *The Studio* (20 June 1900), 48–9.

115 JPC, Stockbook I, p. 9, nos. 1–4.

116 JPC, Design Portfolio 7, file 2 and Stockbook I, p. 10, nos. 1–3, p. 11, no. 23.

117 JPC, Stockbook I, p. 10, no. 44. One of Cooper's earliest octagonal shagreen boxes, completed in August 1901, was bought by Henry Wilson.

118 JPC, Stockbook I, pp. 14, 17, 18, 25.

119 JPC, Stockbook I, p. 31, no. 112: 'Large green oblong very good skin', 25 April 1906; and p. 32, no. 124: 'Octagonal Shagreen Box', December 1906.

120 JPC, Journal I, p. 114.

121 Letter to JPC from Arthur Samuel, 10 March 1903.

122 Letters to JPC from Arthur Samuel, 10 March 1903 and 4 April 1903.

123 JPC, Stockbook I, p. 27, no. 77: 'Shagreen and silver writing box for Arthur Samuel', November 1903. Samuel paid over £31 for this box.

124 Brewer, *Dictionary of Phrase and Fable*, p. 449.

125 JPC, Costing Book I, p. 88 and Stockbook I, p. 28, no. 85. Completed in March 1904, this box appeared as Lot 2973 in Christie's Elveden Hall sale, Norfolk, on 24 May 1984 and as Lot 40 in Sotheby's Robert H. Metzger sale, New York, on 27 October 1995. Lorenzo Colarossi spent 291 hours working on this box. Cooper executed the chasing himself. It cost £23 13*s* 6*d* to make.

126 Letter to JPC from Arthur Samuel, 15 March 1904.

127 JPC, Stockbook I, p. 30, no. 93 and p. 109, no. 384.

128 JPC, Stockbook I, p. 92, no. 149. This box was completed in November 1907.

129 JPC, Costing Book I, p. 68.

130 *Exhibition of British Arts and Crafts 1920–1921 Assembled by the Society of Arts and Crafts* (Detroit, 1920), p. 10.

131 K. Cooper, 'Father, Family and Friends', p. 42.

132 Arts and Crafts Exhibition Society, *Catalogue of the Eighth Exhibition* (London, 1906), cat. nos 308j, 363c, 395e, i–j, l, n–p.

133 R.E.D. Sketchley, 'Metal-Work and Jewellery,' *The Art Journal* (June 1906), 175–6.

134 JPC, Stockbook I, 111, nos 397–400, 403–6 and Stockbook III, p. 6, nos. 600–1.

135 'Fine Craftsmanship', *Morning Post*, 2 October 1924, n. pag.

136 JPC, Stockbook I, pp. 113–17.

137 JPC, Stockbook III, p. 10, no. 691. This box was completed in 1926.

138 JPC, Stockbook I, p. 109, no. 383. This box was completed in 1912.

139 JPC, Stockbook I, pp. 92–113.

140 JPC, Artificers' Guild Book, p. 153 and Stockbook I, p. 111, no. 407.

141 JPC, Stockbook I, p. 113, no. 431. This box was completed on 11 November, 1913.

142 JPC, Exhibition/Approval Book I, pp. 120–1, 156–9. Cooper's shagreen pieces sold particularly well at the Ghent international exhibition of 1913 and at the British arts and crafts exhibition held in Paris in 1914.

143 JPC, Exhibition/Approval Book I, pp. 1–6, and Stockbook I, p. 110, no. 387. Completed in September 1, 1912, the writing cabinet measured H 25.5 × L 31.1 in and was priced at £16 16*s*.

144 JPC, Stockbook I, p. 110, no. 390 and letter to JPC from the Marquess of Lansdowne, 4 February 1913. The piece was completed on 2 May 1913.
145 JPC, Stockbook I, p. 113, no. 432.
146 JPC, Stockbook I, pp. 98–101, 107.
147 JPC, Exhibition/Approval Book I, pp. 77–82 and Christopher Hussey, *The Work of Sir Robert Lorimer* (London, 1931).
148 Letters to JPC from Robert Lorimer, 11 March 1915 and 22 March 1915.
149 JPC, Stockbook II, p. 22, no. 387.
150 Letter to JPC from Arthur Samuel, 6 January 1917.
151 JPC, Costing Book III, n. pag.
152 JPC, 'Description of Design for Proposed Presentation Casket' (unpublished manuscript, 1917), n. pag.
153 JPC, Stockbook III, pp. 5–25.
154 Letter to JPC from Dorothy Hutton, 18 November 1929.
155 JPC, Stockbook III, p. 7, no. 630. This box was completed in 1923.
156 JPC, Stockbook III, p. 14, no. 786. This box was completed September 1927.
157 JPC, Stockbook III, p. 10, no. 691. This box was completed in 1926.
158 JPC, Stockbook III, p. 23 no. 1000. This box was completed February 1932.
159 JPC, Stockbook III, p. 23, no. 1017. This box was completed in 1932.
160 JPC, Stockbook III, p. 8, no. 655, 9, no. 668, p. 15, no. 810, p. 16, no. 852, and p. 19, no. 908. All the pieces were completed between January 1925 and October 1929.
161 JPC, 'Shagreen, Mother-of-Pearl and Tortoiseshell', p. 12.
162 JPC, Sketchbook 72, n. pag.
163 JPC, 'Description of Design for Proposed Presentation Casket', n. pag.
164 The term metalwork in the following discussion refers to pieces made of metal (primarily of silver, copper, or brass) not intended for personal adornment. The term jewellery is used only for items of personal adornment. The term metalware refers to both jewellery and metalwork.
165 JPC, Stockbook I, p. 3.
166 Arts and Crafts Exhibition Society, *Catalogue of the Sixth Exhibition* (London, 1899), p. 93, case P no. 1. For display purposes, a mirror glass was inserted into the frame.
167 JPC, Stockbook I, p. 3, no. 4: 'Silver photo frame', 1899 and no. 1: 'Copper silvered Photo frame violet leaves', September 1901.
168 JPC, Costing Book I, pp. 60–1.
169 JPC, Stockbook I, pp. 52–3 and 57.
170 JPC, Journal I, p. 126 and Stockbook I, p. 3, no. 5: 'M of P buckle silver mounted', 1899–1900.
171 Aymer Vallance, 'Modern British Jewellery and Fans', *Modern Design in Jewellery and Fans* (London, 1902), plate 14.
172 F. Cooper, 'John Paul Cooper and the Arts and Crafts Movement', p. 5.
173 Vittoria Street School for Jewellers and Silversmiths Minutes, vol. 1, 1901–7, Birmingham School of Art Archives, p. 139.
174 JPC, Costing Book I, pp. 2–3.
175 'The Arts and Crafts Exhibition, 1896', *The Studio* 9 (November 1896), 127–9.
176 'Some Recent Examples of the Jeweller's Art in France', *The Studio* 23 (June 1901), 25.
177 Charles Holme (ed.), *Modern Design in Jewellery and Fans* (London, 1902).
178 Arts and Crafts Exhibition Society, *Catalogue of the Seventh Exhibition* (London, 1903), cat. nos. 167a–ii, pp. 253–6.
179 *Der Moderne Stil*, 5, no. 10 (1903), plate 75. JPC, Stockbook I, p. 35, no. 37: 'Silver Copper & M of P Bowl', 1902; no. 43: 'M of P & Silver Candlesticks', 1902. These pieces are rather ambitious and therefore atypical of the simpler, more mundane domestic plate Cooper produced between 1902 and 1906.
180 JPC, 'English Silver and Goldsmiths' Work', paper read to the Art-Workers' Guild, 1 October 1909; 'Lecture on the Chamberlain Casket Executed by Henry Wilson', (unpublished manuscript, 1902); and 'Metal Work', paper read to The Red Rose Guild, March 1929.
181 JPC, 'Lecture on Metal Work', (unpublished manuscript, n.d.), p. 3.

182   JPC, 'Lecture on Metal Work', p. 7.

183   JPC, 'Lecture on Metal Work', p. 2.

184   JPC, 'Metal Work and Jewellery', (unpublished manuscript, n.d.), p. 3.

185   JPC, 'English Silver and Goldsmiths' Work', pp. 5–6.

186   JPC, 'Metal Work', pp. 15–16, 22.

187   JPC, 'Metal Work', pp. 22–23.

188   JPC, 'Lecture on the Chamberlain Casket Executed by Henry Wilson', p. 10.

189   JPC, 'Lecture on Metal Work', p. 8.

190   JPC, 'Lecture on Metal Work', pp. 26–7.

191   JPC, 'Metal Work', p. 22.

192   JPC, 'Ceremonial Goldsmiths' Work', paper read to the Art-Workers' Guild, 4 October 1912, p. 5.

193   JPC, 'Jewellery', paper read to the Women's Guild of the Art, 12 April 1918, pp. 6–7.

194   JPC, 'Lecture on Metal Work', p. 23.

195   J. Paul Cooper, 'Jewellery and Superstition', *Oxted and Limpsfield Signpost*, 1 (March 1928), 85–7.

196   JPC, 'Ceremonial Goldsmiths' Work', p. 5.

197   F. Cooper, 'John Paul Cooper and the Arts and Crafts Movement', p. 6.

198   'Casket by Mr. H. Wilson Presented to The Right Hon. Joseph Chamberlain MP', *Magazine of Art* (1903), 595–7. In reviewing Wilson's casket, the article stated: '. . . we think that Mr. Wilson has adopted something of an affectation in the little irregularities which have been introduced, as well as in the rather summary modelling and rough casting of some of his figures and groups. These contrast somewhat sharply with the highly finished enamels. No doubt all this was deliberately intended, yet we cannot but regard it as a mistake.'

199   F. Cooper, 'John Paul Cooper and the Arts and Crafts Movement', p. 6.

200   JPC, 'Metal Work and Jewellery', p. 4.

201   JPC, 'Lecture on the Chamberlain Casket Executed by Henry Wilson', p. 10.

202   JPC, 'Lecture on the Chamberlain Casket Executed by Henry Wilson', p. 10.

203   JPC, 'Design,' paper read to students at the Birmingham Municipal School of Art, n.d., pp. 3–4.

204   'The Arts and Crafts Exhibition at the Grafton Gallery. Second Notice', *The Studio* 37 (March 1906), 129–30. The exhibition was marked by 'an outburst of enthusiasm and activity on the side of crafts which are ornamental and pleasant, crafts which are certainly useful in an abstract way, as making for beauty, but administrating on the whole to the arts of luxury rather than of use'.

205   'The Arts and Crafts Exhibition at the Grafton Gallery. Second Notice', pp. 132–3, 136.

206   'The Arts and Crafts Exhibition at the Grafton Gallery. Second Notice', pp. 134–6; JPC, Stockbook I, p. 43, no. 108: 'Copper & Silver Pendant', December 1903; p. 45, no. 129: 'Silver pendant with fig. holding lantern & stones,' May 1904; and p. 54, no. 227: 'Silver & Gold Hair ornament set with 5 chrysoprases 2 rubies & 3 opals', 19 November 1905.

207   JPC, Stockbook I, p. 41, no. 83: 'St George & Dragon silver buckle', September 1903 and JPC, 'Lecture on the Chamberlain Casket Executed by Henry Wilson', p. 4.

208   JPC, Stockbook I, p. 6, no. 14, completed December 1902.

209   JPC, Stockbook I, p. 39, no. 65, 'Silver belt squirrel centre', 1903.

210   JPC, Sketchbook 119, n. pag.

211   JPC, Stockbook I, p. 54, no. 229: 'S. Hubert Pendant set with sap. & ameth', 1905.

212   James Hall, *Illustrated Dictionary of Symbols in Eastern and Western Art* (London, 1994), 9.

213   Gerald Massey, *The Logia of the Lord* (London, 1887), pp. 16–17.

214   JPC, Stockbook I, p. 35, no. 35: 'Silver buckle M of P & labradorite', 1902.

215   JPC, Stockbook I, p. 50, no. 184: 'Ring for Miss E.T. 18c gold (her Emerald in top)', 16 February 1905.

216 Information supplied by Margaret Weare, Custodian of the Ellen Terry Memorial Museum.

217 JPC, Stockbook I, p. 50, no. 180, January 1905.

218 Charlotte Gere and Geoffrey Munn, *Artists' Jewellery* (Woodbridge, 1989), pp. 156–7.

219 JPC, Sketchbook 37, 1904, n. pag.

220 Helen Evans and Williaim Dixon (ed.), *The Glory of Byzantium* (New York, 1997), pp. 250–1.

221 JPC, Stockbook I, p. 54, no. 224: 'Silver buckle set with 6 chrysoprases', November 1905.

222 JPC, Sketchbook 34, 1902, n. pag.

223 'The Arts and Crafts Exhibition at the Grafton Gallery. Third and Concluding Notice', *The Studio* 37 (April 1906), 217–18 and JPC, Stockbook I, p. 55, no. 242: 'Silver Teapot', 28 April 1906. In Journal III, on p 176, Cooper mentioned working on this teapot in a letter to his mother: 'I have made a start on your teapot which I want to exhibit if it turns out well.'

224 JPC, Stockbook I, p. 36, no. 49: 'Bonbonnière Coral & Ivory,' begun January 1903 and completed 10 November 1906 and p. 35, no. 39: 'Silver and Ivory Blackberry fruit stand', 19 November 1902 and reworked in 1907.

225 'Suggestions for the Improvement of Sporting Cups and Trophies. Part II', *The Studio* 20 (June 1900), 40–2.

226 JPC, Costing Book II, p. 22.

227 The source of this quotation is unknown. A scrap of paper with this published statement exists among Cooper's personal effects.

228 JPC, Costing Book I, p. 102 and Stockbook I, p. 53, no. 218: 'Brass Cross for Birmingham Cath. Ch.', May 1905. This cross was primarily the work of George Romer who spent 50 hours, Lorenzo Colarossi who spent 295 hours, and William Hazlewood who spent 150 hours executing the piece. S. Cowell, employed in Henry Wilson's studio at the turn-of-the-century, made the base. Cooper himself spent seven weeks chasing the decoration.

229 JPC, 'On the Cross Symbol. Lecture No. I', paper read to students of the Birmingham Municipal School of Art, February 1902, pp. 3–4.

230 JPC, 'On the Cross Symbol. Lecture No. I', p. 8.

231 JPC, Stockbook I, p. 66, no. 350: 'Cooper and Silver Cross', 21 April 1907 and p. 56, no. 256: 'Copper Candlesticks', 17 March 1906.

232 JPC, Stockbook I, pp. 39–48.

233 Jiro Harada, 'Japanese Art and Artists of Today. V. Metal-Work', *The Studio*, 52 (March 1911), 100–101. This article gives a brief outline of Bisei's career.

234 JPC, Stockbook I, pp. 58–66, May 1906– April 1907.

235 JPC, Stockbook I, p. 74, no. 418: 'Silver and Gold brooch set with 5 Moonstones 2 Pearls 7 Tourmalines Ch. on rock in silver', 1908.

236 JPC, Stockbook I, p. 62, no. 317: 'Silver & gold pendant with 113 Burmese rubies 1 Queensland opals 1 opals 6 chrys. 5 sap. 10 aquamarines', 20 December 1906.

237 JPC, Sketchbook 115, p. 56.

238 Marchesa Burlamacchi, *Luca della Robbia* (London, 1900), pp. 42–3. This book is still among Cooper's personal effects.

239 JPC, Stockbook I, p. 81, no. 470: 'Big double gold brooch 15c', 3 December 1908 and 71, no. 400: 'Double 18c Gold brooch 1 moonstone 10 rubies 1 opal 4 emeralds 2 Tourmaline', 23 January 1908.

240 JPC, Costing Book II, pp. 28, 39.

241 JPC, Stockbook I, 53, no. 221: '18c Gold necklace for Vi set with 384 of her pearls', October 1905, and 85, no. 498: '15c gold necklace 17 chrys. 1 sap. 1 rose ruby 5 Ceylon', March 1909.

242 JPC, Stockbook I, p. 69, no. 375: '21 Garnet, 7 Chrys & 7 Pearl 15c Gold Necklace', September 1907.

243 JPC, Stockbook I, p. 55, no. 241: 'Silver Hot Water Jug with Dove & sleeping figure', 8 January 1906 and p. 61, no. 304: 'Hot Water Jug Silver no. 241 altered', October 1906.

244 JPC, Stockbook I, p. 66, no. 354: 'Silver chalice. Sold Leic. Munic. Art Gal.', 1907 and p. 78, no. 450: 'Silver chalice 9⅛ in high set with', 9 September 1908.

245 JPC, Stockbook I, p. 74, no. 417: 'M of P and copper Fruit Stand', 1908 with later gilding.

246 JPC, Stockbook I, p. 66, no. 373, September 1907. Two pairs of these fruit dishes were made, one pair with gilt bowls. The other illustrated pair is now divided between The Detroit Institute of Arts and the Birmingham City Museum and Art Gallery. The stockbook page and costing book entry in Figures 1 and 2 refer to these fruit dishes.

247 JPC, Stockbook I, p. 75, no. 424: 'Silver ink pot with elephant feet', 28 May 1908.

248 JPC, Symbology Notebook, p. 14.

249 JPC, Stockbook II, pp. 2–14.

250 JPC, Stockbook II, p. 3, no. 571: 'Copper Jar stained in No. 4 Jap. Pat.', March 1910.

251 JPC, Sketchbook 52, n. pag.

252 JPC, 'Lecture on Metal Work', p. 28.

253 JPC, Stockbook II, p. 20, no. 809: '18c Gold Pomegranate Necklace', February 1915; no. 819: 'Enamel & silv. box.' 1915; and no. 820: 'Fish Box Enamel & Silver', 1915.

254 'On the Cross Symbol. Lecture No. I', p. 1.

255 JPC, Stockbook II, p. 14, no. 736: '18c (33) Spinel & (3) Coral Pendant "Xmas"', October 1913.

256 JPC, Stockbook II, p. 12, no. 696: 'Silver necklace like no. 690 with azurite lapis ameth. & carb. stained agate', 1912.

257 JPC, Sketchbook 52, n. pag.

258 JPC, Stockbook II, pp. 5–7, 1911.

259 JPC, Stockbook II, p. 5, no. 606: 'Gold brooch 18c? with 2 em. 6 sap.', 11 March 1911 and p. 7, no. 627: '18c Fibula brooch 1³⁄₁₆ diam 5 Em 8 pearls', July 1911.

260 JPC, Stockbook II, p. 9, no. 653: '18c Gold Chain 6 Emer 4 Sap (2 Star Sap) 2 Tourm 3 Pearls', 16 February 1912.

261 JPC, Stockbook II, p. 13, no. 705: Pr. Silver Candlesticks Perseus & Andromeda', January 1913.

262 JPC, Stockbook II, p. 12, no. 823: 'Silver Fruit Bowl', June 1915.

263 JPC, Sketchbook 62, n. pag.

264 JPC, Journal II, pp. 186–7 and Stockbook II, p. 15, no. 740: 'Silv. Bisc. box octag.', October 1913.

265 JPC, Journal II, p. 187.

266 JPC, Stockbook II, p. 9, no. 658: 'Silv. Casket to be Prestd. by Boro' of Leicester to Sir W.W. Vincent', April 1912.

267 JPC, Stockbook II, pp. 6–21, April 1911 – July 1913.

268 Letter to JPC from Robert Lorimer, n.d.

269 JPC, Stockbook II, p. 16, no. 760: 'Cocoanut [sic] bowl'. March 1914 and p. 21, no. 824: 'Cocoanut [sic] bowl', July, 1915.

270 JPC, Stockbook II, p. 20, no. 814: 'Brass Cross for Holloway Col.', 1915.

271 JPC, Stockbook II, p. 23, no. 849: 'Silv. Cross for Four Elms', 27 March 1918.

272 JPC, Costing Book III, n. pag. and letter to JPC from William Hazlewood, 9 October 1916.

273 Letter to JPC from Arthur Samuel, 2 April 1903.

274 JPC, Journal II, pp. 250, 267.

275 JPC, Stockbook II, p. 30, no. 896: '18c G. Pendant Justice,' May 1921 and p. 29, no. 979: 'Cupid Triumphant Silv. Pend.', February 1921.

276 JPC, Stockbook II, p. 32, no. 1020: '18c Gold Neckchain', May 1922 and p. 30, no. 989: '18c Gold Zircon (15) Chain', 14 June 1921.

277 JPC, Stockbook II, pp. 41–64.

278 JPC, Stockbook II, p. 50, no. 1256: 'Sil. Hat Brooch & Pend. for C.R. Ashbee', January 1930; p. 53, no. 1287: 'Silv. Pend. Mrs Ashbee stones supplied', February 1931; and p. 63, no. 1383: 'Sil. Pectoral Cross for Mrs Ashbee', March 1933.

279 JPC, Stockbook II, p. 15, no. 738.

280 JPC, Journal I, p. 19.

281 JPC, Stockbook II, p. 50, no. 1253: Moonstone 18c G. Pend. for Mrs Bowhay given by Lady Sybil Smith', 1929. Lady Sybil Smith, who rented Squerryes Court near Bensom's Hill during summers in the 1920s, knew Thomas Bowhay and was one of his followers. In the 1920s and early 1930s, she bought several pieces of shagreen and metalware from Cooper.

282 JPC, Journal II, pp. 180, 149 and Journal IV, pp. 49–50, 79A.

283 G.F. Kunz, *The Curious Lore of Precious Stones* (Philadelphia and London, 1913) pp. 97–8.

284 Richard Payne Knight, *Symbolic Language of Ancient Art and Mythology* (New York, 1892), ch. 25, pp. 13–14. Cooper owned an 1876 edition of this book.

285 JPC, Stockbook II, p. 56, no. 1308: 'Mermaid bowl', 1931.

286 JPC, Stockbook II, p. 52, no. 1278: 'Silver Bowl Dragon Tree Pattern', September 1930 and no. 1279: 'Silver Bowl Datura', 1930.

287 JPC, Stockbook II, p. 56, nos 1305: 'Indian(?) Carved Coc. bowl, Mounted in Silver', October 1931.

288 JPC, Stockbook II, p. 33, no. 1024: 'Copper string box with brass rings', June 1922 and no. 1026: 'Brass chased self', 1922.

289 JPC, Stockbook II, p. 59, nos 1343–5: 'Sil Vase', 1932.

290 JPC, Stockbook II, p. 42, no. 1175: 'Silver Cross for Oakham Chapel. Old Victorian Jewellery supplied to mount', 1925.

291 JPC, Stockbook II, p. 55, no. 1304A: 'Reliquary for Bernard Shaw', September 1931 and Dan H. Lawrence, (ed.) *Bernard Shaw. Collected Letters: 1911–1925*, vol. 3 (London, 1988), pp. 228–9, 234.

292 Letter to JPC from George Bernard Shaw, 4 May 1931.

293 JPC, Journal IV, pp. 40–1.

294 Letter to JPC from George Bernard Shaw, 18 September 1931.

CHAPTER THREE: ASSESSMENT

1 F. Ernest Jackson, foreword to Three Shields Gallery, *Exhibition of Work by J. Paul Cooper* (London, 1932), p. 2.

2 Henry Wilson, et al., *Memorial of the Late J.D. Sedding* (London, 1892).

3 F. Cooper, 'John Paul Cooper and the Arts and Crafts Movement', p. 4.

4 JPC, Journal IV, p. 173.

5 Letter to JPC from W.R. Lethaby, 17 January 1920.

6 Shelagh Wilson, 'Art Into Industry, The Birmingham Experiment: The Attempt to Unify Art With Manufacturing in the Birmingham Trade 1860–1914', (unpublished MA thesis, Royal College of Art, 1991), ch. 3, pp. 12–17. Correspondingly, Alan Crawford has pointed out that 'W.R. Lethaby proposed to Edward Johnston (1872–1944) that he should teach a lettering class at the Central School of Arts and Crafts in 1897 when Johnston was hardly skilled at all in lettering; Lethaby also started bookbinding classes at the Central School in that year, employing Douglas Cockerell (1870–1945) as the teacher when Cockerell had himself not yet finished his apprenticeship with Cobdon-Sanderson.'

7 *The Athenaeum*, 21 January 1905, n. pag.

8 *Deutsche Goldschmiede-Zeitung*, 14 (April 1911), 143.

9 JPC, Object Photo Book III. On the front and back pages of this book Cooper pasted clippings of various published reviews of his work.

10 W.T. Whitley, 'The Arts and Crafts Society's Exhibition at Grosvenor Gallery', *The Studio*, 57 (January 1913), 293–4.

11 John Betjeman, 'There and Back 1851 A.D. to 1933 A.D. A History of the Revival of Good Craftsmanship', *The Architectural Review* 74 (July–December 1933), 8.

12 JPC, Exhibition/Approval Book I, p. 108.

13 Walter Crane, 'The Arts and Crafts Exhibition Society. To the Editor,' *The Architectural Review* 30 (July–December 1911), 345.

14 'British Arts and Crafts at Ghent. French Official Interest', *The Times*, 20 August 1913, n. pag.

15 *Bulletin Art ancien et moderne*, 2 May 1914, n. pag. and 'Studio-Talk. Paris', *The Studio* 62 (August 1914), 242.

16 Peter Rose, 'It Must Be Done Now: The Arts and Crafts Exhibition at Burlington House, 1916', *Decorative Arts Society Journal* 17 (1993), 3–12.

17 'A Metamorphosed Academy. Arts and Crafts in the Making', *Glasgow Herald*, 7 October 1916, n. pag. and W.T. Whitley, 'Arts and Crafts at the

Royal Academy', *The Studio* 70 (February 1917), 18–20.

18 'The Arts and Crafts at the Royal Academy', *The Nation* 103 (November 1916), 526.

19 'The Arts and Crafts at the Royal Academy', p. 526.

20 'British Arts. Interesting Exhibition at Burlington House', *Star*, 6 October 1916, n. pag.

21 Arts and Crafts Exhibition Society, Executive Committee Minutes, 22 May 1928, National Archive of Art and Design, London, AAD1/61/1980.

22 Arts and Crafts Exhibition Society, Executive Committee Minutes, 11 February 1931, AAD1/61/1980.

23 P. G. Konody, 'Art and Artist. The Royal Academy Winter Exhibition', *The Observer*, 14 January 1923, p. 10.

24 'Crafts Come Into Their Own in Royal Academy Winter Exhibition', *Christian Science Monitor*, 5 February 1923, n. pag.

25 'Notes. London', *The Studio*, 91 (March 1926), 191.

26 'Arts and Crafts. The Importance of Design', *Morning Post*, 16 January 1926, n. pag.

27 Arts and Crafts Exhibition Society, Executive Committee Minutes, 16 January 1930, AAD1/61–1980.

28 Arts and Crafts Exhibition Society, Executive Committee Minutes, 27 January 1930, AAD1/61/1980.

29 Arts and Crafts Exhibition Society, General Committee Minutes, 12 February 1932, National Archive of Art and Design, London, ADD1/62–1980.

30 F.E. Jackson, foreword to *Exhibition of Work By J. Paul Cooper*, pp. 2–3.

31 Charles Marriott, 'Silver and Shagreen. A Novel Exhibition', *The Times*, 31 October 1929, n. pag.; Mr Paul Cooper', *The Times*, 19 March 1931, n. pag.; and 'Shagreen and Silver Work,' *The Times*, 10 October 1927, n. pag.

32 'Art Exhibitions. Shagreen and Silver', *The Times*, 31 October 1929, n. pag.

33 *The Times*, 15 November 1932, n. pag.

34 *The Catalogue of the Exhibition of British Industrial Art in Relation to the Home* (London, 1933), p. iv.

35 'The Exhibition of British Industrial Art in Relation to the Home', *The Studio* 106 (August 1933), 108.

36 T.W. Earp, 'Notes. London. Arts and Crafts', *The Studio* 97 (January 1929), 57.

37 Betjeman, 'There and Back 1851 A.D. to 1933 A.D. A History of the Revival of Good Craftsmanship', p. 4.

38 Lord Gorell, 'Design and the Industrial Revival', *The Architectural Review* 74 (July–December 1933), 2–3.

39 JPC, 'When and Where a Handicraft Expires So Also the Quality of Machine Production in That Country Fails', paper read to the Art-Workers' Guild, 22 November 1929, p. 4. Cooper's paper spoke out against the statement given as its title. This statement appeared as part of the foreword to the 1928 Arts and Crafts Exhibition Society catalogue.

40 JPC, 'When and Where a Handicraft Expires', p. 5.

41 JPC, 'When and Where a Handicraft Expires', p. 8.

42 JPC, 'On Benedetto Croce's Theory of Aesthetics', paper read to the Art-Workers' Guild, 25 March 1922, pp. 5–6.

43 JPC, 'On Benedetto Croce's Theory', p. 19.

44 JPC, 'When and Where Handicraft Expires', pp. 4–5.

45 JPC, 'Modern Metal Work', paper read to the Art-Workers' Guild, 25 March 1922, p. 8.

46 JPC, 'Modern Metal Work', p. 3.

47 JPC, 'Metal Work and Jewellery', (unpublished manuscript, n.d.), p. 4.

48 JPC, Journal I, p. 144.

49 Letter from C.R. Ashbee to Henry Wilson, 16 May 1915, Henry Wilson Archives, Royal College of Art, London.

50 JPC, 'On Benedetto Croce's Theory', p. 19.

51 'Mr Paul Cooper', *The Times*, 19 March 1931, n. pag.

52 JPC, 'Taste', paper read to the Art Workers' Guild, 17 January 1930, p. 7.

53 'Death of Mr J. Paul Cooper', *Westerham Herald*, 6 May 1933, 5.

SELECT
BIBLIOGRAPHY

PRIMARY SOURCES

British Architectural Library, London. Alfred Powell, 'Owen Jones Studentship. Memoir, December 1893', Msfo 1893–(079J)72.03(45).

Cooper Family Archives. Francis Cooper, 'John Paul Cooper and the Arts and Crafts Movement', Letter to Tricia Laurie, February 1979.

——, John Paul Cooper, Personal Papers, Documents, and Correspondence.

——, Kanty Cooper, 'Father, Family and Friends', unfinished manuscript.

Institute of Art and Design. The Birmingham School of Art Archives. Birmingham Municipal School of Art Management Sub-Committee Minutes, vols 6–9 (June 1900–March 1906).

——, School of Art, Margaret Street Registrar, vols 1–2 (1897–1916).

——, Vittoria Street School for Jewellers and Silversmiths Minutes, vol. 1 (June 1901–July 1907).

Royal College of Art, London. The Henry Wilson Archives, Personal Correspondence.

Royal Institute of British Architects, London. Ordinary General Meetings Minutes, vol. 1 (1885–94).

Victoria and Albert Museum, London. National Archive of Art and Design, Arts and Crafts Exhibition Society Papers, Executive Committee Minutes, 1928–31. AAD1/61–1980.

——, Arts and Crafts Exhibition Society Papers, General Committee Minutes, 1917–23, 1929–35. AAD1/53,62–1980.

——, Arts and Crafts Exhibition Society Papers, John Paul Cooper, Letter to H.J.L.J. Massé, July 1900. AAD1/508–E15/71.

——, Arts and Crafts Exhibition Society Papers, John Paul Cooper, 'A Proposal for the Reorganization of the Arts and Crafts Exhibition Society', 1913. AAD1/21–1980.

SECONDARY SOURCES

'Art Exhibitions', *Morning Post*, 19 March 1931, n. pag.

The Art-Journal Catalogue of the Paris Universal Exhibition, London, 1867.

The Art-Journal Illustrated Catalogue of the International Exhibition, London, 1862.

'Art Metal-Work at the Chicago Exhibition', *The Art Journal Supplement* (1893), xxi–xxiv.

'The Arts and Crafts at the Royal Academy', *The Nation* 103 (November 1916), 524–6.

'The Arts and Crafts Exhibition, 1896', *The Studio* 9 (November 1896), 117–134.

'The Arts and Crafts Exhibition at the Grafton Gallery. Second Notice', *The Studio* 37 (March 1906), 129–144.

'The Arts and Crafts Exhibition at the Grafton Gallery. Third and Concluding Notice', *The Studio* 37 (April 1906), 213–29.

'Arts and Crafts. The Importance of Design', *Morning Post*, 16 January 1926, n. pag.

'British Arts and Crafts at Ghent. French Official Interest', *The Times*, 20 August 1913, n. pag.

'British Arts. Interesting Exhibition at Burlington House', *Star*, 6 October 1916, n. pag.

'Casket by Mr H. Wilson Presented to The Right Hon. Joseph Chamberlain M.P.', *The Magazine of Art* (1903), 595–7.

The Catalogue of the Exhibition of British Industrial Art in Relation to the Home, London, 1933.

'"Corri", Legion Steward Was Famous Craftsman', *Sevenoaks Chronicle*, 13 February 1948, p. 4.

'Crafts Come Into Their Own in Royal Academy Winter Exhibition', *Christian Science Monitor*, 5 February 1923, n. pag.

'Death of Mr J. Paul Cooper', *Westerham Herald*, 6 May 1933, p. 5.

Exhibition of British Arts and Crafts 1920–1921 Assembled by the Detroit Society of Arts and Crafts, Detroit, 1920.

'The Exhibition of British Industrial Art in Relation to the Home', *The Studio* 106 (August 1933), 108.

'Fine Craftsmanship', *Morning Post*, 2 October 1924, n. pag.

The Illustrated Catalogue of the Paris International Exhibition, London, 1878.

'The Late Mr W. Jackson', *Leicester Daily Post*, 16 July 1894, n. pag.

'A Metamorphosed Academy. Arts and Crafts in the Making', *Glasgow Herald*, 7 October 1916, n. pag.

'Mr Paul Cooper', *The Times*, 19 March 1931, n. pag.

'Notes. London', *The Studio* 91 (March 1926), 191–2.

'Shagreen and Silverwork', *The Times*, 10 October 1927, n. pag.

'Some Recent Examples of the Jewellers' Art in France', *The Studio* 23 (June 1901), 25–31.

'Studio-Talk', *The Studio* 20 (June 1900), 48–9.

'Studio-Talk. Paris', *The Studio* 62 (August 1914), 237–42.

'Suggestions for the Improvement of Sporting Cups and Trophies. Part II', *The Studio* 20 (June 1900), 37–46.

Anscombe, Isabelle and Gere, Charlotte, *Arts and Crafts in Britain and America*, (London, 1978).

Arts and Crafts Exhibition Society, *Catalogue*, 15 vols, London, 1888–1931.

Bell, Quentin, *The Schools of Design*, London, 1963.

Betjeman, John, 'There and Back A.D. 1851 to A.D. 1933. A History of the Revival of Good Craftsmanship', *The Architectural Review* 74 (July–December 1933), 4–8.

Birmingham Museum and Art Gallery, *Finely Taught. Finely Wrought. The Birmingham School of Jewellery and Silversmithing 1890–1990*, Birmingham, 1990.

Brégor, Alphonse. 'L'Art décoratif à la Walter [*sic*] Art Gallery de Liverpool', *Revue du vrai et du beau* 4 (December 1925), 26.

Brewer, E. Cobham, *Dictionary of Phrase and Fable*, London, 1894.

Burlamacchi, Marchesa, *Luca della Robbia*, London, 1900.

Bury, Shirley, *Jewellery 1780–1910*, 2 vols, Woodbridge, Suffolk, 1991.

Camino, Mary, *Gimson and the Barnsleys*, London, 1980.

Coulson, Anthony J., *A Bibliography of Design in Britain 1851–1970*, London, 1979.

Craig, Edward Gordon, 'Writing in Water-Colour', *Walker's Monthly* 39 (March 1931), 1.

——, *Index to the Story of My Days*, London, 1957.

Crane, Walter, 'Notes on Gesso Work', *The Studio* 1 (May 1893), 45–9.

——, 'The Arts and Crafts Exhibition Society. To the Editor', *The Architectural Review* 30 (July–December 1911), 345.

Day, Lewis F., 'Victorian Progress in Applied Design', *The Art Journal* (June 1887), 185–202.

——, 'Arts and Crafts', *The Art Journal* (November 1893), 330–3.

Earp, T.W. 'Notes. London. Arts and Crafts', *The Studio* 97 (January 1929), 57.

Farleigh, John, *The Creative Craftsman*, London, 1950.

The Fine Art Society Ltd, *Jewellery and Jewellery Design 1850–1930 and John Paul Cooper 1869–1933*, London, 1975.

Frazer, James George, *The Golden Bough. A Study in Magic and Religion*, 3rd rev. edn, 12 vols, London, 1911–15.

Garner, Philippe, 'Unpublished Notes on Gesso by Frederick Marriott', *Bulletin of the Decorative Arts Society 1890–1940* 1 (1975), 28–34.

Gere, Charlotte, 'The Work of John Paul Cooper', *The Connoisseur* 190 (November 1975), 200–8.

——, 'Edward Spencer and the Artificers' Guild', lecture delivered at The Decorative Arts Society Symposium, Art-Workers' Guild, 21 November 1992.

——, and Geoffery C. Munn, *Artists' Jewellery. Pre-Raphaelite to Arts and Crafts*, Woodbridge, Suffolk, 1989.

Gorell, Lord, 'Design and the Industrial Revival', *The Architectural Review* 74 (July–December 1933), 1–3.

Harada, Jiro, 'Japanese Art and Artists of Today. V. Metalwork', *The Studio* 52 (March 1911), 95–105.

Harris A. 'The Technical Commission and Industrial Art', *The Art Journal* (October 1884), 309–12.

Hart, George, *A Dictionary of Egyptian Gods and Goddesses*, London, 1986.

Holme, Charles (ed.), *Modern Design in Jewellery and Fans*, London, 1902.

Houghton, W., *Country Walks of a Naturalist with His Children*, London, 1870.

Hulme, F. Edward, *Symbolism in Christian Art*, London and New York, 1899.

Jopp, Keith, *Corah of Leicester 1815–1965*, Leicester, 1965.

Kaplan, Wendy and Cummings, Elizabeth, *The Arts and Crafts Movement*, New York, 1991.

Knight, Richard Payne, *Symbolic Language of Ancient Art and Mythology*, 1818, New York, 1892.

Konody, P.G., 'Art and Artist. The Royal Academy Winter Exhibition', *The Observer*, 14 January 1923, 10.

Kunz, George Frederick, *The Curious Lore of Precious Stones*, Philadelphia and London, 1913.

Kuzmanović, Natasha, 'The Jewelry of John Paul Cooper', *Jewelry* I (1996–7), 40–51.

——, 'John Paul Cooper (1869–1933): Arts and Crafts Artist', *The Wolfsonian Bulletin* 2 (Spring–Summer 1994), 2–3.

——, 'The Shagreen Work of John Paul Cooper', *The Magazine Antiques* 148 (September 1995), 348–57.

Lambourne, Lionel, *Utopian Craftsmen. The Arts and Crafts Movement from the Cotswolds to Chicago*, Salt Lake City, 1980.

Lethaby, W.R. *Architecture, Mysticism, and Myth*, London, 1892.

Lucas, Geoffrey,. 'Obituary. Walter John Nash Millard', *Journal of the Royal Society of British Architects* 44 (1936–7), 152–3, 247.

MacCarthy, Fiona, *A History of British Design 1830–1970*, London, 1979.

Mackail, J.W., *The Life of William Morris*, 2 vols, London, 1899.

Manton, Cynthia, 'Henry Wilson (1864–1934): His Work and Influence', PhD dissertation, Brighton Polytechnic, 1985.

Marriott, Charles, 'Silver and Shagreen. A Novel Exhibition', *The Times*, 31 October 1929, n. pag.

Massé, H.J.L.J., *The Art-Workers' Guild 1884–1934*, Oxford, 1935.

Massey, Gerald, *The Logia of the Lord*, London, 1887.

Morris, William, *The Letters of William Morris to His Family and Friends*, edited by Philip Henderson, London, 1950.

——, *William Morris By Himself*, edited by Gillian Naylor, Boston, 1988.

Mourey, Gabriel. 'L'Exposition des Arts et Métiers (Arts and Crafts) de la Grande-Bretagne au Pavillon de Marsan', *Art et décoration* 35 (June 1914), 189–204.

Naylor, Gillian, *The Arts and Crafts Movement. A Study of Its Sources, Ideals, and Influences on Design Theory*, Cambridge, Mass., 1971.

——, 'Formative Years of the Arts and Crafts Exhibition Society: 1888–1916', *Craft History* 1 (1988), 1–7.

New Gallery, *Catalogue of a Loan Collection of Antique Furniture, Medieval Tapestries, and Allied Domestic Arts*, Edinburgh, 1917.

Pennell, E.R. and J., *The Life of James McNeill Whistler*, 2 vols, London, 1908.

Pliny the Elder, *The History of the World*, translated by Philemon Holland, 2 vols, London, 1634.

Redgrave, Gilbert R. 'Art Education During the Past Fifty Years', *The Art Journal* (June 1887), 221–4.

Robert Dunthorne & Son, Ltd, *Memorial Exhibition of Silverwork, Shagreen and Water-Colour Drawings by the Late J. Paul Cooper*, London, 1933.

Rose, Peter, 'It Must Be Done Now: the Arts and Crafts Exhibition at Burlington House, 1916', *Decorative Arts Society Journal* 17 (1993), 3–12.

Royal Institute of British Architects, *The Kalender of the Royal Institute of British Architects*, 58th sess. (1893–4), London, 1893.

Rücklin, Rudolf, 'Zu unseren Abbildungen', *Deutsche Goldschmiede-Zeitung* 14 (April 1911), 142–4.

Ruskin, John, *The Nature of Gothic. A Chapter of the Stones of Venice by John Ruskin*, edited by William Morris, Hammersmith, 1892.

——, *The Complete Works of John Ruskin*, 30 vols, New York, 1905.

Shaw, George Bernard, *Bernard Shaw. Collected Letters: 1874–1950*, edited by Dan H. Lawrence, 4 vols, London, 1965–1988.

Stansky, Peter, *Redesigning the World. William Morris, the 1880s, and the Arts and Crafts*, Princeton, 1985.

Summerson, John, *The Architectural Association 1847–1947*, London, 1947.

Three Shields Gallery, *Exhibition of Work by J. Paul Cooper*, London, 1932.

Triggs, Oscar Lovell, *Chapters in the History of the Arts and Crafts Movement*, Chicago, 1902.

Untracht, Oppi, *Jewelry Concepts and Technology*, New York, 1985.

——, *Metal Techniques for Craftsmen*, New York, 1975.

Vallance, Aymer. 'The Arts and Crafts Exhibition Society at the New Gallery, 1893', *The Studio* 2 (October 1893), 3–27.

——, 'British Decorative Art in 1899 and the Arts and Crafts Exhibition. Part III', *The Studio* 18 (December 1899), 179–96.

——, 'The Revival of Tempera Painting', *The Studio* 23 (August 1901), 156–65.

Verneuil, M.P. 'L'Exposition des Arts et Métiers (Arts and Crafts) de la Grande-Bretagne au Pavillon de Marsan', *Art et décoration* 35 (May 1914), 129–60.

Victoria and Albert Museum, *William Morris*, London, 1996.

Walker's Galleries, *An Exhibition of Water-Colour Drawings, Shagreen and Silverwork by J. Paul Cooper*, London, 1931.

Webb, Matthew, 'On Gesso', *The Studio* 13 (August 1894), 153–9.

Whitley, W.T., 'The Arts and Crafts Society's Exhibition at Grosvenor Gallery', *The Studio* 57 (January 1913), 290–302.

——, 'Arts and Crafts at the Royal Academy. Fourth and Concluding Article', *The Studio* 70 (February 1917), 118–29.

Wickre, Bille, 'Collaboration in the Work of Margaret and Frances Macdonald, Charles Rennie Mackintosh, and J. Herbert McNair', PhD dissertation, University of Michigan, 1993.

Wilson, Henry, et al, *A Memorial of the Late J.D. Sedding*, London, 1892.

Wilson, Henry, 'The Arts and Crafts Society: With Especial Reference to Certain Exhibits', *The Architectural Review* 6 (June–December 1899), 209–16.

——, *Silverwork and Jewellery*, London, 1903.

Wilson, Shelagh, 'Art Into Industry, The Birmingham Experiment: The Attempt to Unify Art With Manufacturing in the Birmingham Trade 1860–1914', MA thesis, Royal College of Art, 1991.

INDEX